OXFORD PHILOSOPHICAL TEXTS

George Berkeley

A Treatise Concerning the Principles of Human Knowledge

OXFORD PHILOSOPHICAL TEXTS

Series Editor: John Cottingham

The Oxford Philosophical Texts series consists of authoritative teaching editions of canonical texts in the history of philosophy from the ancient world down to modern times. Each volume provides a clear, well laid out text together with a comprehensive introduction by a leading specialist, giving the student detailed critical guidance on the intellectual context of the work and the structure and philosophical importance of the main arguments. Endnotes are supplied which provide further commentary on the arguments and explain unfamiliar references and terminology, and a full bibliography and index are also included.

The series aims to build up a definitive corpus of key texts in the Western philosophical tradition, which will form a reliable and enduring resource for students and teachers alike.

PUBLISHED IN THIS SERIES:

Berkeley *A Treatise Concerning the Principles of Human Knowledge* (edited by Jonathan Dancy)
Berkeley *Three Dialogues between Hylas and Philonous* (edited by Jonathan Dancy)
Hume *An Enquiry concerning the Principles of Morals* (edited by Tom L. Beauchamp)
Leibniz *Philosophical Texts* (edited by R. S. Woolhouse and Richard Francks)
Mill *Utilitarianism* (edited by Roger Crisp)

FORTHCOMING TITLES INCLUDE:

Frege *Philosophical Writings* (edited by Anthony Kenny)
Hume *A Treatise of Human Nature* (edited by David Fate Norton and Mary J. Norton)
Kant *Groundwork for the Metaphysics of Morals* (edited by Thomas E. Hill and Arnulf Zweig)
Kant *Prolegomena to Any Future Metaphysics* (edited by Günter Zöller)
Locke *An Essay concerning Human Understanding* (edited by S. Nicholas Jolley)
Spinoza *Ethics* (edited by G. H. R. Parkinson)

GEORGE BERKELEY

A Treatise Concerning the Principles of Human Knowledge

EDITED BY
JONATHAN DANCY

Oxford · New York
OXFORD UNIVERSITY PRESS
1998

Oxford University Press, Great Clarendon Street, Oxford OX2 6DP

Oxford New York

Athens Auckland Bangkok Bogota Bombay Buenos Aires
Calcutta Cape Town Dar es Salaam Delhi Florence Hong Kong
Istanbul Karachi Kuala Lumpur Madras Madrid Melbourne
Mexico City Nairobi Paris Singapore Taipei Tokyo Toronto Warsaw

and associated companies in
Berlin Ibadan

Oxford is a trade mark of Oxford University Press

Published in the United States
by Oxford University Press Inc., New York

editorial introduction and apparatus © Jonathan Dancy 1998

British Library Cataloguing in Publication Data
Data available

Library of Congress Cataloging-in-Publication Data
Berkeley, George, 1685–1753.
A treatise concerning the principles of human knowledge /
George Berkeley; edited by Jonathan Dancy.
— (Oxford philosophical texts)
Includes bibliographical references and index.
1. Knowledge, Theory of. I. Dancy, Jonathan. II. Title.
III. Series.
B1331.D38 1997 121–dc21 97–12131
ISBN 978-0-19-875161-8

9 10

Typeset by Best-set Typesetter Ltd, Hong Kong
Printed in Great Britain
on acid-free paper by
CPI Antony Rowe
Chippenham, Wiltshire

Contents

Contents

PART 1

Introductory Material

How to Use this Book

This book contains the text of George Berkeley's *A Treatise Concerning the Principles of Human Knowledge*, commonly known as his *Principles*, together with two letters on philosophical topics sent to Berkeley by the American philosopher Samuel Johnson, and Berkeley's replies. These texts are sandwiched between editorial material of various sorts. After the texts comes a Glossary, and after the Glossary there are Notes to the *Principles* and to the Berkeley–Johnson correspondence. Unfamiliar or obsolete terms, and those in foreign languages, are explained or translated in the Glossary, at the end of the book; whole phrases in foreign languages, usually Latin, are normally translated in the Notes following the Glossary. Sometimes a word used by Berkeley has changed its meaning since his time, in a way that might lead to misunderstanding; such occasions are also signalled in the Notes rather than in the Glossary. But the main purpose of the Notes is to explain anything with which a comparatively inexperienced reader is likely to have difficulty. Not everything can be kept at this level, and sometimes the material given is intended for a more advanced reader. There should be something for everyone, therefore, though not everything in the Notes is for everyone.

Before the texts there is a substantial Editor's Introduction, whose fifteen sections can be seen as falling into five groups. After the Preamble, there is a short life of Berkeley (Section 2). Next come three sections which give a general overview of the contents of the *Principles*. Then there is a section (6) which investigates the passage in which Berkeley gives the main argument for his philosophical position, followed by seven sections dealing with the most important topics covered in the *Principles*. Finally there is a historical section (14) and an account of the Berkeley–Johnson correspondence.

The best way to start with this book is to ignore all the editorial matter at the beginning and just read the text of the *Principles* first. Second best is to read just §§1–34 first, before turning to the editorial material for help. If these approaches are both too daunting, however, start by reading Sections 3, 4, and 5 of the Editor's Introduction; this will give you a reasonable idea of what to expect.

If you are going to sit down to work on the *Principles* in some detail, you should read the Editor's Introduction straight through; the Notes often refer you back to the Introduction, and it would be best to have read that before you begin to use the Notes in earnest.

Once you have become more familiar with the text of the *Principles*, the Analysis of the *Principles* should prove useful in internal navigation.

Where incomplete bibliographical details are given of other works referred to in the Editor's Introduction or in the Notes, or abbreviated titles, full details can be found in the Bibliography.

Editor's Introduction

1. Preamble

The *Principles* is a young man's book. Berkeley had conceived the main ideas in his early twenties, and the book was published when he was 25. He thought that he had found the key to many of the great problems of philosophy—a key so obvious that one only had to open one's eyes to notice it. His mission is to open our eyes, eyes that have become unclear because of the dust thrown up by centuries of mistakes. If we accept Berkeley's help, the problems of philosophy will go away; they will have been solved, and we will be freed to get on with the ordinary business of life. So Berkeley was a young man in a hurry, and his book has all the energy and enthusiasm that goes with that.

The frustrating thing for young men in a hurry is that their elders refuse to be impressed. They refuse to have their problems solved for them. They refuse to admit that Berkeley's key can open anything at all. If this is the cure, they say, we very much prefer the disease; if this has to be the solution, we would rather keep the problems. Since the solution appeared to require them to deny the existence of the material world, one can understand their reluctance.

Berkeley knew he was up against the great weight of intellectual inertia—not to mention the power of common sense. But he was not without hope. For what he was doing was to take something which many had said before him, and extend it. Many had maintained that colours, sounds, tastes, and smells are nothing but sensations, existing in the mind alone. But Berkeley had the nerve to say the same about shape, size, and motion, and to find a way of sustaining this view against the barrage of objections that he knew was bound to come. Of course we are sure that he *is* wrong. Shape and size, we want to say, are not sensations in the mind but real independent qualities of real independent objects. But Berkeley defends his claims with extraordinary skill, using a minimum of resources but marshalling his arguments impeccably. The basic moves are not too difficult to grasp, but the question where, if anywhere, he makes his mistakes is still unsolved.

If Berkeley's key to the problems of philosophy requires us to say about size and shape what others have said about colour and sound, he is

5

standing on the shoulders of his predecessors; his views do not come from nowhere. His originality as a philosopher lies in the fact that he presses harder than anyone before him on the relation between our experience and the supposedly independent world that our experience tells us about. We acquire both the concepts with which we think about the world, and our knowledge of how things actually are around us, by the use of our senses. And we suppose that our senses tell us about a world that exists independently of sense experience—a world that is by and large the same whether we experience it or not, and that has no need to be experienced in order to exist. But Berkeley sees a difficulty here. Everything we see or feel is, as it were, made for the senses. The objects of our senses are, we might say, appearances, and it is only because of this that they are available to experience. But how is it possible, starting from things like that, to construct a conception of something that is not like that at all—the world *beyond* experience, *beyond* appearance? Berkeley argues that it isn't; the only world we can understand is one to which experience is essential, one which is essentially appearance. If something is accessible to the mind, that accessibility is essential to it.

These views of Berkeley are historically important, partly because of what went before, and partly because they were the idealist half of the Kantian synthesis of idealism and realism, and are therefore the first stirrings of the great Idealistic tradition of Kant, Hegel, Fichte, and Schelling. This, however, is not the place to elaborate on that tradition.

Berkeley argues passionately for his views. This passion has two sources. First, he is convinced of them in their own right, as philosophy. Second, he sees them as the best way to defend the Christian religion. In 1734, the year in which the version of the *Principles* that is presented here was published, Berkeley became Bishop of Cloyne in the County of Cork in Ireland. But he had been ordained in 1709, and religious concerns were even nearer to his heart than philosophical ones.

2. Berkeley's Life

George Berkeley was born on 12 March 1685 in Co. Kilkenny in Ireland, into a family about which little is known. His parents were well enough off, however, to send him to one of the leading schools in Ireland, Kilkenny College, at the age of 11. He was a student there for four years, and then entered Trinity College, Dublin, of which he remained a member until 1724. Most of that time, however, was spent abroad, in London or on the

Continent of Europe. For four years, until 1704, he worked for his BA degree, and in 1707 he was elected to a fellowship, a permanent position in the College. His earliest known philosophical writings date from 1707, and his first book, *An Essay towards a New Theory of Vision*, appeared in 1709, running into a second edition in the same year. This was an apparently free-standing enquiry into the nature of vision, a topic of great current interest partly because of rapid development in microscopes and telescopes, and partly because the received theory of vision was admitted to be inadequate. But Berkeley has a further motive for writing this work, which was to solve in advance, as it were, a difficulty that arose for the philosophy he had already developed,[1] and which was to be the subject of his next book. This book was the *Treatise Concerning the Principles of Human Knowledge*, which appeared in 1710. For two years after this Berkeley busied himself with College duties. But he clearly felt that the *Principles* had not had the effect that he had expected,[2] and 1713 saw him taking two measures to remedy this. He moved to London, and took with him the completed manuscript of the *Three Dialogues between Hylas and Philonous*. In the *Dialogues* he presents the views of his *Principles* more accessibly and more persuasively; the text has a much lighter touch, but is still serious. This time Berkeley had a success; where before he had been met with ridicule, now those who disagreed with him at least were more likely to understand and respect the views they rejected. But far more successful was Berkeley himself. He was an instant hit on the London literary scene. He was presented at the Court of Queen Anne by Swift, who clearly approved of him, describing him in the *Journal to Stella* as 'a very ingenious man and a great philosopher'.[3] Steele immediately took him up, and asked him to write for his periodical, the *Guardian*. Berkeley also became friends with Pope, Addison, Gay, and other leading figures. He lived in London for a year enjoying this success, and then we find him leaving for Sicily in 1713 as chaplain to the Earl of Peterborough, who had been appointed Ambassador Extraordinary to Victor Amodeus, King of Sicily. (Swift recommended

---

[1] Berkeley tells us in §43 of the *Principles* that the difficulty was the apparent 'outness' of the things we see; apparent 'outness' was hard to reconcile with his claim that the things we see are ideas in our own minds.

[2] Berkeley's friend Sir John Percival reported to him from London that 'a physician of my acquaintance undertook to describe your person, and argued you must needs be mad, and that you ought to take remedies. A bishop pitied you that a desire and vanity of starting something new should put you on such an undertaking'; see B. Rand *Berkeley and Percival* (Cambridge: Cambridge University Press, 1914), 80–1. Berkeley replied sadly that he was 'not at all surprised to find that the name of my book should be entertained with ridicule and contempt by those who never examined what was in it' (*Works*, viii. 36).

[3] Entry for 12 Apr. 1713.

Berkeley for this post.) In 1714 he was back in London, since the death of Queen Anne led to the recall of the Earl of Peterborough. He hoped to be elected Dean of St Paul's in Dublin.[4] But these hopes came to nothing, and in 1716 he was appointed tutor to St George Ashe, son of a friend of Swift's, in which role he travelled round Europe until 1720.

It is hard to know why Berkeley had left London in 1713, after such success there, let alone why he returned to the Continent for a further four years. The terms of his fellowship at Trinity College, Dublin, allowed no more than sixty-three days' absence in any year. So every two years Berkeley had to ask for permission to be away from Ireland for another two, on the joint excuse of ill health and a desire to promote learning. Did he promote learning? During this second trip to the Continent he wrote the *De Motu* (published in 1721); in this work he applies the general philosophical position laid out in the *Principles* to contemporary problems concerning motion. According to a letter to Johnson, he had also written much of Part II of the *Principles* on his travels in Italy, but lost the manuscript.[5] Beyond that, he seems to have done little to justify taking such an extended leave from Trinity.[6]

Returning to England, and with his income reduced to his salary as Fellow of Trinity, he found the country in the huge financial crisis known as the South Sea Bubble, in which the value of stocks rose to an enormous height before collapsing completely, and many people were ruined. This aroused in Berkeley a lifelong interest in public affairs; in 1721 he published *An Essay towards preventing the ruin of Great Britain*, in which he suggested that the Bubble was merely a symptom of a more general evil, which was the collapse of religion, of morality, and of a sense of the public good. His own fortunes, however, were about to take a turn for the better. In the same year, two months after he had again received permission to be absent for another two years, he was in Dublin again, engaged in duties at Trinity, but now with hopes of a 'good Deanery', i.e. a well-paid senior position in the Church. In 1723 he received a very substantial and entirely unexpected legacy from a lady whom he hardly knew but who had been a good friend of his friend Swift;[7] and in 1724 he finally got the sort of post he had been

[4] A deanship is an eminent position in the Anglican Church, second only to a bishopric. A dean would be in day-to-day charge of a cathedral, or would supervise the affairs of several parishes.

[5] See the quotation at the end of Sect. 13 of this Introduction.

[6] It is fair to say that he was far from being the only Fellow of Trinity who took extended leave in this way. People were more relaxed about such things than they are now.

[7] This is Hester van Homrigh, the Vanessa of Swift's poem *Cadenus and Vanessa*.

looking for. He became Dean of Derry, with an income of about £1,100 a year, compared to about £80 at Trinity.[8] He had now achieved financial security, in a post that left him time to devote himself to thinking and writing. At least, that is what we would have expected him to do. But we would have been wrong. Instead he devoted himself to the practical and political. This was, of course, in keeping with his philosophical views, since the *Principles* Part I ends with the claim that the main purpose of successful philosophy is to turn us away from barren speculations, so that we can devote ourselves to living a truly Christian life (§156). This is the choice that Berkeley made.

It is just as well that being Dean of Derry did not require constant attendance on one's duties,[9] since of the ten years that Berkeley held the post he was in London for at least three and in America for more than another three. Since 1722 he had been putting together ambitious plans for a new college in Bermuda designed to provide a Christian education for young men from America.[10] These plans, which eventually came to nothing, now seem high-minded but patently impractical.[11] The more impractical, however, the greater must have been Berkeley's powers of persuasion. He managed to induce five Fellows of Trinity to agree to renounce their cosy posts in Dublin and commit themselves to becoming teachers in the new college, abandoning their prospects in Ireland. He travelled to London four months after becoming Dean and raised £3,400 (which rose later to

[8] It is difficult to give a precise equivalent of these sums in modern terms. One indicator is that in 1700 an unskilled manual labourer earned about £5 a year; another is that someone who left £500 was deemed to have died rich. So the income Berkeley received as Dean of Derry was really enormous; Swift described the deanship as 'the best preferment among us', meaning the best-paid position in the Irish Church (letter to Lord Carteret, 3 Sept. 1724; quoted in Fraser (ed.), *Life and Letters of George Berkeley*, 102–3).

[9] The deanship involved overseeing the activities of several parishes, as well as the care of the cathedral at Derry. It was one of the most desirable positions in the Irish Church, because of the large income it brought with it. Berkeley delegated his duties, and determined to use his position and the bulk of his income as Dean to further his Bermudan project.

[10] Berkeley made provision both for students of European descent and for native Americans. His main intention was to provide a supply of parish priests and missionaries for the American colonies.

[11] Impractical in two ways, perhaps. First, because one would have thought it plainly impossible to raise the money (though one would have been wrong about this, as everyone was at the time). Second, because Bermuda, isolated in the middle of the Atlantic, hardly seems a sensible choice of a place to which American families would be wanting to send their sons for education. Berkeley's reason for choosing Bermuda was partly its climate and lack of distractions, and partly the fact that it is more or less equidistant from every part of the American seaboard and the West Indies. For once his common sense seems to have deserted him.

£6,000) by public subscription.[12] At a dinner of the Scriblerus Club he was roundly teased for the idea; but he asked to be heard in reply, and when he had finished speaking the members of the Club all leapt to their feet crying 'Let us set out with him immediately.' Then, feeling that private money would be inadequate, Berkeley applied for public funds, which were awarded almost unanimously by Parliament, much to everyone's surprise. With the promise of £20,000 and a Royal Charter giving permission for the college to be founded, everything seemed to be in place. Berkeley married, and in 1728 sailed for the New World with his wife, Anne, to await the promised money. They went, not to Bermuda, but to Rhode Island on the east coast of America, where he bought a farm that was to provide an income for his college. And there they stayed until 1731. But the money was never paid, despite all Berkeley's efforts. Walpole, the Prime Minister, had better uses for such a large sum. In September 1731 Berkeley abandoned the project, and with his wife and son went back to England.

Instead of returning to Derry, Berkeley set up house in London. He was looking for advancement in the Church, and suspected that the best way to get it was to be visible in the place where such advancements were decided. During this period he published slightly revised versions of the *New Theory of Vision*, the *Principles*, and the *Three Dialogues*. He also brought out the *Alciphron; or, The Minute Philosopher* (1732), the main intellectual fruit of his stay in America, in which he defends Christian belief, and *The Analyst* (1734), in which he argues that mathematics contains as much mystery as religion, and religion as much reason as mathematics. He lived in London until 1734, when he was made Bishop of Cloyne, which lies twenty miles from Cork. Berkeley moved there immediately and lived there for the rest of his life. During this period he did not cease to write, but he was also busy with the practical concerns that came with being a bishop. He died in 1753, on a visit to his son in Oxford.

What can we say of such a life? Berkeley was an extraordinary mixture of talents. He was a philosophical thinker of the first order, and able to engage in debate with the leading mathematicians of his day. He was an earnest Christian, and defended his faith with all the intellectual force he could muster. But these characteristics are only half the story. He was convinced that the practical was more important than the theoretical, and he put this belief into practice, first in his American project, and second in the

---

[12] As I have already said, it is extremely hard to give adequate modern equivalents of these sums. But bearing in mind that £20,000 was enough not only to build a college, but also to endow it with funds to pay salaries and maintain the buildings, £6,000 is a very considerable amount.

way he lived at Cloyne. And there was more to him than intellectual ability and practical energy. He was loved and respected for himself. His friend Pope wrote:

> Ev'n in a bishop I can spy desert,
> Secker is decent, Rundel has a heart;
> Manners with candour are to Benson giv'n,
> To Berkley ev'ry virtue under heaven.[13]

A more objective tribute comes from Bishop Atterbury, who was not a personal friend: 'So much understanding, so much knowledge, so much innocence, and such humility, I did not think had been the portion of any but angels until I saw this gentleman.'[14]

3. The Target (or, What Berkeley didn't Believe)

Despite the originality of his views, Berkeley was influenced by many different writers, as we know not only from reading his published work but also from the contents of his private notebooks, now known as the *Philosophical Commentaries*.[15] Some he shared themes with; some he borrowed arguments from; some he largely approved of; and some he thought almost totally wrong. The section below headed 'Berkeley's Intellectual Antecedents' gives details of his debts to his contemporaries and immediate predecessors. But philosophers can be indebted not only to those with whom they agree but also to those with whom they disagree; indeed, they often owe more to the latter than to the former.

We can see the position against which Berkeley was arguing as a sort of party line. As with other party lines, not all members of the party agree with every part of it, and probably all disagree with some part of it. The view that Berkeley rejects is a sort of composite of the views of Locke, of Descartes, of Malebranche, of Newton, and of others who collectively were sometimes referred to as 'the new philosophers'.[16] Broadly, these philosophers agreed that there is a real material world, existing quite independently of the mind. Familiar things like trees, hills, and stones exist 'out there'; we perceive them, but they do not need to be perceived in order to exist. Berkeley called this view 'materialism'. Larger material things like

---

[13] Epilogue to the *Satires*, Dialogue II, lines 70–3.

[14] *Letters by several eminent persons deceased, including the correspondence of John Hughes . . . and several of his friends, with notes* [by J. Duncombe] (London, 1772), ii. 2–3.

[15] *Works*. i.

[16] e.g. by Bayle, in his article on Zeno, note G.

trees and stones are composed of smaller ones, the smaller ones are composed of even smaller ones, and so on down until we reach the ultimate constituents of matter, which are tiny corpuscles. These corpuscles have the properties of size, shape, mobility, and solidity, but no other; these are called 'primary qualities'. The larger objects, being composed of such corpuscles, of course have their own primary qualities. Now we ordinarily speak of trees and stones not only as being large or small, round or square, and so on, but also as being coloured and rough to the touch, as being warmed by the sun and as making a sound when they fall; and we speak of foods as having a certain taste and smell. These further ('secondary') properties have a different place in the picture. The 'primary' qualities are really in the objects, independently of any relation to the mind. A square block of stone that is one metre in height, breadth, and depth has these dimensions in a way that is nothing whatever to do with any relation to us. But the secondary properties are not like this. They are essentially to do with how things look, seem, feel, sound, and taste *to us*.[17]

This position is called 'the distinction between primary and secondary qualities'. With it goes a thought about the nature of the independent world—how the world is 'in itself'. The secondary qualities consist in a relation between the objects and us. What are the objects like *in themselves*, then, or independently of any relation to us? The answer is that in themselves they only have the primary qualities. In this sense the physical world, as the new philosophers conceived it, is a very austere one; *in itself* it lacks all the sensible qualities of colour, touch, smell, sound, and taste—the qualities that make it come alive to us.

We need to add to this picture of the constituents of the material world an account of how change takes place in it. Change occurs when one corpuscle or group of corpuscles strikes another and moves it. This sort of *mechanical* change is the only sort of change we can understand, according to the new philosophers.[18] Now Locke, for instance, is too sane, and too

[17] Although they would all have agreed that the primary and the secondary qualities are different in the way I have described, the new philosophers gave differing accounts of the nature of the secondary qualities. (See Sect. 14 of this Introduction for more detail.) Locke held that they are *powers in the objects* to cause ideas in us; he got this view and the terminology of 'primary' and 'secondary' from his friend Robert Boyle, the chemist. Others held that smell, sound, colour, taste, and feel are not really properties of the outer object at all; they are nothing more than sensations in the mind. This second version is the one that Berkeley attacks in the *Principles* and *Dialogues*. He brought other arguments against Locke's view: that no power can exist in an unthinking thing (see *Principles* §25).

[18] See also my note to §103. Previous philosophy would have seen no difficulty in allowing other forms of causation. Aristotle, for instance, held that there were four sorts of cause: form, matter, efficient causes (the source of the change), and final causes (the purpose of the change);

respectful of contemporary science, not to be somewhat half-hearted in his mechanism. He recognized two awkward phenomena. The first is that of attraction. The moon influences the tides by attraction; this is action at a distance, which cannot be thought of as mechanical. The second is the phenomenon of cohesion. Something holds a lump of lead together as a lump, and not as just a heap of the particles that constitute it. But whatever the force that does this, it is hard to think of it as mechanical. Locke took the view that these two phenomena are and will remain incomprehensible to us.[19]

There is a special feature of Locke's mechanism which is important to the understanding of Berkeley's philosophy of science. Locke supposes that each material object has a set of observable or surface properties, and he asks himself how it comes about that there are groups of objects (all horses, for example) that broadly agree with each other in their surface properties. The answer he offers is that the surface properties flow from an inner structure which is common to all objects in the group. This inner structure is called the 'real essence'. So all horses share a single real essence. Now Locke supposes that these real essences are too small for us ever to be able to discover what they are like. But he says that if we could discover them, we would know without any experiment how objects with one real essence would affect objects with another. His model here is that of the lock and the key. If you know how the lock is set up, and you know the shape and composition of the key (it has got to be hard enough to get the lock to turn, of course), you are already in a position to know whether the key will open the lock or not. You do not *need* to try it to see. Equally, Locke says, if we knew the real essence of hemlock and that of man, we would know 'without trial' that hemlock would kill.[20] (Of course we do know this anyway, but only by trial, i.e. by experience.)

There are two things worth stressing in this story. The first is that, as

see his *Physics* 2. 3. He also held that the form of the house was part of the efficient cause of the house (as an idea in the builder's mind); so he would deny that efficient causes could be conceived of as purely mechanical. There is also the later doctrine of intentional forms, which understands perception as a material object's transmitting an idea or image of itself into the mind of a perceiver. Descartes argues against this doctrine in his *Optics* (*Philosophical Writings*, i. 153–4): 'when a blind man feels bodies, nothing has to issue from the bodies and pass along his stick to his hand [i.e. no *form* passes along the stick]; and the resistance or movement of the bodies, which is the sole cause of the sensations he has of them, is nothing like the ideas he forms of them. By this means, your mind will be delivered from all those little images flitting through the air, called "intentional forms", which so exercise the imagination of philosophers.'

[19] See *Essay* 2. 23. 23–5 , where Locke runs through possible mechanical explanations of cohesion, dismissing them all, and 2. 8. 11 (all non-mechanical causes, including attraction).

[20] Ibid. 4. 3. 25.

Locke sees it, there is a sort of necessity in nature. Natural processes, being mechanical, operate by a sort of inner necessity, one which is founded on relations between the real essences of the objects involved. Second, we truly understand a process when we come to see the necessity that is hidden in the course of events. The purpose of science, then, is to put us into a position where we do see the natural necessity that underlies all change.

This, then, is what the natural world is like. What of our place in it? The new philosophers held that there are two sorts of substance: material and spiritual. Each has its own pack of properties. Material substances have the primary qualities of shape, size, etc., but they do not think or feel. Spiritual substances have the properties of thinking, willing, and feeling, but they do not occupy space. So the two sorts of substance are totally different in every respect; no one thing could possibly have the properties of both. This position is known as Cartesian substance dualism, since Descartes was its most notable advocate.[21] Locke, by contrast, is not very enthusiastic about it, since he cannot think of any reason why God should not have allowed matter to think.[22] But he goes along with it.

These are the views that Berkeley is reacting to. He thinks them all false, and some of them are worse than false; they are meaningless. What Berkeley wants to do is somehow to retain most of the best science of his day, which he attributes to Newton, but to drop the claim that the things whose nature and behaviour that science describes are material things which exist independently of the mind. In advance, one would have thought that this was plainly impossible.

4. Berkeley's Metaphysical Picture

Berkeley's world consists only of minds and their ideas. There are two sorts of mind, created and uncreated; but there are many created ones and only one uncreated one, the mind that is God. Minds are capable of creating ideas for themselves, and of receiving ideas caused in them by other minds. Created minds cannot create new ideas for themselves from

---

[21] See his *Principles of Philosophy* I. 51–5 (*Philosophical Writings*, i. 210–11).

[22] 'We have the ideas of matter and thinking, but possibly shall never be able to know, whether any mere material being thinks, or no . . . It being, in respect of our notions, not much more remote from our comprehension to conceive that God can, if he pleases, superadd to matter a faculty of thinking, than that he should superadd to it another substance with a faculty of thinking' (*Essay* 4. 3. 6).

scratch, but they can create for themselves copies of ideas they have had before, and recombine such ideas in new ways. God alone is capable of creating new ideas from nothing.

Ideas exist in minds; an idea cannot exist otherwise than in a mind perceiving it. Just as there are two sorts of mind, so there are two sorts of idea: those that are received from elsewhere (which must be from another mind) are called *ideas of sense*, since we receive them via the use of our senses; those that a mind causes for itself are called ideas of the imagination. The Uncreated Mind has no ideas of sense since it is not causally affected by anything. All its ideas are ideas it has thought up for itself—products of its own powerful imagination.

All minds are 'active principles' or agents; they act and do things. Ideas are passive; no idea can do anything. Every change is the result of some agency, the effect of some active principle; all change, therefore, is caused by some mind. An idea of the imagination is caused by the mind that perceives that idea; an idea of sense is caused by another mind than the one that perceives it, since it is we that have these ideas but God that causes us to have them.

That is the nature of Berkeley's world. Its most distinctive feature is that it contains no material substance. As we said above, the new philosophers supposed there to be two sorts of substance: material ones which have qualities like shape and size, and spiritual ones which have ideas, think, feel, and will. Berkeley's world makes do with the latter alone. All our talk of *objects* or *things* and their *qualities* is to be reinterpreted in terms of minds and their ideas. Physical things are merely collections of ideas of sense—ideas that we receive from another mind rather than create for ourselves. They are not material things, existing with their primary qualities entirely independently of the mind.

It is worth pausing for a moment here to establish a terminology. Following Berkeley's lead, I will use the terms 'matter', material', 'material substance', and 'materialist' for the things that Berkeley is against. A material thing is something capable of existing entirely independently of the mind. In that sense, then, Berkeley thinks that physical objects such as tables and trees are not material objects; that matter is a philosophical fiction and does not exist; that there is no such thing as material substance; and that materialism is false. Materialism is here the belief that there are material objects. It is not the belief that there are only material objects (though we now use the term to mean something like that). The materialists whom Berkeley is trying to refute held that there are material objects and that there are non-material minds.

Since there is no material substance, there is no room for the distinction between primary and secondary qualities of material things. With the world consisting entirely of minds and their ideas, we cannot expect to explain some of the qualities of material things by appeal to others; there are no material things to have those qualities. All such so-called 'qualities' are really ideas belonging to and existing in minds, and all have equal status. So colour is as real as shape and size; there can be no contrast between colour as essentially related to the mind and shape as a real independent property of physical things. The primary–secondary distinction collapses.

Again, since there are no material things, there is no such thing as mechanical causation. Events that can be explained mechanically are changes brought about by the impulse of one collection of corpuscles on another. If there were any such events, something other than a mind would be capable of acting. But Berkeley holds that minds are the only active things there are (ideas being entirely inert and passive), and so mechanical causation is impossible.

Since there is no mechanical causation, God (the Uncreated Creator) is not to be conceived as a being who, having established the whole system, with laws to govern every change thereafter, somehow wound it up and set it going—for there is no mechanical system of this sort needing to have been set going. Instead, God supports the sensible world—the world of sense—as its daily and continuing cause.

In sum, Berkeley's world is totally different from the supposed material world, the physical universe that functions as a mechanical system with its own laws, operating on minds as they become aware of it, and changed by them as they act in it, but still essentially independent of them.

Does this mean that there are no real things in Berkeley's world? Berkeley vehemently denies this charge (§34). For him, real things are just collections of ideas of sense. These ideas, though they cannot exist independently of all minds, are independent of the particular mind that perceives them, and the independence they have is sufficient for us to pronounce them real. For they are real for the mind that perceives them.[23] Berkeley thus allows that there are real tables, chairs, and trees existing independently of, and so real for, the mind that perceives them. These physical things are real enough for ordinary mortals, and Berkeley does

---

[23] Is Berkeley's reality subjective rather than objective? As he understands reality, real things are subjective, since they consist of ideas, but not *merely* subjective, since they are independent of the mind that is aware of them, and so real for it. One might say that they are both subjective and objective at once.

not at all intend to undermine their claim to reality. His philosophical account of them, however, is that they are not collections of tiny corpuscles, but rather collections of ideas of sense, caused in the perceiving mind by some other mind. The name that Berkeley gives to this position is 'immaterialism'.

This is the main example of Berkeley's claim that his doctrines do not flout common sense; all that they do is to undermine bad philosophy and metaphysics. Ordinary people hold that the ground they are standing on is solid, and Berkeley agrees with them. But philosophers tell them that the ground is a collection of corpuscles with primary qualities, capable of existing independently of all minds whatever, and this is what Berkeley is in the business of denying.

5. What Happens in the *Principles*?

The structure of the *Principles* is not complicated. It falls into three main parts. The first part (§§1–33) lays out Berkeley's own position. The second (§§34–84) considers a series of objections, supposedly rebutting them all. The third (§§86–156) tries to persuade us of the great advantages of adopting Berkeley's views. The whole is preceded by an Introduction, which is largely concerned with mistakes in philosophy that are caused by mistakes about language.

Berkeley's main philosophical view, as we have seen, is in a way a negative one: though there are real things, real trees and fields, there is no such thing as material substance or matter. As a result, his arguments in the first part are all negative. They attempt to convince us either that there is no sense whatever in the notion of material substance, or that there is no reason to believe that there is any such thing. Suppose that these arguments are successful, and that things have gone as well for Berkeley as he hopes in this first section. Still, though we may be convinced that we cannot hold on to the notion of material substance, we are probably not yet convinced that we can do without it either. So Berkeley has yet to show that we can give up material substance without disaster. There are, however, various sorts of disaster. In the remainder of the *Principles* Berkeley considers three main threats. His views may be in breach of common sense; they may be in opposition to established scientific opinions and results; and they may be in opposition to religion. In each of these cases he argues that his philosophy leaves things either no worse, or else notably better, than they were before. In the second part, where he is considering objections, he is still fairly defensive. In the third part, where he is listing advantages, things are rather more positive.

As far as common sense goes, Berkeley's official position is that he has nothing to fear. He claims that the ordinary person will find nothing substantial to disagree with in immaterialism. The notion of material substance is an invention of philosophers, not part of the common-sense picture of the world. On the immaterialist account, the world we live in remains as real and as independent as common sense takes it to be. The worst that can be said is that immaterialism leads to some rather unusual expressions, such as that we are clothed with ideas, and eat and drink them (§38). Berkeley is here not quite as candid as one might like. He is trying to minimize the extent to which immaterialism is paradoxical or outrageous, and he does this by pretending rather unconvincingly that common sense is not at all wedded to the belief that physical things exist independently of the mind. Privately, as we know from his letters, he was well aware that there is something shocking about his views, and he looked for ways in which he could reduce the shock. These ways include an Introduction in which there is no mention of the more outrageous aspects of his philosophy at all.[24]

Where science is concerned, Berkeley tries to argue on two fronts. He attempts to show that contemporary science can perfectly well do without the notion of an independent material world consisting of tiny particles or corpuscles bundled together into the larger things that are more familiar to us (§§50, 60–6). We do not need to think of science as discovering the laws that govern the behaviour of a mechanical universe; we can see it instead as investigating the regular methods by which God makes ideas available to us. What were seen as the intricate internal workings of physical objects (including animals and plants) are not a kind of advanced clockwork. The world of ideas that God makes available to us includes ideas of the sort that we get when looking through a microscope as well as the ones provided by the senses unaided, and both are necessary if we are going to learn as much as possible about how to cope with the world we live in. But still, all that is going on here is that we are learning what ideas to expect next. We do not need to see ourselves as investigating a mechanical and independent reality. In these remarks Berkeley is a precursor of the instrumentalist conception of science, under which the business of science is not

---

[24] Berkeley wrote to his friend Percival, on 6 Sept. 1710, 'For this reason it was I omitted all mention of the non-existence of matter in the title-page, dedication, preface and introduction [of the *Principles*], that so the notion might steal unawares on the reader, who possibly would never have meddled with a book that he had known contained such paradoxes' (*Works*, viii. 36).

to discover inner workings, but merely to describe regularities in the phenomena in an explanatory way.

Thoughts such as these concern contemporary science in general. But towards the end of the *Principles* Berkeley discusses some more detailed matters. First, he tries to deal with the fact that Newton explicitly argued that there is such a thing as absolute space, time, and motion, existing independently of the mind (§110). According to Newton, as well as relative motion, which happens when one object moves relative to another, there is such a thing as absolute motion, which would happen, in the absence of relative motion, if the whole of creation were to be moving in absolute space. Berkeley suggests that this is an unnecessary mistake, and that Newtonian science can get along better without the notions of absolute space, time, and motion. In particular, it can get along better because it will enable us to avoid the mistaken view that finite space is infinitely divisible (§125). He also considers the nature of arithmetic, which he claims has become over-involved in high theory because of supposing there to be such things as numbers, abstract objects that are neither numerals such as 1, 2, 3, . . . , nor names such as 'one', 'two', 'three', . . . , nor yet the things we use those signs and names to number (e.g. the cars in London). Finally, he considers directly the idea that finite space is infinitely divisible, and argues first that this is false, and second that it is not required for the proof of any scientific theorem.

Religious considerations are never far from Berkeley's mind, though they are explicitly discussed in the *Principles* only in §§25–33, 82–4, and 134–56. Berkeley has to show that there is nothing in the Bible that is at odds with his views; this is dealt with very briefly in §§82–4. Indeed, Berkeley is fond of extracting quotations from the Bible that he can present as supporting his views rather than as undermining them. Beyond that, he has two main messages. The first is that the belief in matter is a leading cause of atheism, for it not only distracts people from recognizing the omnipresence of God, but causes them to think that God is more or less redundant to the operations of nature (§35, 66, 92–4). The second is that immaterialism provides a completely convincing and new proof of God's existence (§§25–33, 145–51). We know that the things we see (the ideas of sense) are not caused by our minds; there must therefore be some other cause, which must be a mind of incredible power, and this is certainly God.

As well as thoughts about common sense, science, and religion, there is a fourth area in which Berkeley recognizes that he might be thought vulnerable, but which is really one in which he triumphs. This is in the defeat of scepticism. Unsubtle thinkers might (and did) suppose that Berkeley's world is one in which we are restricted to knowledge of our ideas, with no possibility of discovering the real nature of external things. In fact, however, things are quite the other way around. Immaterialism puts us in a position in which we are directly aware of the real nature of the things around us, since they consist entirely of ideas, which are directly present to us. There is no gap between appearance and reality, since reality is appearance. Sceptical attacks on the possibility of human knowledge are therefore annihilated at the start.[25]

The title-page of the *Principles* reads:

A TREATISE concerning the PRINCIPLES of *Human Knowledge*. Part I. Wherein the chief Causes of Error and Difficulty in the *Sciences*, with the grounds of *Scepticism, Atheism,* and *Irreligion,* are inquired into.

These are indeed the matters that are discussed in the text, and on which Berkeley claims complete triumph.

The Introduction to the *Principles* is discussed in Sections 7–8 below, religion in Section 9, scepticism in Section 11, and science in Section 12.

6. The Arguments of *Principles* §§1–24

One can feel the excitement with which Berkeley wrote the beginning of the *Principles*. The book as a whole is that of a young man in the grip of a great idea which he is struggling to control, and at its outset he is trying to hold that idea in check, and to let it out into the light with the sort of explosion that he thinks and hopes it will cause. Sometimes his writing is so compressed that we wish he had given us more than the bare outlines that we have. But the great conclusion that he is driving us towards is exciting enough to give us an incentive to help him out—to clarify things where they need it, and to expand things where they need more elaboration than he gives them.

---

[25] There are two ways of annihilating sceptical attacks: by refuting the reasoning that leads to scepticism, or by proving scepticism false. Berkeley is not very careful about this distinction, but in fact he takes himself to have done both, as we can see in two passages in the *Dialogues*. For the first: 'Or can you produce so much as one argument against the reality of corporeal things, or in behalf of that avowed utter ignorance of their natures, which doth not suppose their reality to consist in an external absolute existence?' (p. 258). For the second: 'Wood, stones, fire, water, flesh, iron, and the like things, which I name and discourse of, are things that I know. And I should not have known them, but that I perceived them by my senses . . . Away then with all that scepticism' (p. 230).

By the time we reach §24, an enormous amount has been achieved. Berkeley has already established the central elements of his metaphysical scheme, and saved us from the errors of materialism. All that remains for him to do is to show how the scheme yields an argument for the existence of God (§§25–33).

The argumentation of §§1–24 is complex, however. After two introductory paragraphs, Berkeley produces in §§3–7 two arguments tending to the same conclusion, that 'there is not any other substance than *spirit*' (§7). There is a longer argument to this conclusion (§§3–6) and a shorter one (§7). The shorter one is easy to understand. Material substance is defined as 'an inert, senseless substance, in which extension, figure, and motion, do actually subsist' (§9). But the sensible qualities, including extension (i.e. size), figure (i.e. shape), and motion, are all merely ideas or sensations, and such things cannot exist in an unthinking substance; they can only exist in a mind or thinking substance. So there can be no such thing as material substance. All bearers of sensible qualities must be minds.

The first argument, with which in a way Berkeley seems much better pleased, is also much harder to understand fully. Berkeley claims that we have only to consider the issue, and we will immediately recognize that what it is for a sensible thing or quality to *exist* is for it to be perceived. Sounds, colours, shapes, and smells are sensible things, and Berkeley asserts without hesitation, 'There was an odour, that is, it was smelled; there was a sound, that is to say, it was heard; a colour or figure, and it was perceived by sight or touch' (§3). The same is true of the collections of sensible qualities that we more ordinarily call 'things', such as houses, mountains, and rivers. We want to say that such things can exist unperceived. But such things are all combinations of ideas, and clearly as such they cannot exist unperceived (§4).

In the next paragraph Berkeley offers a diagnosis of how we come to make this error—the error of thinking that sensible things can exist unperceived.[26] The explanation he offers is that we are misled by supposing that, though of course we never come across any sensible thing existing unperceived, we can still distinguish in our minds their existence from their presence to a mind. Having 'abstracted' existence from being perceived in this way, we suppose that sensible things can have the existence without the being perceived. But this is a mistake. It is in fact impossible to conceive of a sensible thing distinct from the perception of it.

In the final paragraph of the argument Berkeley hammers his point

---

[26] For further diagnosis, see §56.

home. He appeals once more to introspection: just try to separate in your own mind the existence of a sensible thing from its being perceived, and you will find that you fail.

So what are we to make of the arguments of §§3–7? There is a general difficulty in understanding the nature of Berkeley's appeal to the difficulties of abstraction, but this I leave until the next section for separate treatment. Beyond that, the broad thrust of the two arguments I have mentioned is that sensible things are manifestly incapable of existence outside the mind. The longer argument differs from the second, shorter one in concentrating on the question what it is for a sensible thing to *exist*. (The shorter one says, 'Well, whatever we mean by a sensible thing's existing, such things are ideas and so cannot do it outside a mind.') So—what is it for sensible things to exist? It is obviously crucial that this question concerns 'sensible things'. Sensible things are things of which we are capable of being aware, just as they are; the nature of a sensible thing is the way it is *for sense* (for the *senses*). And Berkeley thinks it inconceivable that, when you stand before a mountain and consider the way the mountain presents itself to your senses, *that thing* could exist other than as perceived. Concentrate on what is presented to you in sense, and ask yourself whether what is presented is capable of existing unpresented—and your answer will immediately be no. The sensible thing is incapable of existing outside a mind.[27]

The argument in §4 attempts to reinforce this point by appeal to something already established but not used in the argument of §3 as I have just expressed it, namely that sensible things are combinations of ideas. The thought seems to be roughly this: 'It is incoherent to hold that sensible things can exist unperceived—and if you don't see that, remember that they are ideas, and that it is a contradiction to say that an idea can exist unperceived.' Now if we are already persuaded that they are ideas or sensations, we will certainly agree that what it is for them to exist is for them to be perceived. But we will equally certainly want to know the reason for claiming that sensible things are ideas or sensations. This question is all the more pointed when we realize that for Berkeley 'sensible things' includes rivers, mountains, and trees. Has he just taken this point for granted?

Berkeley was careful to introduce the claim explicitly right at the beginning, in §1: 'collections of ideas constitute a stone, a tree, a book, and the like sensible things'. But we might still ask what gives him the right to

---

[27] Of course we want to say that there is more to the mountain than the way it presents itself to us; but Berkeley will reply that that more, whatever it is, is not a sensible thing. He is only talking about the sensible.

make the claim, which looks as if it is one that a materialist would deny. That question, however, affects the shorter argument (of §7) more than the longer one. The core of the longer argument is to be found in §3, and it does not appeal to the claim that sensible things are ideas or sensations at all. It is, as I have suggested, *reinforced* by the point made in §4, that since sensible things are ideas, they are plainly incapable of existence outside the mind. But this is only reinforcement of something that has been established independently. So if we are looking for Berkeley's basic move, we should concentrate on §3.

After the two arguments that there is only one substance, i.e. spirit, Berkeley spends §§8–15 demolishing what he knows will be the standard reply to what he has said so far. This is that, even if everything we immediately perceive is an idea, we can still come to know about things beyond our ideas—and these things, which are not ideas, will have an existence outside the mind. We get to know about these things because the ideas we perceive represent them to us. In sight, we perceive a visual idea, but the idea is an idea *of* a tree, which represents the tree to us. So in having the idea I am coming to know of the presence of the tree. My ideas or sensations inform me in this way about a world that does not consist of ideas or sensations; and even though the ideas can only exist in a spiritual substance, the world they inform me about is quite different. It is a world of material substances, with suitable properties.

Berkeley's first attack on this position is aimed at the notion of representation that it uses. He takes it that ideas can only represent 'things whereof they are copies or resemblances' (§8). For an idea to be an idea *of* a tree, the idea must resemble that tree. But the only things that an idea can resemble are other ideas. This claim is called Berkeley's 'Likeness Principle'. He offers us two reasons in its support. The first is that we cannot conceive a likeness without conceiving of the two things we suppose to be like each other—in which case the likeness will be between two ideas of ours. The second is different: 'I appeal to any one whether it be sense, to assert a colour is like something which is invisible; hard or soft, like something which is intangible; and so of the rest' (§8). This appeal should be taken carefully. The position Berkeley is attacking here is one that does not draw the distinction between primary and secondary qualities. That distinction surfaces in the next paragraph, and is dealt with there. The position he is attacking here holds that *all* our ideas that represent do so by resembling physical things in one way or another. An idea that represents something as brown, then, must be like a brown thing—it must itself be brown. So we have the brownness of the idea, and the brownness of the physical thing

23

that we see. What is that second brownness like? It must be either perceivable or unperceivable. If it is perceivable, it is an idea—in which case one idea here is resembling another, as the Likeness Principle holds, and we do not have ideas resembling things of quite another sort. If it is unperceivable, we get the ludicrous result that the colour we perceive resembles a quality that is intrinsically invisible. This is ludicrous because nothing like colour could be intrinsically invisible. Nor could the sort of hardness and softness we know—sensible hardness and softness—be anything like something intangible.

The expected reply to this is that our ideas can resemble physical things in respect of the primary qualities, even if not of the secondary qualities.[28] So a perceived redness cannot resemble redness-as-it-is-in-the-object, but a perceived roundness can resemble roundness-as-it-is-in-the-object. To put it another way, a round object is just the way we think of it and perceive it to be when we think of it or perceive it as being round; the same is not true for redness. This is an attempt to restrict the account of representation to the primary qualities. But it is a failure. Berkeley argues in §§9–10 that we cannot abstract the primary from the secondary in the way that this picture requires:

For my own part, I see evidently that it is not in my power to frame an idea of a body extended and moved, but I must withal give it some colour or other sensible quality which is acknowledged to exist only in the mind. In short, extension, figure, and motion, abstracted from all other qualities, are inconceivable. Where therefore the other sensible qualities are, there must these be also, to wit, in the mind and no where else.   (§10)

There then follows a series of rather unconnected remarks designed to show that Locke's primary qualities, extension, shape, and number, are all in some sense relative, and hence incapable of existence outside the mind (§§11–13). After that, Berkeley returns to the primary–secondary distinction. He has already argued that the primary qualities cannot be conceived as existing apart from the secondary ones, and so must be in the mind, where the secondary qualities are. Now he argues that the very arguments that prove that secondary qualities are sensations and exist only in the mind will show the same of the primary ones. This is important, because it is our first sight of a *direct* argument to the effect that certain sensible qualities are ideas or sensations in the mind—the point that seemed to be missing earlier on. But Berkeley immediately follows it with the acknowledgement that the arguments he is referring to do not really prove that

---

[28] See e.g. Locke's *Essay* 2. 8. 15–18.

sensible qualities exist only in the mind; they prove only that we do not know by sense which of the apparent colours of an object is the real colour. For the proof that colour cannot exist except in the mind, he throws us back to what is gone before.

There then follow two sections (§§16–17) in which Berkeley introduces some quite independent thoughts about the notion of material substance. A material substance is a thing with qualities. But what exactly is the relation between the 'thing' and the qualities? We speak happily of the thing 'having' the qualities; but when we ask ourselves what sort of 'having' this is, no obvious answer suggests itself. We can 'have' all sorts of things: illnesses, friends, pasts, memories, books, and so on. Which if any of these is like the relation between substance and properties (or, as Berkeley calls them here, 'accidents')? In Berkeley's day, philosophers spoke of a *substratum* or 'support' of qualities such as extension.[29] But he points out that there is no way of understanding the relation between the supposed support and the qualities it supports. What is this relation of 'supporting'? Nobody can say anything intelligible about it. Berkeley's own system, which makes do with spiritual substance and ideas, has no such trouble. The relation between minds and their ideas is perfectly comprehensible: the mind perceives ideas.

§§18–20 concern our ability to come to know anything about material substances, if they were to exist. Here Berkeley argues that we must either know the existence of material things by sense or by reason; i.e. we must either perceive them, or have some other reason to believe that they are there. Our senses tell us nothing about things existing outside the mind; so it must be reason. But there can be no reason to believe that there is such a thing as matter, since all agree that it is possible we might have all the ideas we now enjoy, even if matter did not exist. What is more, we cannot claim that, despite that possibility, it is easier to explain our ideas and sensations if we admit that matter exists, since nobody can think of any way in which material (or indeed physical) things could produce ideas in minds. So the production of ideas and sensations in minds is no easier to explain with matter than without it.

§21 mentions some incidental advantages of doing without material substance, and it is followed by three important sections, §§22–5, which attempt to sum up what has gone before, in a way that appears to add

[29] See e.g. Locke's *Essay* 2. 23. 2: 'So that if anyone will examine himself concerning his *notion of pure substance in general*, he will find he has no other *idea* of it at all, but only a supposition of he knows not what support of such qualities which are capable of producing simple ideas in us; which qualities are commonly called accidents.'

something new at the same time. Berkeley repeats the claim he made in his first argument, that all one has to do is to consider the question carefully, and one will immediately see that no sensible thing can exist unperceived. This, he says, is his central view. To refute him, all you have to do is to show that you can conceive 'it possible for one extended moveable substance, or in general, for any one idea or any thing like an idea, to exist otherwise than in a mind perceiving it', and he will allow that such things exist. His main point, then, is not that we don't understand the notion of substance or substratum, nor that we have no positive reason to believe that material substance exists. It is that the notion of a material substance existing independently of any relation to the mind is unintelligible.

Unfortunately Berkeley's critics have not been much impressed by the great argument designed to show the truth of immaterialism all at once, often called the 'Master Argument'. The argument is that to think of something existing unthought of, or to conceive it existing unconceived, is a 'manifest repugnance' or a 'contradiction'. But Berkeley does not make it very clear why one cannot do these things. He provides more details in the First Dialogue (p. 200), where Philonous represents Berkeley's position:

PHILONOUS. If you can conceive it possible for any mixture or combination of qualities, or any sensible object whatever, to exist without the mind, then I will grant it actually to be so.

HYLAS. If it comes to that, the point will soon be decided. What more easy than to conceive a tree or house existing by itself, independent of, and unperceived by any mind whatsoever? I do at this present time conceive them existing after that manner.

PHILONOUS. How say you, Hylas, can you see a thing which is at the same time unseen?

HYLAS. No, that were a contradiction.

PHILONOUS. Is it not as great a contradiction to talk of *conceiving* a thing which is *unconceived*?

HYLAS. It is.

PHILONOUS. The tree or house therefore which you think of, is conceived by you.

HYLAS. How should it be otherwise?

PHILONOUS. And what is conceived, is surely in the mind.

HYLAS. Without question, that which is conceived is in the mind.

PHILONOUS. How then came you to say, you conceived a house or tree existing independent and out of all minds whatsoever?

HYLAS. That was I own an oversight . . .

Berkeley is drawing an analogy between the attempt to conceive of something existing unconceived and the attempt to see something existing unseen. One cannot see something unseen, since one is seeing it oneself, and one cannot think of something unthought of, because one is thinking of it oneself.

If this is really Berkeley's point, it is a failure; the analogy is flawed. It is true that I cannot conceive of something while nobody is conceiving of it. But I can conceive of things *as* having properties that (as I am well aware) they have not got. I can conceive of a short person, for instance, as being tall. I do not, in doing this, make the contradictory supposition that he is both tall and short; I am not, ridiculously, trying to think of a short person as being tall as well. I conceive, of a person who is in fact short, that he is tall instead of short. (I might do this by saying, 'He would have hit his head on that door.') Similarly, we would say, I can conceive, of a tree that is in fact being conceived (by me), that it is not being conceived. The 'not being conceived' here is not a description of the thing that I am conceiving, but of *how* I am conceiving of it. So the fact that I cannot see something that is not being seen by anybody does nothing to show that I cannot conceive of something unconceived. I am not trying to conceive of something while nobody is conceiving of it. I am conceiving of it *as* existing unconceived, which is all that is required.

However, that may not be Berkeley's point. The passage in the First Dialogue may have misled us. His point may rather be that I cannot conceive of something that is now present to me as (capable of) existing unperceived or unconceived; see the sentence 'to make out this, it is necessary that you conceive [the objects of your thought] existing unconceived or unthought of, which is a manifest repugnancy' (*Principles* §23). But if this is his point, it is little more than a recapitulation of the first, longer argument of §§3–6. For 'the objects of your thought' refers to things like trees in a park or books in a closet. This would mean that the 'Master Argument' adds nothing substantial to what has gone before, and throws us back once again to §3.

So this is the general structure of §§1–24:

Ideas and minds. §§1–2
First argument against material substance: for sensible things, to exist is to be perceived. §§3–6
Second argument against material substance: sensible things are ideas, which can only exist in a mind. §7
The Likeness Principle; we cannot have an idea of something that is not

an idea. Attempts to use the primary–secondary distinction to get round this fail. Only an illegitimate abstraction could persuade us that primary qualities could exist either singly or together in the absence of secondary ones. §§8–15

The concept of a material *substance* or *substratum* is unintelligible. §§16–17

There is no reason to believe in the existence of material substance (not even an argument to the best explanation). §§18–20

A posteriori[30] arguments against material substance. §21

Summary of the above. Berkeley's Master Argument. §§22–4

One final question: Berkeley speaks often in his notebooks, the *Philosophical Commentaries (PC)*, of a 'New Principle' that he has discovered, and that lies at the centre of his attack on material substance. The argumentation of §§1–24 is complex; if we knew what the New Principle was, it would help us to put things into some kind of shape. Sadly, Berkeley is not as helpful as he might be. He writes at one point of 'the Principle, i.e. that neither our ideas nor anything like our ideas can possibly be in an unperceiving thing (*PC* §379: *Works*, i, p. 46). This is a mixture of the argument of §7 and the Likeness Principle of §8. Elsewhere he writes ''tis on the Discovering of the nature & meaning & import of Existence that I chiefly insist. This puts a wide difference betwixt the Sceptics and me. This I think wholly new. I am sure 'tis new to me' (*PC* §491). I think this tells us that the leading thought in Berkeley's attack on materialism was, not surprisingly, the one he put first, namely the argument about what it is for a sensible thing to exist, in §3. But, equally, this is the argument that is the hardest to understand.

7. Berkeley's Attack on the Doctrine of Abstract Ideas

Perhaps the greatest mystery of the *Principles* is the relation between the Introduction and the main text. The broad outlines of what is supposed to be going on are clear enough. Berkeley argues in the Introduction that abstraction of a certain sort (or of certain sorts) is impossible. And he links this to a more general theme about the relation between language or words and thought. In the *Principles*, he appeals to the impossibility of abstraction at several crucial places. The more general theme does not

---

[30] For Berkeley, an 'a posteriori' argument against a doctrine is an argument that it has unfortunate consequences; see the note to §21.

appear so explicitly except in the discussion of arithmetic and the infinite divisibility of space (§§131–4). All this is clear enough. But once one tries to tell this story in greater detail, things become murkier.

In the Introduction Berkeley starts by distinguishing between two distinct sorts or uses of abstraction. The first, which we might call singular abstraction, is like this (Intro. §7):

> But we are told, the mind being able to consider each quality singly, or abstracted from those other qualities with which it is united, does by that means frame to it self abstract ideas. For example, there is perceived by sight an object extended, coloured, and moved: this mixed or compound idea the mind resolving into its simple, constituent parts, and viewing each by it self, exclusive of the rest, does frame the abstract ideas of extension, colour, and motion. Not that it is possible for colour or motion to exist without extension: but only that the mind can frame to it self by *abstraction* the idea of colour exclusive of extension, and of motion exclusive of both colour and extension.

I call this singular abstraction because the suggestion is that we frame the idea of a single quality and consider it all by itself, even though it is quite incapable of occurring alone but must always be joined with others. The quality concerned is still the quality of a particular thing—the size of this object, for instance. But Berkeley goes on in the next section to say that, having framed the abstract ideas of the size of this thing, the size of that, and so on, we are supposed to be able to construct by abstraction from these the doubly abstract idea of size in general—what he calls a 'most abstract idea'. We do this by leaving out what is different between one size and another, and retaining only what is common to each. These are the sorts of idea that he will be concerned with in the *Principles*.

The second sort (or use) of abstraction, which we can call compound abstraction, does not involve concentration on a single quality in the same way as the first does, but it does involve abstracting what is different and being left only with what is common. Abstraction of this sort is required if we are to understand general terms such as 'book', 'chair', 'horse', and 'man'. Locke, who was Berkeley's explicit target on this point, held that for each such term there is a general idea, created by abstraction. Abstraction of either sort is subtraction; in creating the abstract general idea of man, what we do is to start from the particular ideas we have of individual men—of Peter, James, and John—and form an idea of the respects in which they are similar to each other by leaving out of the ideas of each any feature that is not common to all. If we carry on this process long enough, we will achieve an idea of those features that are common to all men, and this will be the abstract general idea of man. It will be a bit strange, since all men have some colour and height, though there is no colour or height that all men have. So the abstract general idea of man is of something that is coloured but has no particular colour, has some height or other but no particular height, and so on.

But Berkeley says that abstracting of this sort is just impossible (Intro. §10):

I deny that I can abstract one from another, or conceive separately, those qualities which it is impossible should exist so separated; or that I can frame a general notion by abstracting from particulars in the manner aforesaid. Which two last are the proper acceptations of *abstraction*.

The reason for saying this comes just before:

whatever hand or eye I imagine, it must have some particular shape and colour. Likewise the idea of man that I frame to my self, must be either of a white, or a black, or a tawny, a straight, or a crooked, a tall, or a low, or a middle-sized man. I cannot by any effort of thought conceive the abstract idea above described. And it is equally impossible for me to form the abstract idea of motion distinct from the body moving, and which is neither swift nor slow, curvilinear nor rectilinear; and the like may be said of all other abstract general ideas whatsoever.

This is not much to go on. What is Berkeley really objecting to? There are basically two different stages in singular abstraction, both of which are at issue in the creation of the 'most abstract idea' of motion, and both of which he rejects. The first is the creation of an idea of motion 'distinct from the body moving', i.e. of motion distinct from extension and figure. The second is the creation of an idea of motion that is neither swift nor slow (since some motion is swift and some slow). This second stage is involved over and over again in compound abstraction; we use the abstract idea of colour that is neither red nor blue etc., that of height that is neither tall nor short, and so on, in constructing the idea of man. In Berkeley's view, both stages are impossible.

He offers us two thoughts to persuade us of his position. The first involves an attempt to describe the supposed abstract idea of motion in such a way as to deprive it of content. It must be abstracted 'not only from the body moved, but likewise from the figure it describes, and all particular directions and velocities' (Intro. §8), 'neither walking, nor flying, nor creeping' (Intro. §9), 'neither swift nor slow, curvilinear nor rectilinear' (Intro. §10). Do you really think, he asks, that you have an idea of motion left when all these determinant features have been abstracted? And this appeal is supported by the claim that one cannot abstract from each other 'or conceive separately, those qualities which it is impossible should exist so separated'. So if we ask why we cannot form the abstract idea of motion as described, Berkeley tells us that it is because there can be no such thing as motion, as conceived in that idea. And for similar reasons, there can be no such idea as the abstract idea of colour, and so there can be no such thing as the abstract idea of man.

Why is Berkeley so insistent that we cannot conceive apart properties that cannot exist apart? The most probable answer is that he saw no difference between the question what is possible and the question what is conceivable.[31] So if I hold that I can conceive *A* existing apart from *B*, but that *A* cannot exist apart from *B*, I am effectively contradicting myself.[32] Berkeley could reinforce his view with the thought that, in whatever way I am capable of conceiving things, God is certainly capable of creating them. It follows that if someone does make this contradictory claim, he must be wrong, either about the impossibility of what he conceives, or about his ability so to conceive it. And Berkeley says that there is a ready explanation for his being wrong about the latter, which is that he has confused the ability to think of *A* without thinking of *B* with the ability to form a conception of *A* which is not at the same time a conception of *B*. (See the next section.)

Let us leave on one side for the moment the question whether Berkeley is right about this, and pursue the debate in the way that he pursues it. Why did anyone think that there were such abstract ideas? Locke thought that without these ideas there would be two things that we could not explain. The first of these is the way in which we understand and use general terms. The difficulty arises in the following way. All meaningful terms (at least all of a certain sort) stand for ideas. If I understand a term, I know the relevant idea. Names like 'Julius Caesar' and 'London' stand for the ideas of Caesar and of London respectively. What ideas do general terms like 'man' and 'city' stand for? It cannot be the ideas of any particular men or cities—those of Caesar and of London, for instance. For that would mean that the term 'man' would have the same meaning as the term 'Julius Caesar', since they both stand for the same idea; the term 'city' would have the the same meaning as the term 'London', which cannot be right. So we need some new ideas for the job. Locke and others thought

---

[31] See here, and in general on abstraction and abstract ideas in Berkeley, Winkler *Berkeley: An Interpretation*, ch. 2.

[32] Locke does seem to claim to conceive apart things that cannot exist apart, in a passage quoted by Berkeley in Intro. §13: 'For example, does it not require some pains and skill to form the general idea of a triangle . . . for it must be neither oblique not rectangle, neither equilateral, equicrural, not scalenon, but *all and none* of these at once. In effect, it is something imperfect that cannot exist . . .'.

that we could create these new ideas by abstracting from the old ones—by carving bits off the ideas of London, Paris, New York, etc. so to leave an idea only of what is common to all cities.

There is a second reason for supposing that general ideas must be abstract. This concerns communication. Suppose that there were only particular ideas of this or that city. Each of us, according to our experience, would have different ones. So when I say, 'There is a green hill far away, without a city wall', the idea of a city in my mind may well not be the idea raised in yours when you hear me. But this seems to undermine the possibility of communication. For me to succeed in communicating with you, I must call up in your mind ideas like those in mine. And whether I can do this will be very dubious, in most cases, if the ideas involved are ideas of particular cities; it will depend on whether we happen to think of the same city. If, however, there is an abstract general idea of a city, there is a good chance that this will be common to all those with reasonable experience of cities; and this restores the possibility that the idea I express in speaking about cities will be the one raised in your mind by what I say. Communication becomes possible again.

So there are two reasons for thinking that general ideas need to be formed by abstraction. Berkeley thinks that both of them are mistaken. He holds that a perfectly non-abstract idea, the idea of a particular man, can stand for all men whatever; and he also, more contentiously, holds that thought does not require the constant occurrence of ideas in the thinker's mind, and that therefore communication does not require the speaker to raise a matching idea in the hearer's mind (Intro. §§19–20).

On the first of these, he argues first that we can draw a line in a geometric proof, and use that line to stand for all lines whatever. Let us agree for the moment that the person giving the proof must have some idea of a line in his mind. But that idea need not be a special one formed by abstraction; it can perfectly well be the ordinary idea of this line on the paper before us. Just as this *line* can stand for all lines whatever in my proof, so the *idea of this line* can stand for all lines whatever in my mind. All that is necessary for this to happen is that I consider only the features of this line that do not distinguish it from others. I can do this in my mind, and I can do it in my proof. I do not need to create a new idea by abstraction. Selective attention to a non-abstract idea will do the trick.

Even to say this is to admit something that Berkeley wants to question, namely that every time we use a meaningful term the (or a) relevant idea must occur in our mind. He thinks that the claim that all use of language is accompanied by a corresponding pattern of ideas in the minds of speaker and hearer is just false. It doesn't happen, and it needn't happen (Intro. §19). Berkeley points out something often forgotten, that communication of ideas is not the 'chief and only end' of speech. 'There are other ends, as the raising of some passion, the exciting to, or deterring from an action', etc. (Intro. §20), and we don't pursue these ends by attempting to raise in our hearers ideas just like ours. Since that is not necessary for these purposes, why suppose that it is necessary for communication?

But at this point we want to ask what account Berkeley does give of the relation between language and thought. What is it to hear and understand the sentence 'London is a city', if it is not for the relevant ideas to occur in one's mind? Locke's account of the matter would be that the idea of London should occur in one's mind, somehow linked to the quite different idea of a city. One may be suspicious of this constant mental accompaniment of significant speech, but what does Berkeley have to put in its place?

Let us return to the first point, that general thought does not require abstract general ideas. Commentators have found two things to criticize about this claim. The first is to say that Berkeley's own theory (now called the theory of selective attention) is no different from the theory that Locke held.[33] Locke's texts are not perfectly clear on the point, however, and my own view is that Berkeley is justified in his reading of Locke. The second and better criticism is that Berkeley begs the question in saying, as he effectively does, that I make an idea of a particular line general by using it to stand for all things of the same sort. What determines exactly *which* things this idea stands for? Locke had an answer to this question. He could say that the abstracted general idea of a line stood for all objects that it *fully* resembled. Berkeley cannot say this, because for him the idea of the line before him fully resembles only that individual line. But if we say that the idea of the line can stand for objects that it does not 'fully resemble', it is in danger of resembling, and so standing for, far too many wrong things—it resembles the smear on the other side of the paper, for instance, since they

---

[33] See J. L. Mackie, *Problems from Locke* (Oxford: Oxford University Press, 1976), ch. 1, and Winkler, *Berkeley: An Interpretation*, ch. 2. 2. I have represented Locke as claiming that the abstract idea of man is a *new* idea, created for the purpose by abstraction from old ones. See e.g. *Essay* 3. 3. 6: 'and *ideas* become general by separating from them the circumstances of time and place and any other *ideas* that may determine them to this or that particular existence. By this way of abstraction they are made capable of representing more individuals than one: each of which, having in it a conformity to that abstract *idea*, is (as we call it) of that sort.' Mackie suggests that the abstract idea is just an idea of one or more particular men, considered in a certain light. See ibid. 3. 3. 7: 'Wherein they make nothing new, but only leave out of the complex *idea* they had of *Peter* and *James*, *Mary* and *Jane* that which is peculiar to each, and retain only what is common to them all.' If Mackie is right, Berkeley's view is closer to Locke's than he supposes.

both share the quality of 'being on this piece of paper'. So which of the things that the idea of the particular line resembles does it stand for? To ask the same question in another way, which objects is the geometric proof a proof about?

In the case of the proof, there may be an answer to this question. Berkeley said that the line used in the proof stands for everything that resembles that line in the respects mentioned in the proof. But even if this serves to tell us what the idea of that line stands for, it fails to tell us how general terms function in other contexts, where there is nothing like proof going on. If I say 'Men are wonderful', I should have in my mind the determinate idea of some man. Suppose it happens to be my next-door neighbour. What I say is not said about him especially, of course. Even though I am using my idea of him, I am not using it to stand for him in particular. Can we say that I am using it to refer to all things 'of the same sort' as him? Not without begging the question, since he is of many sorts.

So Berkeley's rejection of the reasons for needing abstract general ideas involves him in problems. But he closes the Introduction by extracting a general message from the preceding discussion. He suggests that people have been drawn into accepting the need for abstract ideas by making mistakes about language. The sort of mistake he has in mind is that of supposing that every significant word, having its own meaning, must have its own idea. Instead, he suggests, 'there is no such thing as one precise and definite signification annexed to any general name, they all signifying indifferently a great number of particular ideas' (Intro. §18). Philosophers have been misled by language. Berkeley recommends, therefore, both to himself and to others, that so far as possible they do their thinking without language: 'whatever ideas I consider, I shall endeavour to take them bare and naked into my view, keeping out of my thoughts, so far as I am able, those names which long and constant use hath so strictly united with them' (Intro. §21). Whether this is either possible or desirable is extremely dubious; nor is it obvious that what happens in the *Principles* is much affected by it.

8. Abstract Ideas in the *Principles*

I now return to consider Berkeley's attempt to show that abstract ideas are impossible. The crucial sentence is 'I deny that I can abstract one from another, or conceive separately, those qualities which it is impossible should exist so separated' (Intro. §10). What exactly is being denied here?

Let us take one of the examples that Berkeley uses, that of motion, and consider four things that might be meant by the claim that he denies—the claim that one can form the abstract idea of motion distinct from the body moving:

(1) I can consider the motion of an object without considering its shape and size.

(2) I can conceive of an object as moving without conceiving of it as having a shape or size.

(3) I can conceive of an object as moving but lacking a shape or size.

(4) I can conceive of there being motion but no body moving.

Lurking in the background is a fifth claim, which, as I suggested earlier, Berkeley did not really distinguish from the fourth:

(5) There could be motion but no body moving.

Berkeley wants to deny all of these except the first. The first is just selective attention. He writes (in a passage added in the second edition), 'a man may consider a figure merely as triangular, without attending to the particular qualities of the angles, or relations of the sides' (Intro. §16). This does nothing to show that one can form the abstract idea of a triangular figure with angles of no particular size. So the first is true, but all the others are false. If (5) were true, (4) would be, and so would (3) and (2).

The same is true for colour. Berkeley would say that one can attend to the fact that an object is coloured without attending to its particular colour, but that this does not show that one can conceive of an object as coloured without conceiving of it as red or as blue or whatever. There is a notable passage in *Principles* §10 where he argues that we cannot abstract extension and the other primary qualities from colour and the other secondary ones: 'it is not in my power to frame an idea of a body extended and moved, but I must withal give it some colour or other sensible quality'. By analogy, in the case of colour he would presumably say, 'I cannot frame an idea of a coloured body, but I must withal make it a red one or a blue one or a body of some other particular colour.' So the crucial gap in all these cases is that between (1) and (2) above.

One might reasonably wonder whether there really is an enormous difference between (1) and (2). To persuade oneself that the difference is real, consider the distinction between examining a photograph, concentrating on one feature—say, the indistinct figure in the background—and cutting that figure out and looking at it alone. In the first case, we are engaged in selective attention—as we are when, in a crowded room, we are able to focus on the conversation of the person we are talking to, picking out her words from the surrounding hubbub. Berkeley would say that the second case is more like (2), and that we cannot do to complex ideas what we can do to photographs.

Let us suppose that Berkeley is right: we can selectively attend to features which we cannot 'conceive separately'. What is the relevance of this claim to what happens in the *Principles*? Berkeley appeals to the impossibility of abstraction in the *Principles* in arguing against the following claims:

> The existence of sensible things is one thing, their being perceived another. §3
> The existence of a mind is one thing, and its perceiving another. §98
> One can conceive of the primary qualities abstracted from all others. §10
> One can conceive of extension, motion, number, and unity existing without the mind. §§11–13
> One can conceive of time as 'duration in abstract'. §97
> One can conceive of justice and virtue abstracted from all particular persons and actions. §100
> One can conceive of pure space, exclusive of all body. §116
> Extension is infinitely divisible. §125
> One can conceive of the powers or acts of the mind prescinded from mind itself and from their objects and effects. §143

What baffles commentators here is how Berkeley can suppose that what he has to say about abstraction will show all these claims to be false. Nobody can bring to light the required connection between the impossibility of abstraction and the non-existence of matter, to take the most glaring example. It seems probable, however, that Berkeley is not trying to use his doctrines about abstraction to show all these claims false, which would explain why he shows no signs of achieving this. In my view his appeals to abstraction have a rather different purpose. I suggest that in each of the cases above he appeals to what he has established about abstraction to explain why people have adopted these mistaken views, not to show that those views are mistaken.[34] He argues, in each case, that two things cannot exist separately, but that we have mistakenly come to suppose that they can because we mistakenly take ourselves to have performed an abstraction that is in fact illegitimate and hence impossible. We have supposed that because we can think about size without thinking

[34] Here I abandon some views about abstraction expressed in my *Berkeley: An Introduction*, ch. 3.

about shape, we can conceive of something as having a certain size without conceiving of it as having some shape, and so on. But we are mistaken, because nothing could be like that.

To confirm this, we should notice a change that Berkeley made in the second edition of the *Principles*. I am suggesting that in each case, one can think about *A* without thinking about *B*, but one cannot conceive of *A* without conceiving of *B*. To put it another way: I can focus my attention on this or that aspect of my conception, and away from other aspects; but those others will still remain part of my conception—of how I am conceiving of things—even though I am not focusing my attention on them (i.e. thinking about them). It is because this is what he wants to say, I suggest, that Berkeley removed the original final sentence of §5: 'In truth, the object and the sensation are one thing, and cannot therefore be abstracted from each other.' He removed this sentence because it goes just too far; it makes it appear that one cannot even think about one without thinking about the other. I can think about a sensible thing, e.g. a mountain, without thinking about its relation to a mind. But this does nothing to show that I can conceive of a mountain existing unconceived.

If this were right, Berkeley would have to produce special arguments in each case to show that the relevant *A* cannot exist without the relevant *B* (i.e. to show the falsehood of the relevant version of (5)) and so on backwards to the falsehood of the relevant version of (2). For his appeals to the impossibility of abstraction will do nothing to show that the *A* and the *B* cannot exist separately; at best, they will only show why we mistakenly thought otherwise. I leave it to the reader, however, to determine where and whether Berkeley actually provides us with the further arguments that are needed.

9. The Existence of God

In my account of Berkeley's metaphysical system, I announced that for him there are created minds, and one uncreated one. Later we will see how it is that we come to have a conception of a mind—first of ourselves and then of others. For the moment we leave that problem aside, and ask merely how we know that any mind other than ourself exists. Berkeley's general answer to this question is that we know other minds 'by their operations, or the ideas by them excited in us' (§145). Now Berkeley is not very interested in other created minds, but he is very interested indeed, as a committed Christian, in the one Uncreated Mind.

Berkeley felt that the materialist conception of the world kept God at far too great a distance from us. It leads us to think of God as hidden behind the world he has created rather than as revealed in it; he is at best the product of an inference. For Berkeley, this was not the way in which the Holy Scriptures (the Bible, that is) thought of things at all. He wanted a God who is close to us at every moment of the day, in everything we do. And his system provides exactly that. God is present to us in every waking moment, since every experience we have is an idea caused in us by him. So the God whose existence he sets out to prove is 'a being whose spirituality, omnipresence, providence, omniscience, infinite power and goodness, are as conspicuous as the existence of sensible things' (*Dialogues* p. 257). His favourite quotation from the Bible speaks of a God 'in whom we live, and move, and have our being' (Acts 17: 28).

The argument that establishes the existence of such a God is a causal one. All ideas need both a perceiver and a cause. Ideas of the imagination are perceived by the mind which causes them. But ideas of sense are not caused by the minds that perceive them, as we know perfectly well. 'But whatever power I may have over my own thoughts, I find the ideas actually perceived by sense have not a like dependence on my will' (§29). They must therefore be caused by some other mind, since only minds can be causes. What must that other mind be like? By its works we shall know it, and those works are the infinite detail and richness of the natural world. A mind that can create such ideas must be of infinite power, and the regularity with which the world operates, which is so vital to human ability to predict the future and so prepare for it, is evidence of the infinite goodness of its Creator. For the world could have been created random and unpredictable.

In these ways Berkeley puts together a proof of the existence of the Christian God, a causal proof that starts from the observed nature of the world we live in and argues to the existence of God as cause. Berkeley's proof is not the only proof of this sort. Indeed, proofs of God come in groups or families. An example of what is called a 'cosmological' argument for God can be found in Newton: 'it is not to be conceived that mere mechanical causes could give birth to so many regular motions [as those of the moons and planets] . . . This most beautiful system . . . could only proceed from the counsel and dominion of an intelligent and powerful Being.'[35] 'Arguments from design' make a different appeal to the intricacy,

---

[35] General Scholium added to book 3 of Newton's *Principia*; see *Newton's Philosophy of Nature*, 42. Richard Bentley's Boyle sermons of 1692 also contained an elaborate cosmological argument, based on Newtonian premises. The difference between Newton's cosmological argument and an argument from design is that the former says, 'We could not

detail, and orderliness of the natural world; they claim that just as a watch bears evidence of a creating intelligence, so (but to a far greater extent) the world bears evidence of its Creator. Berkeley's proof is different from these, even though he does make his own appeal to the intricacy of the created world. For Berkeley, we know already that there is a mind capable of creating ideas in us, because we are not the cause of the ideas of sense; we cannot determine what we are to see and feel. The intricacy and complexity of these ideas of sense come in when we try to discover the nature of that Creator, which we do by considering the nature of what he created. The difference, then, between Berkeley's proof and the others is that for the latter, the complex nature of the world is evidence for the *existence* of a creating intelligence, whereas for Berkeley it is evidence for the *nature* of that intelligence, whose existence has already been established. For them, if the world had been very different, there would have been no argument to God at all; Berkeley's proof, by contrast, starts from the mere fact that there is a world.

There is one weakness in Berkeley's proof, which to some extent it shares with the others. This is that, even if we agree that ideas of sense need a cause and that only minds can be causes, we surely want to know what it is that tells us that one and the same mind is the cause of all the ideas of sense. Might there not be several very powerful minds, all at work at once? If this is possible, Berkeley's argument is not yet an argument for the unique Christian God; it would be compatible with various forms of polytheism. He never considers this difficulty, but presumably he would try to argue that the nature of the created world (i.e. of the ideas of sense) bears the marks of a single creator rather than those of a committee. (See the way he appeals to the harmony of the created world in §63.)

Perhaps the crucial features of God as he emerges in Berkeley's philosophy are his omnipresence and the ease with which we can discover him. The argument to his existence is not complex or subtle, but simple and direct; and he is present to us in everything we see. It is not just that God lies behind what we see; he manifests himself to us in the world. This point begins to emerge in §§60–6, especially §65, where Berkeley introduces his doctrine that one natural event is not so much the cause of another as the sign that it will happen next. What sort of sign are we talking about here? Berkeley often expresses his point by saying that natural events are the

have got from chaos to an ordered world like this if there had been no creating intelligence', while the latter says, 'We see signs of design in the world, as in a watch, and design requires a designer.'

language in which God speaks to us, forewarning us of what is to come.[36] This enables him to put a special slant on his argument for the existence of God. We know of God's existence as certainly as we know of the existence of someone who is speaking to us now (§147; the point is more explicit in *Alciphron*).

So much, then, for the argument as we have it in the *Principles*. But there is an interesting development of it in the *Dialogues*, where what was a purely causal argument becomes something more interesting. Berkeley writes in the Second Dialogue (p. 212):

seeing [sensible things] depend not on my thought, and have an existence distinct from being perceived by me, *there must be some other mind wherein they exist.* As sure therefore as the sensible world really exists, so sure is there an infinite omnipresent spirit who contains and supports it.

This takes us beyond anything there was in the *Principles*. It is not just that my ideas of sense must be caused by another mind, though they exist in mine. Since they are independent of my will, their existence is distinct from mine. But, being ideas, they must depend on some mind for their existence, and the mind they depend on in this way must be one in which they exist. So the *Dialogues* version of the argument concludes not only that my ideas of sense are not caused by me, but also that they must exist in the mind that caused them.

However, the next time Berkeley expresses the argument it comes out slightly differently (pp. 214–15):

It is evident that the things I perceive are my own ideas, and that no idea can exist unless it be in a mind. Nor is it less plain that these ideas or things by me perceived, either themselves or their archetypes, exist independently of my mind, since I know myself not to be their author . . . They must therefore exist in some other mind, whose will it is they should be exhibited to me.

The difference lies in the phrase 'either themselves or their archetypes'. An archetype is an original, and what Berkeley is referring to by the use of this phrase is that my ideas of sense might not be identical with ideas in God's mind, but merely copies. It is clear that in the text of the *Dialogues* he was trying not to come down on either side of this debate.[37] But it might seem that in the passage from p. 212 quoted above he fails, as in the final passage in which this argument occurs, which also has something of its own to add (pp. 230–1):

---

[36] See *New Theory of Vision* §§143, 147, *Principles* §43 and 108–9, *Theory of Vision Vindicated* §40, and *Alciphron* 4. 7 and 4. 12.

[37] For another occurrence of the phrase 'they or their archetypes', see *Dialogues* p. 240.

it is plain they have an existence exterior to my mind, since I find them by experience to be independent of it. There is therefore some other mind wherein they exist, during the intervals between the times of my perceiving them: as likewise they did before my birth, and would do after my supposed annihilation. And as the same is true, with regard to all other finite created spirits; it necessarily follows, there is an *omnipresent eternal Mind* . . .

The addition this time is the thought about continuity. Berkeley is not arguing here that what we see necessarily continues to exist when we are not looking, for he was of course aware that some things are destroyed, e.g. when we eat them. His point is that if I see the same thing again after a gap, what I see has continued to exist all the while, in the mind that causes it to occur as an idea in me. The availability of this sort of continuity is just a side-effect of the *Dialogues* claim (if that is what is really being said) that ideas of sense exist in the mind that causes them.[38] So it looks as if, despite his attempt to sit on the fence, Berkeley has committed himself here to the claim that in perception we share ideas with God. This means that the development of his argument for God in the *Dialogues* increases the sense in which, in perception, we are in direct contact with God.

10. Physical Reality

There are real things for Berkeley, then, and these things are collections of ideas of sense. As such they are incapable of existing out of all minds whatever. There is no such thing as 'the world as it is in itself'—the world as it exists out of all relation to minds. Of course, we might say, there are many objects which for most of the time are not present to any created mind. But this need not mean that they cease to exist. God, as a permanent, all-aware mind, underpins their existence.

This last thought, however, concerns the question whether it is true that real things cease to exist when no created mind is aware of them. And there is a prior question to that, which we need to address first. This is, what is it for a physical thing to exist? In early paragraphs of the *Principles*, Berkeley's official view seems to be the one that we would expect, given his doctrine that all sensible things and qualities are ideas or collections of ideas. This is that for such things to exist is for them to be present to some

---

[38] If this is right, the causal argument in the *Principles* leads naturally to thoughts about distinctness and independence, and so to thoughts about continuity. Thoughts about continuity, then, are not a separate and slightly disreputable addition, as suggested by Jonathan Bennett in his *Locke, Berkeley, Hume: Central Themes* (Oxford: Oxford University Press, 1971), ch. 7.

mind.[39] The link between reality and awareness is here very tight. But Berkeley slips on frequent occasions from this view to one which allows a looser link between physical existence and minds. This looser view would have it that for a physical thing to exist is for it to be *able* to be present to some mind, not for it actually to be doing so.[40] Both conceptions of physical existence require a relation to a mind; so both involve a rejection of realism, which conceives the existence of a physical thing in terms of its taking its place in the mind-independent spatio-temporal matrix which constitutes the natural world.

The looser view is called phenomenalism, the tighter one idealism. And it seems that Berkeley really needs to make up his mind between them. The question how we are to conceive of physical existence is too pressing to shirk.

We might be tempted to appeal to God to get us out of this difficulty. The thought would be that since God eternally perceives every possible idea, no idea is merely perceptible, but all are actually perceived. But though this is true, it does not prevent us from having to choose between phenomenalism and idealism. To think otherwise is to have failed to observe a relevant distinction. To see this, consider the notion of continuity. What is it for a physical thing to exist continuously? Suppose that we have an answer to this question, which tells us what continuity is. We then face the question whether anything does in fact exist continuously. In our answer to *this* question we might appeal to the existence of God; it is only because God exists that anything does have continuous existence, for God's is the only truly continuous awareness. But this would not mean that we have appealed to God in our account of continuous existence itself. The appeal to God only came in at the second stage.

The same is true for the concept of physical existence. We have to face up to the question how to conceive of physical existence. (This is after all the question that Berkeley raises so forcefully in §3.) Suppose we decide that existence for a physical thing (idea of sense) requires actual awareness in some mind. We then ask whether anything exists when created minds are not aware of it. To *this* question our answer might be that they do, but

---

[39] For expressions of this view, see §§1, 3, and 6. The slogan '*esse* is *percipi*' means 'to be is to be perceived'.

[40] The classic example here is §3: 'meaning thereby that if I was in my study I might perceive it, or that some other spirit actually does perceive it'. See also §58 and *Dialogues* p. 252, where Berkeley says that physical things begin to exist when they become perceptible to created beings.

only because there is an uncreated mind aware of it all the time. (See §§6 and 48.) This answer, which looks very like Berkeley's official answer, takes things in the right order. It determines the requirements for existence first, and then asks whether and under what conditions they are satisfied. The appeal to God comes in only at the second stage.

So—does physical existence require actual or only potential awareness? The interesting thing is that Berkeley seems so completely unimpressed by this question. It seems very much as if he does not think it matters, since he appears to express both views without seeing any difference between them. But why not? One possibility is that he does not think we can achieve a concept of a merely possible idea—an idea that is available for perception, but not actually being perceived. In the Third Dialogue he asks, rhetorically: 'And what is perceivable but an idea? And can an idea exist without being actually perceived?' (p. 234). He could perhaps argue that we could only achieve the concept of a perceivable but unperceived idea as a result of an illegitimate abstraction. We would need, impossibly, to abstract the 'being perceived' from the idea, which is impossible. We can, of course, think about an idea without thinking about its presence to a mind; but this does nothing to show that there could be an idea that is not present to a mind.

But even if this does explain Berkeley's lack of interest in the question whether physical existence requires actual or only possible awareness, it does nothing to tell us what the answer is. Do physical things exist when not perceived by created minds? We should expect to find an answer to this question, if anywhere, in the long passage in the Third Dialogue in which Berkeley tries to show that his views are compatible with the biblical account of the Creation (Gen. 1). The problem for him is that, as the Bible has it, the physical world was created before God created any animals or humans to perceive it. How can this be so, if the existence of sensible things is their being perceived? There seems to be no room for an intermediate stage. Berkeley's solution is (p. 252):

All objects are eternally known by God, or which is the same thing, have an eternal existence in his mind: but when things before imperceptible to creatures, are by a decree of God, made perceptible to them; then are they said to begin a relative existence, with respect to created minds.

This *seems* to tell us that there are, as it were, three stages of existence. There is eternal existence in the mind of God. There is relative existence (perceptibility), which starts at the Creation, before there are any created minds to do the perceiving. Finally, there is what we might call actual or real existence, which requires actually being perceived by a created mind. But this three-stage picture is not attractive. It has the consequence that real existence is gappy. We can perhaps say that the things we see *exist* when we are not aware of them; but the existence they then have is not real existence, but only second-stage, relative existence. Is that really good enough for Berkeley? Many Berkeleians would feel that something significant has been lost here.

We should ask ourselves, then, whether the third stage was well called 'real existence'. Now it is not as if there is no justification for using that name. The justification lies in the thought that, for Berkeley, reality and independence are closely linked. At its starkest, the claim is that to be real is to be independent of the mind. Berkeley, of course, does not believe anything as extreme as that. But he might well believe that for a physical thing to be real is for it to be independent of the mind that perceives it. If there is *this* link between reality and independence, then nothing is real for God, and physical things cease to be real when they cease to be perceived by created minds. For created minds are the only ones of which physical things are independent. They remain potentially real, of course, when we cease to be aware of them. But they cease to be actually real, as we might put it.

Finally, then, we should look at the main passage where Berkeley lays out his conception of reality, in *Principles* §33:

The ideas of sense are allowed to have more reality in them, that is, to be more strong, orderly, and coherent than the creatures of the mind; but this is no argument that they exist without the mind. They are also less dependent on the spirit, or thinking substance which perceives them, in that they are excited by the will of another and more powerful spirit: yet still they are *ideas* . . .

If Berkeley here understands reality *entirely* in terms of strength, orderliness, and coherence, then he can say that physical things remain real when we are not perceiving them; there will be no gaps in reality, and our problem of the nature of the existence of physical things will have been solved. But he only has to understand reality *partly* in terms of independence for the gaps to reappear. And it does seem from §33 that he has a mixed conception of reality, in which independence features alongside thoughts of strength, orderliness, and coherence. If so, there remains a serious problem for him. The reality of physical things will be at least diminished when we are not aware of them.

11. Scepticism

Berkeley's main argument against material substance is that it is inconceivable; we cannot achieve a concept of something existing out of all relation to a mind. He is so convinced of this that he is willing to let the rest go by the board (§22):

Insomuch that I am content to put the whole upon this issue; if you can but conceive it possible for one extended moveable substance, or in general, for any one idea or any thing like an idea, to exist otherwise than in a mind perceiving it, I shall readily give up the cause: and as for all that *compages* of external bodies which you contend for, I shall grant you its existence, though you cannot either give me any reason why you believe it exists, or assign any use to it when it is supposed to exist. I say, the bare possibility of your opinion's being true, shall pass for an argument that it is so.

Despite this, however, Berkeley does think that if there were material substances, we could know nothing whatever about them, whereas on his view our knowledge of the things around us is everything that we could wish. Are both these claims true?

There are three aspects to the ignorance imposed on us by materialism: those that the materialists themselves recognized, those of which they were aware but which they thought they could escape, and those that they failed to notice. All this can be detailed with respect to Locke's account of the natural world investigated and, we hope, revealed by science.

Locke held that the macroscopic properties and behaviour of physical things are the effect of their internal structure, which he called their 'real essence'. Unfortunately, in his view, real essences were to be found at a level far too minuscule for us to discern them. So we could never come to understand fully how things work, or why they behave the way they do.[41]

Locke also held that the only sort of way in which we could conceive of one object operating on another was mechanically. He knew, of course, that contemporary physical theory announced at least two non-mechanical forms of causal operation: gravity and cohesion (this is what explains why one cannot pull a piece of metal apart; the bits are somehow stuck together). We can think of both of these as aspects of a common phenomenon, attraction. Since we will, on Locke's own showing, never be able even to conceive of attraction, its nature and operation must for ever lie beyond us.[42]

[41] See §§101–2, Intro. §2, and the relevant notes for references to Locke.
[42] See §103 and the note.

These things, then, Locke recognized. He viewed them as unfortunate limitations of human cognitive powers. For Berkeley they are more the unfortunate consequences of a mistaken philosophical theory. 'We have first raised a dust, and then complain, we cannot see' (Intro. §3).

The second sort of ignorance is sometimes referred to as the 'veil of perception'. This is the thought that perception places a veil of ideas between us and the physical world, a veil that either distorts that world or at least makes it impossible for us to know how things are on the other side. This gives us two unanswerable questions. First, is there anything on the other side of the veil at all? Second, if there is, what is it like?

Locke did not really take these questions very seriously. He argued that we have all the certainty we need for our purposes, and that if it was futile to ask for more, it was also unnecessary.[43] But this did not impress Berkeley. He wanted something more solid than that.

In §§18–19 Berkeley argues that on the materialist hypothesis, nothing in our ideas (the veil) can reveal either the existence or the nature of material things to us. The senses reveal nothing but sensory qualities, so that if we can come to know of anything other than that, it must be by inference from what we perceive—by reason, as Berkeley puts it. But no such inference can succeed, since 'it is granted on all hands . . . that it is possible we might be affected with all the ideas we have now, though no bodies existed without, resembling them'. What is more, the existence of this material world would explain nothing. It is common even for our own contemporaries to claim against Berkeley that the existence of the material world is the best explanation of the course of our experience. But he has seen this one coming (§19): 'for though we give the materialists their external bodies, they by their own confession are never the nearer knowing how our ideas are produced: since they own themselves unable to comprehend in what manner body can act upon spirit, or how it is possible it should imprint any idea in the mind'.

---

[43] *Essay* 4. 11. 8: 'But yet, if after all this anyone will be so sceptical as to distrust his senses and to affirm that all we see and hear, feel and taste, think and do during our whole being is but . . . a long dream, . . . if he pleases he may dream that I make him this answer, that *the certainty of* things existing *in rerum natura*, when we have *the testimony of our senses* for it, is not only *as great* as our frame can attain to, but *as our condition needs*. For our faculties being suited not to the full extent of being, nor to a perfect, clear, comprehensive knowledge of things free from all doubt and scruple, but to the preservation of us, in whom they are, and accommodated to the use of life: they serve to our purpose well enough if they will but give us certain notice of those things which are convenient or inconvenient to us.'

Of course this depends on what we are trying to explain. If we are appealing to the existence of material things to explain the course of experience, Berkeley has a point. But what if we say that we are trying to explain the changes we observe, rather than our observations and experiences of those changes? Would the existence of material things be required for *that* explanation? Berkeley does not answer that question here, but elsewhere he claims that there are no physical phenomena that require us to suppose a world existing outside the mind (§§58–9).[44] He also considers one particular experiment that Newton claimed as evidence in favour of the existence of absolute space (the water in the bucket, §114), and pronounces it irrelevant.

So much, then, for attempts to reach beyond the veil of perception. They all fail. But there remains an even more dramatic ignorance. We are supposing at the moment that there are real material things, and asking how we can come to know this fact, or to know what those things are like. The veil of perception introduces only a weak form of scepticism, since it leaves us supposing that though the physical world may be as it appears, it may not; and nothing in our experience can help us to decide. But there are stronger arguments around. We see these in full detail only in the *Dialogues* pp. 175–94. They are referred to in *Principles* §§14–15. These arguments derive from the Greek sceptical tradition known as Pyrrhonism. Pyrrho, who lived *c.*365–270 BC, left no writings, but his views have been reported to us by Sextus Empiricus (late second century AD). Sextus argued that we are quite incapable of deciding which of the ways in which things appear are the way they really are. He concluded from this that we should abandon the attempt to find out how things really are, and live by the appearances. Now he did not conceive of the appearances as ideas in the mind, as Berkeley and Locke did; appearances for the Pyrrhonists are not mental events or objects, but just the ways things look and seem.[45] Pyrrho left it an open question whether things really are one of the ways in which they look or not; he said it was a question we are quite incapable of deciding. But Berkeley argued that, at least for the materialists, no material substance can be the way it looks.

For a material substance to be the way it looks, it would have actually to have one of the sensible qualities we can experience it as having. Those

[44] Of course he has in reserve the claim that material things, being inert, cannot cause anything anyway.
[45] See M. Burnyeat, 'Can the Sceptic Live his Scepticism?', in M. Schofield, M. F. Burnyeat, and J. Barnes (eds.), *Doubt and Dogmatism* (Oxford: Clarendon Press, 1980), 20–53.

qualities are the primary qualities of shape, size, number, and motion, and the secondary qualities of colour, sound, taste, smell, and feel (touch). In the *Dialogues* Berkeley takes these qualities one by one and argues that all these sensible things are no more than sensations or ideas in the minds of perceivers. Given this, he can say that material substances can have none of the qualities they appear to have. It is not that we don't know which of those qualities they actually have; we do know that they actually have none of them. Whatever qualities they do have, then, are qualities of which we know nothing at all.

But although Berkeley refers to these arguments at *Principles* §§14–15, he immediately discounts them by saying that they prove only that we do not know by sense which of the sensible qualities the outward objects possess. It must be, I think, that in the interval between the publication of the *Principles* and the *Dialogues*, he came to see that there was more to Pyrrhonist arguments than he had originally thought. Let us suppose that we do not know by sense which sensible qualities material things really possess. Do we know it by reason, then? Pyrrho was up to this reply. He argued that reason is incapable of helping us out here. Let us admit, as Berkeley argues in *Dialogues* pp. 188–90, the same thing can look bigger or smaller, depending on how far away we are when we view it. Which of its apparent sizes is its real size? The senses alone are incapable of answering this question. Can reason do it? Pyrrho argued that there would be no more reason in favour of one way of answering the question than of another, so that reason is as useless here as the senses are. Berkeley seems to have come to agree, since his conclusion in the *Dialogues* is that all the apparent sizes are equally real, so that none of them can be *the* real size. If so, there can be no real size at all.[46]

All this, however, is premissed on materialism. Are things better once we adopt Berkeley's immaterialism?

For Berkeley, there can be no veil of perception. Real things cannot be hidden behind appearances, since appearances (ideas of sense) *are* real things. What is more, there are no unanswerable questions about what qualities real things can have, all sensible qualities having been taken away from them. For the sensible qualities are all there is to real things. There is no difficulty about conceiving how reality is in itself, or which of its apparent qualities are its real qualities. All these problems derived from materialism.

But surely, we want to say, Berkeley has to admit that some of the ways

---

[46] On Pyrrhonism in general, see Annas and Barnes (eds.), *The Modes of Scepticism*.

things appear to be are misleading; things often appear to have qualities other than their real ones. How are we to know which are which? Don't all the old problems come back in? Berkeley's answer to this question is impressive. He maintains that we cannot be mistaken about an idea of sense. Each such idea appears exactly as it really is. But such ideas can be misleading, not in the sense that they can be false, but in the literal sense that they can mislead. When I see a bent oar in water, what I see is really the way it looks, i.e. bent. But I may be misled by what I see and so suppose falsely that if I were to act in a certain way, I would have certain other experiences (e.g. that if I took the oar out of the water, it would still look bent).[47] So perceptual illusion is possible, though a sensible thing cannot look other than it is. We may not be able to be wrong about the nature of our ideas, but we can draw mistaken inferences from them about which other ideas we are likely to have. And we guard against making mistakes of this sort by taking care, by doing science, and in general by coming to understand better the way the natural world works, i.e. the regular methods of its Creator.

Finally, we have no problem with real essences. There are no inner workings of material things, too small for our poor capacities to discern them. For material things are not machines; they are collections of ideas, and as such have no mysterious interior. They are as they appear. Nor is there any difficulty about attraction. We only felt that this was beyond our comprehension because we took ourselves to be discussing the operations of material substances, and we could not conceive of these as other than mechanical. But once we recognize that the only cause of natural events is the will of God, we are going to find this particular sort of natural event no harder to make sense of than any other.

This reply is not yet sufficient. If there are no inner mechanisms, there are still the appearances of such things, at least at the levels revealed by microscopes. Why should it look as if there are mechanisms when there are none? And we should not forget that the inner mechanisms were what provided the detailed explanation of why things go on the way they do, which in a way is the most satisfying part of science. If Berkeley takes these away, what can he put in their place? The direct appeal to the will of God seems too bland, too all-encompassing, to do their job. To understand Berkeley's position on these points, we need to introduce rather different considerations, and turn to his account of science.

---

[47] Perhaps the clearest statement of his view is at *Dialogues* p. 238.

12. Berkeley and the Progress of Science

In denying real essences, Berkeley escapes sceptical problems only to create others in their place. The crucial feature of the world as conceived by contemporary science was its inner intricacy. Scientific investigation was revealing more and more intricate and detailed workings as it delved further and further into the structures of things. Now on the mechanical philosophy we understand perfectly why there are such inner details to be found. Just as the hands of a clock would not go round were it not for the machinery hidden inside, so macroscopic material change is conceived as the result of the workings of microscopic mechanisms, without which nothing would happen at all. But on Berkeley's picture it seems hard to account for all that detail. It can be serving no mechanical purpose, because ideas are passive and not capable of causing anything. The physical world goes the way it goes not because of the internal workings of a great machine but simply because that is how God determines that it should go. But why would God need to bother with inner 'mechanisms'? He doesn't need to make a mechanism to get the hands of the clock to go round; he can make the hands move directly (§62). So the very existence of all the intricate detail seems to impugn the glory and power of God, rather than to increase that glory as we might have hoped.

Now Berkeley has an official answer to this problem, which he addresses squarely in §§60–6. This is that though we cannot think of one idea as able to cause another, we can think of one idea as the sign of another. 'The fire which I see is not the cause of the pain I suffer upon my approaching it, but the mark that forewarns me of it' (§65). God sets up for us a system of signs, which by experience we can learn to read. The dark clouds overhead are a sign of impending rain, and if we know this we can organize our lives better. The point of this idea, of course, is that the intricate detail revealed in the natural world by science is just more and better signs, which, when we come to understand them properly, will enable us to cure diseases, build better bridges, and travel more safely. It is merely more evidence of God's benevolence that he has made these signs available to us.

In this way we can also show how scientific knowledge is related to ordinary knowledge. We ordinary mortals can read some signs reasonably well and predict to some extent what will happen to us; the scientific community can read more signs and so make better predictions—both more reliable and more precise. In this sense, scientific knowledge of the natural world is better than ordinary knowledge. What is more, the sense in which perceptual knowledge is perfect, so far as it goes, is no hindrance to this result. What is perfect is our knowledge of the individual idea of sense. Our knowledge of what this idea signifies may yet be very imperfect, and normally will be until supported by science.

Berkeley does not restrict himself to suggesting that science provides us with the tools for increasingly accurate predictions. If this were all, his approach would do no more than appeal to the useful regularities in nature, and suppose that these are held in place by the goodness of God. He does say this, of course, but he says more. The crucial extra is the idea that one experience is not just a useful clue to what will happen next. Useful clues are signs, certainly. But not all signs are part of a language. What distinguishes Berkeley's signs is that they are linguistic signs. As a sign, each natural event is an utterance of God's; God speaks to us, and as we learn more we understand better what he is saying, i.e. what the signs he is giving us mean.

Originally Berkeley only thought of *visible* signs (ideas of sight) as the Language of God.[48] His reason for the restriction to the visible lies in the difference he discerns between linguistic and non-linguistic signs. He described this later (*Alciphron* 4. 12; see also 4. 7):

all signs are not language: not even all significant sounds, such as the natural cries of animals, or the inarticulate sounds and interjections of men. It is the articulation, combination, variety, copiousness, extensive and general use and easy application of signs (all which are commonly found in vision) that constitute the true nature of language. Other senses may indeed furnish signs; and yet those signs have no more right than inarticulate sounds to be thought a language.

The crucial features here are articulation and combination, for these are the ones that Berkeley will use to explain the revealed intricacy of the world. His first move was to claim that 'visible figures represent tangible figures much after the same manner that written words do sounds' (*New Theory of Vision* §143). For this analogy to hold, the (signifying) visible must be composed of sufficiently variable elements to be able to capture each relevant variation in the (signified) tangible, just as words are composed of a sufficient stock of letters to be able to capture all relevant variation in the sounds for which they stand.

This version of the analogy won't work for the *Principles*; for there the focus is no longer the contrast between visible and tangible.[49] Berkeley

---

[48] *New Theory of Vision* §§143, 147; *Principles* §43.

[49] Berkeley seems to have reverted to his earlier position, in *Theory of Vision Vindicated* §§40–3 and *Alciphron* (see the passage quoted from *Alciphron* in the text). This probably explains

seems to generalize the claim that visible ideas are a language to include all the ideas of sense; see §65, where he includes the audible: 'the noise that I hear is not the effect of this or that motion or collision of the ambient bodies, but the sign thereof. Secondly, the reason why ideas are formed into machines, that is, artificial and regular combinations, is the same with that for combining letters into words.' But the overall idea is the same. The physical world is a genuinely linguistic system, whose elements are variously combined and concatenated in much the sort of way that letters and words are, so that they should be capable of carrying detailed messages. Just as a limited number of letters can be used to create an infinite variety of messages, so a limited number of physical elements can be combined for the same purpose. The whole is thus an informational system, in which God, of his goodness, speaks to us about what we can expect in the future.[50] And scientists can be conceived as the grammarians of this system, who understand how the individual elements combine to generate this or that meaning in the particular case, and are thus able to know better what is being said (see the first-edition version of *Principles* §108).

This, then, is Berkeley's account of science and of the intricacy of the natural world. But there remains one further problem for him. His system of natural signs is an excellent tool for prediction, as we have seen. But science is not only interested in prediction; scientists also aspire to *explain why* things happen the way they do. The mechanists achieved this wonderfully. In the classic example of the clock, we come to understand why the hands *must* move once we discover the nature of the mechanism that drives them. There comes a point where we can see that if the mechanism is functioning properly, the hands have *got* to move; they can't help but move. Here our explanation is working so well that we have a sense of a necessity in nature. It is not just that the hands will move, and that we can know this in advance; they *must* move. Now we have understanding and explanation, as well as prediction. But without the idea of a natural necessity (the hands having to move) we would not have achieved this.

What sort of explanation can be offered by Berkeley? In particular, can he offer us this sense of necessity in nature? It seems not. Everything happens because God wills that it should. But God might equally well have

the alterations he made in the relevant passages in the second edition of the *Principles*, which seem intended to weaken the claim that all sensible ideas are linguistic signs.

[50] See §65: 'By this means abundance of information is conveyed unto us, concerning what we are to expect from such and such actions . . .'. There is no reason to suppose that God does not also speak of the past (e.g. archaeology, geology).

determined differently. So the course of nature is arbitrary; there is no necessity in the case at all. 'There is nothing necessary or essential in the case, but it depends entirely on the will of the *governing spirit*, who causes certain bodies to cleave together . . . ; and to some he gives a quite contrary tendency to fly asunder, just as he sees convenient' (§106). And on this account explanation is stymied; at the end of the day all that we can say is that this is how things do happen, but give no reason why they should (other than God's free choice, which would have explained any other hypothesis equally well).

If this is right, Berkeley's account of science leaves science less well off than he found it. And he would not be indifferent to this result. The title-page of the *Principles*, which I have already referred to, runs: 'A Treatise concerning the Principles of *Human Knowledge*. Part I. Wherein the chief Causes of Error and Difficulty in the *Sciences*, with the grounds of *Scepticism, Atheism,* and *Irreligion,* are inquired into . . .'. So his account of science needs to work well, and there is a point at which it begins to fail.

So—can Berkeley provide a sense in which science explains without imputing necessary connections between distinct natural events, or does he in fact offer necessary connections of a new type, and rest his explanations on them? He might be thought to be attempting the first in §107:

> considering the whole creation is the workmanship of a *wise and good agent*, it should seem to become philosophers [i.e. scientists], to employ their thoughts (contrary to what some hold[51]) about the final causes[52] of things: and I must confess, I see no reason, why pointing out the various ends, to which natural things are adapted, and for which they were originally with unspeakable wisdom contrived, should not be thought one good way of accounting for them, and altogether worthy a philosopher.

To explain an event by appeal to its 'final causes' is to explain it teleologically. And teleological explanations may be full and complete, even if the events so explained are still thought of as arbitrary. So here there is complete explanation without necessity. Berkeley also *appears* to deny necessary connections in §106: 'There is nothing necessary or essential in the

---

[51] The new scientists vaunted themselves on the exclusion of final causes and admitting only efficient causes, which for them meant mechanical ones. Descartes wrote, 'When dealing with natural things we will, then, never derive any explanations from the purposes which God or nature may have had in view when creating them, and we shall entirely banish from our philosophy the search for final causes' (*Principles of Philosophy* i. 28, in *Philosophical Writings,* i. 202).

[52] The final cause of an action is the end intended by the agent; the final cause of a natural event is the end it tends to promote. If natural events are divine utterances, and so actions, these two accounts must be combined.

case, but it depends entirely on the will of the *governing spirit*'—though, as I argue in the note to that passage, there is more than one way of reading this sentence. In fact there are many denials of necessary connections in his work, especially in the *Alciphron*. In all of these, however, he seems to be wanting to establish that the informational system is not *founded* on prior necessary connections, there being none to be found.

There are, however, two ways of supposing that despite these denials Berkeley was in a position to suppose that there is indeed necessity in the natural world. The first appeals to the idea that the relation between an all-powerful will and its chosen acts is necessary; there is no possibility but that things should happen as that will determines. If so, every natural event is necessary. Malebranche held that this was the only conceivable sort of necessity.[53] Such necessity is not a relation between distinct natural events, but it might serve the purposes of explanation for all that. It will do so especially well if we take the view, as Malebranche did, that the created world is the best possible as a whole. If so, and if God's nature requires him to create the best, the natural world is becoming necessary in an increasingly strong sense.

Second, admitting that the system itself is arbitrary is quite compatible with supposing that once it is established, there will be necessity available within it. The obvious analogy here is with language: the choice of words or of script is arbitrary, but within this arbitrarily chosen system there are (linguistic) necessities. And this is just what Berkeley seems to be saying at one point (*New Theory of Vision* §143): 'It is indeed arbitrary that, in general, letters of any language represent sounds at all: but when that is once agreed, it is not arbitrary what combination of letters shall represent this or that particular sound. I leave this with the reader to pursue, and apply it in his own thoughts.' On this basis, we might hope to build a new sense of a natural necessity—one in which the necessity is semantic.

13. The Nature of Spirits

Berkeley distinguishes carefully between the question what conception we have of a physical thing and the question what reason we have to believe that there are any such. (He is much more interested in the first of these than in the second.) He ought similarly to distinguish between two separate philosophical stories about minds: the first will describe our con-

---

[53] *Recherche* 6. 2. 3.

ception of a mind, and the second will tell us what right we have to believe that any such thing exists. In a sense this is just what he does, though the matter is complicated by the fact that according to him we acquire our conception of a mind from some feature of what it is to be one. So the second story is to some extent pre-empted by the first. But after that things go on smoothly. Having acquired a conception of what it is to be a mind from my own case, I acquire a conception of a mind other than me by thinking of it as something that is like me but not me (§145).

The first story is interesting. Berkeley supposes that minds are active principles or beings which operate on ideas. How does such a being come to have a conception of itself? The official answer, the best account of which is given in a passage added to the *Dialogues*, is that the mind, an active being, *as such* reflects itself to itself. 'The being of my self, that is, my own soul, mind or thinking principle, I evidently know by reflexion' (p. 233). We would do well, of course, to enquire carefully what sort of reflection this might be, and indeed how a mind might be thought capable of reflecting itself to itself (are we supposed to think of a mirror here?). And we should also be interested in the idea that what is reflected is an agent, and that it is in acting that one creates a reflection for oneself. But however all this might be, it is important first to notice the difference between Berkeley's approach here and that of Descartes. For Descartes, I know my own existence because it is impossible for me to doubt it; the proof is an intellectual proof of an intellectual being.[54] For Berkeley, the proof lies not in thought but in agency.

There are difficulties here for Berkeley because the mind is not *wholly* active, nor is all its activity of the same sort. The first of these derives from his claim that in perception we are in some degree passive; it is only in the imagination that we are wholly active. So our first question should be how an impurely active being is completely revealed to itself in acting. Won't our passive side be left out of the picture (the reflection)? But there is a worse difficulty than this, for even if we confine ourselves to our active side, we have two different sorts of agency to consider. The first is the one of which Berkeley talks so often, which occurs when by a mere act of will we call up ideas in the imagination (§29). The second is what we would more naturally think of as agency, when we move around the natural world and act in it. Actions in this second sense are physical actions rather

[54] See Descartes's Second Meditation. The contrast between Descartes's views and Berkeley's is not quite as stark as I have here suggested, because for Descartes judging and doubting are actions (see his *Principles of Philosophy*, I. 32–4). But it is not that feature of them that Descartes appeals to in his proof of his own existence.

than mental ones. And Berkeley has the gravest difficulties in making room for physical actions in his system. The problem derives from the fact that a physical movement is a natural change in the world, and as such must be caused by God; it is a real thing, and so an idea of sense, and so not caused by the created beings that perceive it. But if our physical movements are caused by God rather than by us, it would seem that he has more claim to be the agent here than we do. How then can we restore our sense that it is *we* who move our bodies—that we are physical agents? The more we insist that we are the cause, the less our bodily movements retain the status of a real thing; ideas that are caused by the mind in which they exist are termed 'ideas of the imagination'; and for Berkeley this means that they are not real things.

I know of no satisfactory answer to this puzzle. Berkeley seems to have set things up in such a way that he has little or no room for manœuvre. Since he does not really address the problem directly, it is hard to know what he might have come up with (but see the discussion in *Dialogues* pp. 236–7). One possibility would be to appeal to joint agency—to the idea that God combines with us so that together we can do what neither of us could have done alone (such as lifting this boulder). The problem with this idea, of course, is to establish a sense in which what we do together God could not have done without my help.

Let us return to the problem that he does recognize and try to deal with, concerning our ability to acquire a conception of ourselves. The touchy point is whether a mind is something of which there can be a conception at all, or whether, as a conceiver, a mind lies necessarily at the conceiving end of the conceiving process and never at the other end (that of the thing conceived). This is a general philosophical worry, but the point is especially difficult for Berkeley because of two claims he makes. The first is that an idea can resemble only another idea, and the second is that ideas are passive and minds active. No idea can therefore resemble a mind in any respect in which it is active; and so it turns out to be impossible to have an idea of a mind. If to have a conception of a mind is to have an idea of it, then, we cannot attain a conception of a mind.[55]

This is Berkeley's attempt to deal with this matter: 'the words *will, soul, spirit*, do not stand for . . . any idea at all, but for something which is very different from ideas, and which being an agent cannot be like unto, or represented by, any idea whatsoever. Though it must be owned at the same

---

[55] Berkeley is so firm on this point that he thinks we cannot have an idea of something in which agency is even partly concerned. This is why he denies that we can have any idea of a relation (§142).

time, that we have some notion of soul, spirit, and the operations of the mind, such as willing, loving, hating, in as much as we know or understand the meaning of those words' (§27; cf. also §§142, 145–8; note also the changes made in these passages in the second edition of the *Principles*, which are detailed in the footnotes). The point here is that we can come to understand the meaning of the word 'mind' without this depending on an ability to acquire an idea of a mind (or a conception of the mind, or any-thing else that functions in the sort of way that ideas function). Berkeley is at least consistent here. He has not bound himself to the doctrine that every significant name stands for an idea; indeed he denies it explicitly in the Introduction §§18–20. But we can reasonably expect from him an account of what it is to understand the meaning of a word other than by acquiring the relevant idea. And Berkeley's text is apparently devoid of any such account.[56] Here again we are left to our own devices, just when we need Berkeley's help.

Berkeley is clearly conscious of this as a problem that needs careful handling; to that end, he added a discussion of it to the third edition of the *Dialogues* (pp. 232–4). The way the point is put there is by contrasting the notions of material and spiritual substance. As Hylas puts it, as there is no more meaning in spiritual substance than in material substance, 'the one is to be exploded as well as the other'. This, however, is a slightly different point. There are two difficulties for Berkeley, not just one. The first we have already seen. It is that an idea cannot resemble a mind, and that we seem therefore prevented from acquiring an idea of a mind. The second is that Berkeley's objection to material substance is equally effective against spiritual substance. The first problem might remain even if the second could be dispelled. And unfortunately Berkeley restricts himself in this passage to arguing against the second; his final remark on the subject is that 'there is therefore upon the whole no parity of case between spirit and matter'. The point he makes is that the very concept of material substance is incoherent, unlike the concept of spiritual substance. Presumably this is because, if sensible qualities are ideas, material substance (defined as something which is not a mind and which possesses sensible qualities) is impossible. Our concept of spiritual substance, however, as a being which has various powers including that of perceiving ideas, is not incoherent for the same reason—nor for any other reason.

Whether this Berkeleian riposte is successful will depend on exactly what we take his main argument against material substance to be. If the

---

[56] For a general discussion of Berkeley's theory of meaning, with this point very much in mind, see Flage, *Berkeley's Doctrine of Notions*.

argument is just the one I have given in the previous paragraph, Berkeley will escape the difficulty. But we should remember that Berkeley takes the defence of material substance to be partly informed by the mistaken doctrine of abstract ideas. And there is a danger that his defence of spiritual substance is subject to the same complaint. The move from a conception of myself to that of other such beings seems to involve abstracting from my conception of myself certain features and then replacing them with others of a like nature. And the process seems likely to involve, in its intermediate stage, the temporary construction of an illegitimately abstracted conception of a person who is nobody in particular.[57]

But whether Berkeley is successful on this preliminary point is in the end irrelevant to our main worry, which is still that we cannot have an idea of a spiritual substance, and that therefore we cannot understand what we are claiming when we claim that such a thing exists. It seems to me that Berkeley fails to provide the material needed to solve this problem, and that as far as the debate in the *Dialogues* goes Hylas is right to conclude, 'Notwithstanding all you have said, to me it seems, that according to your own way of thinking, and in consequence of your own principles, it should follow that you are only a system of floating ideas, without any substance to support them' (p. 233). For if the only thing we can conceive is an idea, and if minds are specifically different from ideas, we cannot conceive of minds.

We should remember, however, that we only have Part I of the *Principles*; Part II, which we could have expected to contain much more on the nature of the mind, was never completed, if we are to believe Berkeley:[58] 'As to the Second Part of my treatise concerning the *Principles of Human Knowledge*, the fact is that I had made a considerable progress in it; but the manuscript was lost about fourteen years ago, during my travels in Italy, and I never had leisure since to do so disagreeable a thing as writing twice on the same subject.'

14. Berkeley's Intellectual Antecedents

The four names that appear most often in the *Philosophical Commentaries* (Berkeley's own working notebooks) are those of Locke, Newton, Descartes, and Malebranche. The same is true of the *Principles* and *Three*

---

[57] In ch. 9 of my *Berkeley*, I suggest in much greater detail that this appeal to abstraction is indeed required .

[58] Letter to Samuel Johnson, 25 Nov. 1729 (p. 175 below).

Dialogues, except that for some reason Locke is only referred to once by name—but his influence is still plainly there throughout. The overall story, as I see it, of how Berkeley stands in relation to the work of these four men is roughly as follows. Malebranche represents an intellectual tradition that stretches back to the scholastics and eventually to St Augustine. Descartes and Locke represent a distinctive philosophical position, informed by the new science. Newton was the new science personified. Berkeley was deeply impressed by Newton's work, and wanted to give it pride of place in his philosophical picture. But he wanted to overturn much of the philosophy of Locke and Descartes, and return us (always still informed by the new science) more nearly to the ways of Malebranche and his tradition.

The time-scale for all this is as follows. René Descartes (1596–1650) published his *Meditations on First Philosophy* in 1641 and his *Principles of Philosophy* in 1644. The seminal work of Nicolas Malebranche (1638–1715), *De la recherche de la verité* (The Search after Truth) appeared in 1674–5. John Locke (1632–1704) published his *Essay Concerning Human Understanding* in 1690, and it immediately ran through several editions in which Locke made significant changes. Isaac Newton's *Principia Mathematica* appeared in 1687.

In charting these matters, I will lay out the views of Descartes, Malebranche, and Locke on three subjects: the distinction between primary and secondary qualities, material and spiritual substance, and scepticism.

Descartes held that, as well as God, the uncreated substance, there were two sorts of created substance: mind and matter. These are quite different from each other; matter is extended and unthinking, and mind is unextended and thinks.[59] Descartes was no sceptic, but he used sceptical arguments in order to isolate the point at which they break down; this would be a fixed point from which he could move to rebuild in sounder form what he had previously dismantled. We know of our own existence because we cannot doubt it without proving it; so this gave him his fixed point. We know of God because only God could be the source of our idea of God. We know of matter because once we have proved the existence of God we need no longer doubt the existence of the material world, for God is no deceiver.[60]

Descartes drew a standard distinction between two sorts of qualities

---

[59] See his *Principles of Philosophy* I. 51–4.
[60] This is all in his *Meditations* I, 2, and 6.

(the terminology of 'primary' and 'secondary' comes later, in Boyle; but I will take advantage of it now). The primary qualities were extension, figure, motion, position, duration, number; the secondary ones were colours, odours, sounds, tastes, and the tactile qualities (e.g. roughness and smoothness). He held that our ideas of the primary qualities are perfectly clear and distinct, and that this enables them to be the ones with which true science is concerned. Our ideas of primary qualities are like, or at least able to be like, those qualities as they are in the objects (i.e. the way in which a thing appears, with respect to the primary qualities, may be the way it actually is). But our ideas of secondary qualities cannot be like the ways the objects in the world are; they are mere sensations, which do not represent the nature of outer things at all:

there are many other features, such as size, shape and number which we clearly perceive to be actually or at least possibly present in objects in a way exactly corresponding to our sensory perception or understanding. And we so easily fall into the error of judging that what is called colour in objects is something exactly like the colour of which we have sensory awareness.[61]

So far, then, for Descartes there are ideas of primary qualities and ideas of secondary qualities, but only the primary qualities are as they appear to us. The secondary qualities exist in the object, certainly, but only as powers or dispositions that physical things have, in virtue of their primary qualities, to cause sensations (e.g. ideas of colour) in the mind. He writes:

Now I have given an account of the various sizes, shapes, and motions which are to be found in all bodies; and apart from these the only things which we perceive by our senses as being located outside us are light, colour, smell, taste, sound and tactile qualities. . . . these are nothing else in the objects—or at least we cannot apprehend them as being anything else—but certain dispositions depending on shape, size and motion.[62]

Malebranche. There were various problems for Descartes, but among those that attracted most attention was the problem of interaction—the question how mind and matter can influence each other if they are so different. We know (or think we know) that our bodies move because we will that they should, and that a pain will occur if we cut ourselves with a knife. How is this possible? Malebranche saw this difficulty as related to a more general problem how physical things could be said to be causes. He argued that they could not. It was not just that they are inert—the point that Berkeley makes much of. It was also that there was no conceivable neces-

---

[61] *Principles of Philosophy* I. 70.   [62] Ibid. 4. 199.

sary connection between one physical event and another; and for Malebranche there can be no causation without a necessary connection.[63] There is, of course, a necessary connection between the will of God and changes in the world. So the only possible cause is God. As such a cause, God can act so as to move our bodies when we will to move, and to affect our minds when the world collides with us. He also acts to cause a physical event when suitable physical conditions occur. Within this picture the interaction problem fails to arise, since there is no difficulty at all in supposing God capable of affecting either minds or matter on suitable occasions.

This view of Malebranche's was called Occasionalism, since it supposes that what we ordinarily think of as the cause of an event is more the occasion for God to cause that event. Berkeley discusses the view in *Principles* §§67–80.

In this respect, then, Malebranche did not accept Descartes's mechanistic science of nature. Descartes thought of the natural world as a system of second causes, with God the primary efficient cause.[64] For Malebranche, the idea of a second cause is unintelligible.[65] But he still thought extremely highly of Descartes's work, especially of his insistence that we have clear ideas only of the primary qualities, so that a true science can only be concerned with these. (This thought underpinned the idea of a mathematical physics, partly because the primary qualities are all quantifiable.[66]) Malebranche distinguished between ideas and sensations. Ideas are mental representations of outer things, representations which are broadly correct in the sorts of way in which they present the world to us; such things are not perceived by sense, but by pure intellect. Sensations, the objects of our senses and not of our intellect, are mere modifications of our minds, which do not represent the nature of outer things at all. The secondary qualities are mere sensations,[67] modifications of the mind caused in us by God, for our own good. Things are different, however, with the primary qualities. The sizes and shapes of physical things as we experience them are a sort of mixture of idea and sensation. There is one aspect to them which concerns their relation to us as perceivers; it is this aspect that we use to distinguish one object from another, and it is this that varies

[63] *Recherche* 6. 2. 3 at p. 450: 'a true cause as I understand it is one such that the mind perceives a necessary connection between it and its effect'.

[64] 'We should . . . consider him as the efficient cause of all things' (*Principles of Philosophy* 1. 28).

[65] See his Fifteenth Elucidation (the one that concerns *Recherche* 6. 2. 3).

[66] At least those on Descartes's list of the primary are all quantifiable. But see n. 75 below.

[67] See e.g. *Recherche* 3. 2. 5.

according to our distance from the thing we see and the angle we see it from; all this is mere sensation. There is another aspect which is idea, however, in virtue of which, despite the admixture of sensation, we are capable of experiencing the primary qualities of physical things.

Like Descartes, however, Malebranche thought that as well as the sensations of colour etc., it was possible to think of colour as a modification of matter; though Descartes understood this dispositionally while Malebranche, it seems, did not:

> If by heat, colour, flavour, you mean such and such a movement of insensible parts, then fire is hot, grass green, sugar sweet. But if by heat and the other qualities you mean what I feel near fire, what I see when I see grass, and so forth, then fire is not hot at all, nor is grass green, and so forth, for the heat we feel and the colours we see are only in the soul. . . . The terms *sweet*, *bitter*, *salty*, *tart*, *acid*, and so on; *red*, *green*, *yellow*, and so on; such and such an odour, flavour, colour, and so on, are therefore all equivocal . . .[68]

How do we come by the intelligible idea of extension? Malebranche thinks that, though in some sense that idea is present in every experience of the things around us, we are for various reasons unable to acquire or create that idea for ourselves. God has it, however; so we can only get it if God is willing to share his idea with us. This does not mean merely that once we have got the idea from God, we can get on by ourselves. Our experience is no more capable of representing intelligible extension to us than it was before. We can only experience the primary qualities if God is willing *on each occasion* to share with us his idea of the extension and other primary qualities of the things before us. This is the doctrine that *we see all things in God*; the mixture of idea and sensation that occurs when we experience a primary quality is a mixture of a modification of our mind, the sensation, and a modification of God's, the idea.[69]

Berkeley's attitude to Malebranche's Occasionalism was that it made the material world redundant, since it was deprived of causal powers. Why did God bother to create it at all? (§67–75; see also *Dialogues* pp. 219–20). As for seeing all things in God, Berkeley distances himself from this at Dialogues p. 215: 'I do not say, I see things by perceiving that which represents them in the intelligible substance of God. This I do not understand; but I say, the things by me perceived are known by the understanding, and produced by the will, of an infinite spirit.'

On scepticism, Malebranche criticized Descartes's method of showing

---

[68] Ibid. 6. 2. 2.
[69] See ibid. 3. 2. 6. Berkeley refers to this doctrine at *Principles* §86.

that we have knowledge of outer things. His criticism is *ad hominem*, i.e. it depends on something else that Descartes held; this is that we make mistakes only when we decide to accept a belief when we do not have clear and distinct ideas. Malebranche argues that although we have a clear idea of what extension is, we have no clear idea that something extended exists. Since we are capable of deciding not to believe that there are extended things, and since our idea in this case is not clear and distinct, we might be wrong in believing that there are extended things without this meaning that God is a deceiver. It is we that have exceeded our rights and powers, not God who has abused us.[70]

Malebranche himself held that our experience provides a sort of 'natural revelation' of the existence of bodies, but only to the extent that it makes it probable that they exist. To convert that probability into sufficient certainty, Malebranche appealed to the Genesis description of the Creation. This position would clearly not satisfy Berkeley, for two reasons. First, it is evident that the problem itself derives from Malebranche's admission of material substance. Immaterialism puts quite a different perspective on the situation. Second, Berkeley thinks that his views are quite compatible with the Genesis account of the Creation, as he argues in *Dialogues* pp. 250–6.

Locke. Berkeley had to study Locke's Essay as a student at Trinity College, Dublin, and it is possible to see his metaphysical writings as a response to (and almost total rejection of) Locke's views; but, as we have already seen, that would be an exaggeration. Of particular interest here are the matters on which Locke differed from Descartes. The first of these was that Locke was willing to contemplate the possibility of a thinking material substance. He wrote: 'We have the *ideas* of *matter* and *thinking*, but possibly shall never be able to know whether any mere material being thinks or no: it being impossible for us . . . to discover whether Omnipotency has not given to some systems of matter, fitly disposed, a power to perceive and think.'[71]

Second, Locke was not very much impressed by sceptical arguments. He seems not really to have cared very much about them. His general position was that we can be certain enough about things in the physical world for our own limited purposes, and it was pointless to ask for more.[72] He

---

[70] *Elucidations* 6, pp. 572–4.   [71] *Essay* 4. 3. 6.

[72] In *Essay* 4. 11. 3 Locke wrote: '*The notice we have by our senses of the existing of things without us* . . . is an assurance that *deserves the name of knowledge*. If we persuade ourselves that our faculties act and inform us right concerning the existence of those objects that affect them, it cannot pass for an ill-grounded confidence: for I think nobody can, in earnest, be so sceptical as

was much more impressed, however, by the question whether we can know the inner workings of physical things (their real essences, as he called them), which he held to be largely impossible. This was partly because we were not going to get microscopes powerful enough, and partly because even if we did we could not even conceive of the necessary connections there must be between mechanical inner workings and surface secondary properties like colour.[73] As a result Locke failed to show that science yields knowledge.[74] Berkeley, by contrast, takes sceptical problems about ordinary perceptual knowledge far more seriously, and argues that science gives us knowledge of the natural world that is no less secure than our knowledge of what others are saying to us.

On the distinction between primary and secondary qualities, Locke produces in *Essay* 2. 8. 9 ff. a complex account which is heavily influenced by his friend the chemist Robert Boyle (1627–91), but which is still in substantial respects very close to that of Descartes.[75] Locke held that secondary qualities such as colour, taste, etc. exist in the physical object as powers to cause certain ideas in the perceiving mind, powers which the object has in virtue of its primary qualities. Boyle had written, 'So, if there were no sensitive beings, those bodies that are now the objects of our senses would be but *dispositively*, if I may so speak, endowed with colours, tastes, and the like, and *actually* but only with those more catholic affections of bodies—figure, motion, texture, etc.'[76]

Given this unanimity, something has to be said about the fact that Berkeley records 'the modern philosophers' as saying that secondary qualities are nothing but sensations in the mind, where Descartes, Boyle, and Locke agree that they are dispositions or powers in the object. It is possible that this is just an error on Berkeley's part, and if so it is perhaps the result

to be uncertain of the existence of those things which he sees and feels. . . . This is certain: the confidence that our faculties do not herein deceive us is the greatest assurance we are capable of concerning the existence of material beings.' See more generally ibid. 4. 11. 3–10.

[73] See ibid. 2. 31. 6; also 4. 6. 7–16, esp. 4. 6. 7: 'Because our understandings can discover no conceivable connexion between any *secondary quality* and any modification whatsoever of any of the primary ones'.

[74] In general, Locke thought that science only yields probability, and 'the highest probability amounts not to certainty, without which there can be no true knowledge' (ibid. 4. 3. 14).

[75] It should not be forgotten, however, that Locke included solidity in his list of primary qualities. For Descartes, a material object was a mobile shape of a certain size; as a result, he denied the possibility of a void, or empty space, for an empty but circumscribed space was just what he called a material thing. For Locke, a material object was not just a mobile outline; the outline had to be filled. Locke also thought of texture (the arrangement of microscopic corpuscles on the surface of a macroscopic body) as a primary quality, as Boyle did.

[76] *The Origins of Forms and Qualities*, in *Selected Philosophical Papers of Robert Boyle*, 34.

of reading Pierre Bayle's *Dictionnaire historique et critique* (published 1697–1702), as we know that Berkeley had done. (Bayle is the fifth philosopher who should be mentioned in any list of influences on Berkeley.) Bayle says, in section G of his entry on Zeno: 'The new philosophers . . . teach that [sounds, odours, heat and cold, hardness and softness, heaviness and lightness, tastes and colours, etc.] are perceptions in our soul, and that they do not exist at all in the objects of our senses.'[77] It is probable, however, that Berkeley was not simply misreading the tradition he was attacking. First, there is Malebranche, who often speaks as if colours are sensations in the mind. Second, there are other writers to be considered than just the ones I have mentioned. There is Galileo, for instance, in whose *Assayer* we find remarks extraordinarily close to those of Locke's *Essay* 2. 8. 9, followed by the claim that tastes, colours, odours, etc., considered as qualities inherent in external objects, are merely names; properly considered, they reside entirely in the sentient subject, and Galileo is happy to call them sensations:

I think that if ears, tongues, and noses were removed, shapes and numbers and motions would remain, but not odours or tastes or sounds. The latter, I believe, are nothing more than names when separated from living beings, just as tickling and titillation are nothing but names in the absence of such things as noses and armpits. . . . many sensations which are supposed to be qualities residing in external objects have no real existence save in us, and outside ourselves are mere names.[78]

The real point is that what is common to all these writers is the view that secondary qualities *as we know them in perception* are modifications of our own sensibility, not real qualities of outer things. Since Berkeley, in his discussions of these matters, is only concerned to argue that we cannot conceive of *sensible* qualities existing outside the mind, he can rest content with this, and leave out any reference to the secondary qualities *as they exist in the objects*, since our senses tell us nothing of that. But this does not mean that he has nothing to say about those occult qualities; his view is, of course, that since matter is inert, it can have neither powers nor

---

[77] This passage is in Bayle's *Dictionary*, 364–5. Bayle goes on to suggest that the arguments that show colours etc. to be 'perceptions in the soul' show the same of extension—that objects 'in themselves' have no extension. Berkeley pursues this suggestion at great length in the First Dialogue.

[78] *The Assayer*, in *Discoveries and Opinions of Galileo*, 276–7. In general, on the history of the primary–secondary distinction, see Sir William Hamilton's learned discussion in the second volume of his edition of *The Works of Thomas Reid, D.D.* (Edinburgh: MacLachlan & Stewart, 1863), note D, pp. 825–45.

dispositions (§25). The idea that matter has the power to affect the mind in these sorts of ways is therefore incoherent in itself, and broken-backed because nobody can explain how matter can affect the mind at all (§19).

At the end of the day, the picture that Berkeley wants to put in place of Locke's is, as I said, more akin to that of Malebranche and the scholastic tradition than it is to the the work of Descartes and Locke. These matters are not so easy to detail. The clearest trace of the scholastic tradition in Berkeley's work is his view that in perception we share ideas with God. This is a later version of St Augustine's doctrine of divine illumination, according to which God is the interior light of the human soul. A vision of things as they really are is present in us by virtue of the light that is in us, namely God; it cannot be extracted from sense-experience alone.[79] This view is also clearly related to Malebranche's conception of seeing all things in God. Similarly, in my view Berkeley wants to retain a sense that there is natural necessity in the world.[80] He cannot do it in Locke's mechanistic way, as we saw, and he is worried (as Duns Scotus was[81]) by the thought that nothing can be necessary if God could have ordained things otherwise—or, to put it the other way round, that if there were natural necessities, they would constitute a constraint on the power of God. I suggested earlier that he hoped to find a sense in which there is internal necessity in the system of nature, which is entirely due to God's free choice; and that this was connected to his conception of the world as a book or text written by God for us to read. (See §109.)

Newton. Newton's work in physics and mathematics was of a different order altogether, and in general Berkeley had nothing but admiration for what Newton had achieved. He wrote in his notebooks, 'I see no wit in any of them but Newton, the rest are mere triflers' (*PC* §372). Newton's work raised three different sorts of problem for Berkeley. The first was a general problem how to make sense of the new science without matter. How can there be a real physical science without real physical things to investigate? These matters were discussed in Section 12. The second was a more particular difficulty derived from Newton's distinction between relative and absolute space, time, and motion. The problem here was that Newton

---

[79] For a discussion of this doctrine and its later history, see N. Kretzmann, A. Kenny, and J. Pinborg (eds.), *The Cambridge History of Later Medieval Philosophy* (Cambridge: Cambridge University Press, 1982), ch. 21.

[80] The alternative view would be that he would be satisfied with the necessity deriving from the fact that every natural event was the effect of the will of an all-powerful God; see the discussion of necessity at the end of Sect. 12 above.

[81] See John Duns Scotus, *De Primo Principio*, ch. 4, conclusion 5 in *A Treatise on God as First Principle*, ed. A. Wolter (Franciscan Herald, 1966), 91.

explicitly asserted that absolute space exists outside the mind and has no relation to sensible things (see §110). Berkeley is forced to deny that this is possible, and to hold that Newtonian science does not require it. He argues directly against the intelligibility of absolute motion, supposing that if that fails there will be no call for absolute space. He also argues that the idea of absolute space is the result of an illegitimate abstraction (§116). The third concerned the nature of infinitesimals in mathematics, and the infinite divisibility of finite extension, which are treated at some length in §§123–32. Berkeley thinks that the doctrine that a finite length contains an infinite number of infinitely small parts has made mathematics and geometry excessively abstruse and theoretical. He thinks, moreover, that one is likely to be persuaded of it if one believes in abstract general ideas and the real existence of sensible lines (§125). Berkeley has much more to say about these things in *The Analyst* (1734). In the *Principles* he confines himself to arguing that the *idea* we have of any line does not consist of innumerable parts, and there are no other lines than these. Any belief to the contrary is the result of a mistaken conception of general ideas.

15. The Berkeley–Johnson Correspondence

These four letters, written in 1729–30, not long before Berkeley's return to England, give us an intriguing glimpse of private philosophical debate between two of the leading philosophers of the day. Samuel Johnson (1696–1772) is thought of as the father of American philosophy.[82] He studied at Yale, and taught there for a few years, and in 1754 became the first President of King's College, New York (now Columbia University). In 1752 his *Elementa Philosophica* appeared (published in Philadelphia by Benjamin Franklin), dedicated to and much influenced by Berkeley. At the time these letters were written Johnson was 33 and Berkeley was 44. Johnson was in Stratford, Connecticut, about 100 miles from Berkeley's home in Newport, Rhode Island, where Berkeley had bought a farm intended to support his college in Bermuda.

The letters we have are only a part of a larger correspondence between the two men, but the others that we have, which were written on or after Berkeley's return to England, are less concerned with philosophical

---

[82] This Samuel Johnson is not to be confused with the Samuel Johnson who is commonly called Dr Johnson, the English writer and author of the famous Dictionary, and subject of James Boswell's *Life of Johnson*.

matters. Johnson paid several visits to Berkeley in Newport, and seems to have become something of a family friend.

At the time of his correspondence with Johnson, Berkeley had not yet published the revised editions of the *Principles* and *Dialogues*; these only appeared in 1734. But it would be fanciful to suggest that the main changes introduced at that time were particularly due to Johnson's questioning. The matters on which Johnson concentrates do not seem to be ones on which Berkeley was persuaded to change his mind.

In his first letter Johnson asks a series of questions, some of which he is raising more on behalf of some friends of his, and some of which express difficulties that he himself found with elements of Berkeley's philosophy. Some of the questions in the first letter are not very troublesome for Berkeley, who deals with them effectively in his first reply. Strangely, however, he hardly responds to Johnson's own questions at all. And those were the better questions. This gives Johnson the opportunity for his second letter, which is very much more effective, and which supports his earlier criticisms and questions with detailed (though inaccurate) citations from Berkeley's works. Berkeley is now forced to respond.

There are three matters that concern Johnson. The first concerns the nature of the supposed archetypes of our ideas in the mind of God, and the consequences of supposing that our ideas of sense resemble their divine archetypes. These consequences include answers to the question whether two people can see the same thing, and whether the thing I see can be identical with the thing I touch. In his questioning here Johnson gives a much more explicit account of the relation between our ideas and God's than any that is found in either the *Principles* or the *Dialogues*. Berkeley does not reject that account, but merely says that he does not object to calling the ideas in the mind of God archetypes of ours. This is not really a very helpful response.

The second thing worrying Johnson is Berkeley's rejection of Newton's absolute space, time, and motion. He wants to retain these ideas, partly out of a general respect for Newtonian science. But he is keen to do so within the broad constraints of Berkeley's system. The way in which he tries to do this is to conceive of infinite absolute space and infinite absolute time as expressions of God's infinite properties—his immensity and eternity. Johnson suggests that Berkeley in fact agrees with him about this, though he may differ from Newton in his way of explaining himself. Berkeley, however, does not want to say anything like this at all. For him space is an object for the mind, not an attribute or modification of any mind, not even God's. God's awareness of infinite space is an infinite version of our awareness of finite spaces around us. So space is an idea of sense (for us).

The third matter on which Johnson questions Berkeley is the nature of the mind and the relation between the mind and its actions. Berkeley had maintained that for a mind to exist is for it to perceive (*Principles* §98). Johnson is keen to retain a distinction between that which perceives and the perceivings that it engages in, i.e. a mind distinct from its actions. In reply, Berkeley picks holes in one of Johnson's arguments, taken from Locke, but beyond that does little more than suggest that Johnson should think harder about whether supposing the mind to exist separately from its actions requires an illegitimate use of abstraction.

Overall the tone Berkeley adopts is very much that of the senior figure in the debate, trying to brush Johnson off with a few brusque waves of the hand, while Johnson is the gadfly, persistently buzzing around Berkeley and trying to get some response out of him. The whole debate is conducted according to the rules governing polite society of the day. The delicacy with which Johnson points out that Berkeley has simply failed to address the most important questions in his first letter is particularly enjoyable.

The Text Printed in this Edition

The text of the *Principles* printed here is as it appears in volume ii of the full nine-volume edition of *The Works of George Berkeley, Bishop of Cloyne*, by A. A. Luce and T. E. Jessop (London: Nelson & Sons, 1948)—which I refer to as *Works*. The four letters between Berkeley and Johnson, also reprinted here, are from the same volume of *Works*. I am very grateful to Thomas Nelson & Sons for permission to reproduce these texts. In the case of the Berkeley–Johnson correspondence, I am also grateful to Columbia University Press, which holds the copyright; these were first published in *Samuel Johnson: His Career and Writings*, edited by H. and C. Schneider (New York, 1929).

The Luce–Jessop text is that of the second edition of the *Principles*, which was published in 1734 bound together with the third edition of the *Dialogues*. Berkeley made some changes to the texts of both works for the 1734 editions, and they are generally taken to represent his mature thought. Significant differences between the first and the second edition of the *Principles* are noted here at the foot of the relevant page rather than in the Notes. I have made very minor corrections and changes to the Luce–Jessop text, which is itself partially modernized. For instance, I have italicized *phenomena* where Berkeley did (he was not consistent). But I have not further modernized the text; I have, for example, left Berkeley's 'any thing', 'some thing', and 'it self'.

In addition to the footnotes to the text that indicate changes from earlier editions, and which are marked in the text by superscript roman letters 'a', 'b', 'c', and so on, there are a very few footnotes of Berkeley's own, e.g. at §82, marked by an asterisk. Endnotes are marked with superscript arabic numerals.

Berkeley helpfully numbered the paragraphs of the *Principles*. So reference to the *Principles* is by paragraph: e.g. to §34 or *Principles* §34. (Any otherwise unattributed reference in the present volume will be to the *Principles*.) Reference to Berkeley's Introduction to the *Principles*, which also has numbered paragraphs, will be, for example, to Intro. §15.

References to Other Works by Berkeley

References to Berkeley's other works will be made to them as they appear in *Works*. In particular, page references to the *Three Dialogues between Hylas and Philonous* are to the pages of the *Works* edition (also in *Works*, volume ii). Modern editions of the *Dialogues* tend to have the *Works* page numbers printed by the side of the text, so that people with different editions can have a common system of reference. My Oxford University Press edition of the *Dialogues*, which reprints the text given in *Works*, volume ii, follows this practice; so someone who has both volumes will be able to work from one to the other. I have also followed this practice for the text of the Berkeley–Johnson correspondence.

Berkeley's *Philosophical Commentaries*, to which I occasionally refer, are the private notebooks he made while working on the material that became the *Principles*. These were not intended for publication, but were rediscovered by A. C. Fraser and published in his 1871 edition of Berkeley's works. They are printed in *Works*, volume i.

Bibliography and Further Reading

Berkeley's Main Philosophical Works

1709   *An Essay towards a New Theory of Vision* (repr. 1710 and twice in 1732).

1710   *A Treatise Concerning the Principles of Human Knowledge* (repr. 1734).

1712   *Passive Obedience.*

1713   *Three Dialogues between Hylas and Philonous* (repr. 1725, 1734).

1721   *De Motu* (repr. 1752).

1732   *Alciphron; or, The Minute Philosopher.*

1733   *The Theory of Vision, Vindicated and Explained.*

1734   *The Analyst.*

1735   *A Defence of Free-thinking in Mathematics.*

1744   *Siris: A Chain of Philosophical Reflections and Enquiries Concerning the Virtues of Tar-water.*

Works of Berkeley: Modern Editions

LUCE, A. A., and JESSOP, T. E. (eds.), *The Works of George Berkeley, Bishop of Cloyne*, 9 vols. (London: Nelson, 1948–57). The classic edition; vol. i includes Berkeley's private notebooks (the *Philosophical Commentaries*).

ADAMS, R. M. (ed.), *George Berkeley: Three Dialogues between Hylas and Philonous* (Indianapolis: Hackett, 1979). Has a good short introduction.

AYERS, M. (ed.), *George Berkeley: Philosophical Works; including the Works on Vision* (London: Dent, Everyman, 1993). Has an excellent introduction, and contains a large number of central Berkeleian texts in accessible form, including the *Philosophical Commentaries*, largely taken from the Nelson edition above.

DANCY, J. (ed.), *Three Dialogues between Hylas and Philonous* (Oxford: Oxford University Press, 1998). This is a companion volume to the present edition of the *Principles*, and contains similar editorial material. A limited amount of material is common to the two Editor's Introductions (Section 2 and parts of Section 14).

WINKLER, K. P. (ed.), *George Berkeley: A Treatise Concerning the Principles of Human Knowledge* (Indianapolis: Hackett, 1982). Has a helpful introduction.

Biographical Works

LUCE, A. A., *The Life of George Berkeley, Bishop of Cloyne* (London: Nelson, 1949) is the standard biography.

Bibliography

FRASER, A. C. (ed.), *Life and Letters of George Berkeley, D.D.* (Oxford: Clarendon Press, 1871) is also interesting.

Works by Berkeley's Predecessors and Contemporaries: Modern Editions

ARNAULD, ANTOINE, *The Art of Thinking*: trans. with intro. by J. Dickoff and P. James (Indianapolis: Bobbs-Merrill, Library of Liberal Arts, 1964).

BAYLE, PIERRE, *Historical and Critical Dictionary: Selections*, trans. with intro. and notes by Richard Popkin (Indianapolis: Bobbs-Merrill, Library of Liberal Arts, 1965). Contains Bayle's articles on Pyrrho, Spinoza, and Zeno.

BOYLE, ROBERT, *Selected Philosophical Papers of Robert Boyle*, ed. S. Stewart (Manchester: Manchester University Press, 1979).

DESCARTES, RENÉ, *The Philosophical Writings of Descartes*, 2 vols., trans. J. Cottingham, R. Stoothoff, and D. Murdoch (Cambridge: Cambridge University Press, 1985).

GALILEO GALILEI, *The Discoveries and Opinions of Galileo*, trans. Stillman Drake (New York: Doubleday Anchor, 1957).

HUME, DAVID, *A Treatise of Human Nature*, ed. L. A. Selby-Bigge, rev. P. H. Nidditch (Oxford: Clarendon Press, 1978).

LOCKE, JOHN, *Essay Concerning Human Understanding*, ed. P. H. Nidditch (Oxford: Clarendon Press, 1975).

MALEBRANCHE, NICOLAS, *The Search after Truth* and *Elucidations of the Search after Truth*, ed. and trans. with comm. by T. M. Lennon and P. J. Olscamp (Columbus: Ohio State University Press, 1980). Contains Malebranche's *Recherche de la verité* in full in a modern translation.

NEWTON, ISAAC, *Newton's Philosophy of Nature*, ed. H. S. Thayer (New York: Hafner, 1953).

PASCAL, BLAISE, *Pensées*, ed. L. Lafuma (Paris: Editions du Seuil, 1962).

Books about Berkeley's Philosophy

DANCY, J., *Berkeley: An Introduction* (Oxford: Blackwell, 1987).

FLAGE, D. E., *Berkeley's Doctrine of Notions: A Reconstruction Based on his Theory of Meaning* (New York: St Martin's Press, 1987).

GRAYLING, A. C., *Berkeley: The Central Arguments* (London: Duckworth, 1986). Presents an advanced and detailed interpretation of Berkeley.

JESSEPH, D. M., *Berkeley's Philosophy of Mathematics* (Chicago: University of Chicago Press, 1993). Almost the only serious work on this topic.

PITCHER, G., *Berkeley* (London: Routledge, 1977). Contains a substantial discussion of the works on vision.

TIPTON, I. C., *Berkeley: The Philosophy of Immaterialism* (London: Methuen, 1974).

Bibliography

URMSON, J. O., *Berkeley*, Past Masters (Oxford: Oxford University Press, 1982). Short but lively.

WINKLER, K. P., *Berkeley: An Interpretation* (Oxford: Clarendon Press, 1989). A serious work of Berkeleian scholarship.

Collections of Articles about Berkeley

FOSTER, J., and ROBINSON, H. (eds.), *Essays on Berkeley: A Tercentennial Celebration* (Oxford: Clarendon Press, 1985).

MARTIN, C. B., and ARMSTRONG, D. M. (eds.), *Locke and Berkeley* (London: Macmillan, 1968).

MUEHLMANN, R. G. (ed.), *Berkeley's Metaphysics: Structural, Interpretive and Critical Essays* (University Park: Pennsylvania State University Press, 1995).

SOSA, E. (ed.), *Essays on the Philosophy of George Berkeley* (Dordrecht: Reidel, 1987).

STEINKRAUS, W. E. (ed.), *New Studies in Berkeley's Philosophy* (New York: Holt Rinehart, Winston, 1966).

TURBAYNE, C. (ed.), *Berkeley: Critical and Interpretative Essays* (Minnesota: Minnesota University Press, 1982). Contains the only recent bibliography of works on Berkeley.

Articles about Berkeley

AYERS, M. R., 'Substance, Reality and the Great, Dead Philosophers', *American Philosophical Quarterly*, 7 (1970), 38–49.

BURNYEAT, M., 'Idealism and Greek Philosophy: What Descartes Saw and Berkeley Missed', in G. Vesey (ed.), *Idealism Past and Present*, Royal Institute of Philosophy Lectures, xiii (1982).

CRAIG, E. J., 'Berkeley's Attack on Abstract Ideas', *Philosophical Review*, 77 (1968), 425–37.

CUMMINS, P. D., 'Berkeley's Likeness Principle', in Martin and Armstrong (eds.), *Locke and Berkeley*.

—— 'Hylas' Parity Argument', in Turbayne (ed.), *Berkeley: Critical and Interpretative Essays*.

FOSTER, J., 'Berkeley on the Physical World', in Foster and Robinson (eds.), *Essays on Berkeley*.

GALLOIS, A., 'Berkeley's Master Argument', *Philosophical Review*, 83 (1974), 55–69.

GARBER, D., 'Locke, Berkeley, and Corpuscular Scepticism', in Turbayne (ed.), *Berkeley: Critical and Interpretative Essays*.

HAUSMAN, A., 'Adhering to Inherence: A New Look at the Old Steps in Berkeley's March to Idealism', *Canadian Journal of Philosophy*, 14 (1984), 421–42.

POPKIN, R. H., 'Berkeley and Pyrrhonism', in M. Burnyeat (ed.), *The Sceptical Tradition* (Berkeley: University of California Press, 1983).

TAYLOR, C. C. W., 'Action and Inaction in Berkeley', in Foster and Robinson (eds.), *Essays on Berkeley*.

Bibliography

WILLIAMS, B. A. O., 'Imagination and the Self', in his *Problems of the Self* (Cambridge: Cambridge University Press, 1973).

Other Useful Works

ANNAS, J., and BARNES, J. (eds.), *The Modes of Scepticism: Ancient Texts and Modern Interpretations* (Cambridge: Cambridge University Press, 1985). Classical Pyrrhonism: texts and helpful commentary.

JOLLEY, N., *The Light of the Soul* (Oxford: Clarendon Press, 1990). A sympathetic examination of Malebranche's notion of 'seeing all things in God'.

McCRACKEN, C. J., *Malebranche and British Philosophy* (Oxford: Oxford University Press, 1983). Contains a chapter on Malebranche and Berkeley.

Analysis of the *Principles*

This section gives a brief breakdown of the contents of the *Principles*, paragraph by paragraph.

Introduction

The Principles Part 1

THE ARGUMENTS FOR IMMATERIALISM (§§3–24)

PART 2

The Texts

A TREATISE CONCERNING THE PRINCIPLES OF HUMAN KNOWLEDGE

Wherein the Chief Causes of Error and Difficulty in the Sciences, with the grounds of Scepticism, Atheism, and Irreligion, are inquired into.

THE PREFACE

What I here make public has, after a long and scrupulous inquiry, seem'd to me evidently true, and not unuseful to be known, particularly to those who are tainted with scepticism, or want a demonstration of the existence and immateriality of GOD, *or the natural immortality of the soul. Whether it be so or no, I am content the reader should impartially examine. Since I do not think my self any farther concerned for the success of what I have written, than as it is agreeable to truth. But to the end this may not suffer, I make it my request that the reader suspend his judgment, till he has once, at least, read the whole through with that degree of attention and thought which the subject matter shall seem to deserve. For as there are some passages that, taken by themselves, are very liable (nor could it be remedied) to gross misinterpretation, and to be charged with most absurd consequences, which, nevertheless, upon an entire perusal will appear not to follow from them : so likewise, though the whole should be read over, yet, if this be done transiently, 'tis very probable my sense may be mistaken ; but to a thinking reader, I flatter my self, it will be throughout clear and obvious. As for the characters of novelty and singularity, which some of the following notions may seem to bear, 'tis, I hope, needless to make any apology on that account. He must surely be either very weak, or very little acquainted with the sciences, who shall reject a truth, that is capable of demonstration, for no other reason but because it's newly known and contrary to the prejudices of mankind. Thus much I thought fit to premise, in order to prevent, if possible, the hasty censures of a sort of men, who are too apt to condemn an opinion before they rightly comprehend it.*

The Preface was omitted from the 1734 edition.—Ed.

INTRODUCTION

1   Philosophy being nothing else but the study of wisdom and truth, it may with reason be expected, that those who have spent most time and pains in it should enjoy a greater calm and serenity of mind, a greater clearness and evidence of knowledge, and be less disturbed with doubts and difficulties than other men. Yet so it is we see the illiterate bulk of mankind that walk the high-road of plain, common sense, and are governed by the dictates of Nature, for the most part easy and undisturbed. To them nothing that's familiar appears unaccountable or difficult to comprehend. They complain not of any want of evidence in their senses, and are out of all danger of becoming *sceptics*. But no sooner do we depart from sense and instinct to follow the light of a superior principle, to reason, meditate, and reflect on the nature of things, but a thousand scruples spring up in our minds, concerning those things which before we seemed fully to comprehend. Prejudices and errors of sense do from all parts discover themselves to our view ; and endeavouring to correct these by reason we are insensibly drawn into uncouth paradoxes, difficulties, and inconsistences, which multiply and grow upon us as we advance in speculation ; till at length, having wander'd through many intricate mazes, we find our selves just where we were, or, which is worse, sit down in a forlorn scepticism.

2   The cause of this is thought to be the obscurity of things, or the natural weakness and imperfection of our understandings. It is said the faculties we have are few, and those designed by Nature for the support and comfort of life, and not to penetrate into the inward essence and constitution of things.[1] Besides, the mind of man being finite, when it treats of things which partake of infinity, it is not to be wondered at, if it run into absurdities and contradictions ;[2] out of which it is impossible it should ever extricate it self, it being of the nature of infinite not to be comprehended by that which is finite.

3   But perhaps we may be too partial to our selves in placing the fault originally in our faculties, and not rather in the wrong use we make of them. It is a hard thing to suppose, that right deductions from true principles should ever end in consequences which cannot be maintained or made consistent. We should believe that God has dealt more bountifully with the sons of men, than to give them a strong desire for that

knowledge, which He had placed quite out of their reach. This were not agreeable to the wonted, indulgent methods of Providence, which, whatever appetites it may have implanted in the creatures, doth usually furnish them with such means as, if rightly made use of, will not fail to satisfy them. Upon the whole, I am inclined to think that the far greater part, if not all, of those difficulties which have hitherto amused philosophers, and blocked up the way to knowledge, are entirely owing to our selves. That we have first raised a dust, and then complain, we cannot see.

4   My purpose therefore is, to try if I can discover what those principles are, which have introduced all that doubtfulness and uncertainty, those absurdities and contradictions into the several sects of philosophy ; insomuch that the wisest men have thought our ignorance incurable, conceiving it to arise from the natural dulness and limitation of our faculties. And surely it is a work well deserving our pains, to make a strict inquiry concerning the first principles of *human knowledge*, to sift and examine them on all sides : especially since there may be some grounds to suspect that those lets and difficulties, which stay and embarrass the mind in its search after truth, do not spring from any darkness and intricacy in the objects, or natural defect in the understanding, so much as from false principles which have been insisted on, and might have been avoided.

5   How difficult and discouraging soever this attempt may seem, when I consider how many great and extraordinary men have gone before me in the same designs : yet I am not without some hopes, upon the consideration that the largest views are not always the clearest, and that he who is short-sighted will be obliged to draw the object nearer, and may, perhaps, by a close and narrow survey discern that which had escaped far better eyes.

6   In order to prepare the mind of the reader for the easier conceiving what follows, it is proper to premise somewhat, by way of introduction, concerning the nature and abuse of language. But the unravelling this matter leads me in some measure to anticipate my design, by taking notice of what seems to have had a chief part in rendering speculation intricate and perplexed, and to have occasioned innumerable errors and difficulties in almost all parts of knowledge. And that is the opinion that the mind hath a power of framing *abstract ideas* or notions of things. He who is not a perfect stranger to the writings and disputes of philosophers, must needs acknowledge that no small part of them are spent about abstract ideas.[3] These are in a more especial manner, thought to be the object of those sciences which go by the name of *Logic* and *Metaphysics*, and of all that which passes under the notion of the most abstracted and sublime learning, in all

which one shall scarce find any question handled in such a manner, as does not suppose their existence in the mind, and that it is well acquainted with them.[4]

7   It is agreed on all hands, that the qualities or modes of things do never really exist each of them apart by it self, and separated from all others, but are mixed, as it were, and blended together, several in the same object. But we are told, the mind being able to consider each quality singly, or abstracted from those other qualities with which it is united, does by that means frame to it self abstract ideas. For example, there is perceived by sight an object extended, coloured, and moved : this mixed or compound idea the mind resolving into its simple, constituent parts, and viewing each by it self, exclusive of the rest, does frame the abstract ideas of extension, colour, and motion. Not that it is possible for colour or motion to exist without extension : but only that the mind can frame to it self by *abstraction* the idea of colour exclusive of extension, and of motion exclusive of both colour and extension.

8   Again, the mind having observed that in the particular extensions perceived by sense, there is something common and alike in all, and some other things peculiar, as this or that figure or magnitude, which distinguish them one from another ; it considers apart or singles out by it self that which is common, making thereof a most abstract idea of extension, which is neither line, surface, nor solid, nor has any figure or magnitude but is an idea entirely prescinded from all these. So likewise the mind by leaving out of the particular colours perceived by sense, that which distinguishes them one from another, and retaining that only which is common to all, makes an idea of colour in abstract which is neither red, nor blue, nor white, nor any other determinate colour. And in like manner by considering motion abstractedly not only from the body moved, but likewise from the figure it describes, and all particular directions and velocities, the abstract idea of motion is framed ; which equally corresponds to all particular motions whatsoever that may be perceived by sense.

9   And as the mind frames to it self abstract ideas of qualities or modes, so does it, by the same precision or mental separation, attain abstract ideas of the more compounded beings, which include several coexistent qualities. For example, the mind having observed that Peter, James, and John, resemble each other, in certain common agreements[5] of shape and other qualities, leaves out of the complex or compounded idea it has of Peter, James, and any other particular man, that which is peculiar to each, retaining only what is common to all ; and so makes an abstract idea wherein all the particulars equally partake, abstracting entirely from

and cutting off all those circumstances and differences, which might determine it to any particular existence. And after this manner it is said we come
by the abstract idea of *man* or, if you please, humanity or human nature ;
wherein it is true, there is included colour, because there is no man but has
some colour, but then it can be neither white, nor black, nor any particular
colour ; because there is no one particular colour wherein all men partake.
So likewise there is included stature, but then it is neither tall stature nor
low stature, nor yet middle stature, but something abstracted from all
these. And so of the rest. Moreover, there being a great variety of other
creatures that partake in some parts, but not all, of the complex idea of
man, the mind leaving out those parts which are peculiar to men, and
retaining those only which are common to all the living creatures, frameth
the idea of *animal*, which abstracts not only from all particular men, but
also all birds, beasts, fishes, and insects. The constituent parts of the
abstract idea of animal are body, life, sense, and spontaneous motion. By
body is meant, body without any particular shape or figure, there being no
one shape or figure common to all animals, without covering, either of
hair or feathers, or scales, &c. nor yet naked : hair, feathers, scales, and
nakedness being the distinguishing properties of particular animals,
and for that reason left out of the *abstract idea*. Upon the same account
the spontaneous motion must be neither walking, nor flying, nor
creeping, it is nevertheless a motion, but what that motion is, it is not easy
to conceive.

10   Whether others have this wonderful faculty of *abstracting their
ideas*, they best can tell : for my self I find indeed I have a faculty of imagining, or representing to my self the ideas of those particular things I have
perceived and of variously compounding and dividing them. I can imagine
a man with two heads or the upper parts of a man joined to the body of a
horse. I can consider the hand, the eye, the nose, each by it self abstracted
or separated from the rest of the body. But then whatever hand or eye I
imagine, it must have some particular shape and colour. Likewise the idea
of man that I frame to my self, must be either of a white, or a black, or a
tawny, a straight, or a crooked, a tall, or a low, or a middle-sized man. I
cannot by any effort of thought conceive the abstract idea above
described. And it is equally impossible for me to form the abstract idea of
motion distinct from the body moving, and which is neither swift nor slow,
curvilinear nor rectilinear ; and the like may be said of all other abstract
general ideas whatsoever. To be plain, I own my self able to abstract in one
sense, as when I consider some particular parts or qualities separated from
others, with which though they are united in some object, yet, it is possible

they may really exist without them. But I deny that I can abstract one from another, or conceive separately, those qualities which it is impossible should exist so separated ; or that I can frame a general notion by abstract-ing from particulars in the manner aforesaid.[6] Which two last are the proper acceptations of *abstraction*. And there are grounds to think most men will acknowledge themselves to be in my case. The generality of men which are simple and illiterate never pretend to *abstract notions*. It's said they are difficult and not to be attained without pains and study. We may therefore reasonably conclude that, if such there be, they are confined only to the learned.

11   I proceed to examine what can be alleged in defence of the doctrine of abstraction, and try if I can discover what it is that inclines the men of speculation to embrace an opinion, so remote from common sense as that seems to be.[7] There has been a late deservedly esteemed philosopher,[8] who, no doubt, has given it very much countenance by seeming to think the having abstract general ideas is what puts the widest difference in point of understanding betwixt man and beast. 'The having of general ideas, (*saith he*) is that which puts a perfect distinction betwixt man and brutes, and is an excellency which the faculties of brutes do by no means attain unto. For it is evident we observe no footsteps in them of making use of general signs for universal ideas ; from which we have reason to imagine that they have not the faculty of *abstracting* or making general ideas, since they have no use of words or any other general signs. *And a little after.* Therefore, I think, we may suppose that it is in this that the species of brutes are discriminated from men, and 'tis that proper difference wherein they are wholly separated, and which at last widens to so wide a distance. For if they have any ideas at all, and are not bare machines (as some would have them) we cannot deny them to have some reason. It seems as evident to me that they do some of them in certain instances reason as that they have sense, but it is only in particular ideas, just as they receive them from their senses. They are the best of them tied up within those narrow bounds, and have not (as I think) the faculty to enlarge them by any kind of *abstraction.*' *Essay on Hum. Underst.* B.2. C.11. Sect. 10. and 11. I readily agree with this learned author, that the faculties of brutes can by no means attain to *abstraction*. But then if this be made the distinguishing property of that sort of animals, I fear a great many of those that pass for men must be reck-oned into their number. The reason that is here assigned why we have no grounds to think brutes have abstract general ideas, is that we observe in them no use of words or any other general signs ; which is built on this sup-position, to wit, that the making use of words, implies the having general

ideas. From which it follows, that men who use language are able to abstract or generalize their ideas. That this is the sense and arguing of the author will further appear by his answering the question he in another place puts. 'Since all things that exist are only particulars, how come we by general terms ?' *His answer is*, 'Words become general by being made the signs of general ideas.' *Essay on Hum. Underst. B.3. C.3. Sect. 6.* But it seems that a word becomes general by being made the sign, not of an abstract general idea but, of several particular ideas, any one of which it indifferently suggests to the mind. For example, when it is said *the change of motion is proportional to the impressed force*, or that *whatever has extension is divisible* ; these propositions are to be understood of motion and extension in general, and nevertheless it will not follow that they suggest to my thoughts an idea of motion without a body moved, or any determinate direction and velocity, or that I must conceive an abstract general idea of extension, which is neither line, surface nor solid, neither great nor small, black, white, nor red, nor of any other determinate colour. It is only implied that whatever motion I consider, whether it be swift or slow, perpendicular, horizontal or oblique, or in whatever object, the axiom concerning it holds equally true. As does the other of every particular extension, it matters not whether line, surface or solid, whether of this or that magnitude or figure.

12   By observing how ideas become general, we may the better judge how words are made so. And here it is to be noted that I do not deny absolutely there are general ideas, but only that there are any *abstract general ideas* : for in the passages above quoted, wherein there is mention of general ideas, it is always supposed that they are formed by *abstraction*, after the manner set forth in Sect. 8 and 9.[9] Now if we will annex a meaning to our words, and speak only of what we can conceive, I believe we shall acknowledge, that an idea, which considered in it self is particular, becomes general, by being made to represent or stand for all other particular ideas of the same sort. To make this plain by an example, suppose a geometrician is demonstrating the method, of cutting a line in two equal parts. He draws, for instance, a black line of an inch in length, this which in it self is a particular line is nevertheless with regard to its signification general, since as it is there used, it represents all particular lines whatsoever ; for that what is demonstrated of it, is demonstrated of all lines or, in other words, of a line in general. And as that particular line becomes general, by being made a sign, so the name *line* which taken absolutely is particular, by being a sign is made general.[10] And as the former owes its generality, not to its being the sign of an abstract or general line, but of all

particular right lines that may possibly exist, so the latter must be thought to derive its generality from the same cause, namely, the various particular lines which it indifferently denotes.

13   To give the reader a yet clearer view of the nature of abstract ideas, and the uses they are thought necessary to, I shall add one more passage out of the *Essay on Human Understanding*, which is as follows. '*Abstract ideas* are not so obvious or easy to children or the yet unexercised mind as particular ones. If they seem so to grown men, it is only because by constant and familiar use they are made so. For when we nicely reflect upon them, we shall find that general ideas are fictions and contrivances of the mind, that carry difficulty with them, and do not so easily offer themselves, as we are apt to imagine. For example, does it not require some pains and skill to form the general idea of a triangle (which is yet none of the most abstract comprehensive and difficult) for it must be neither oblique nor rectangle, neither equilateral, equicrural, nor scalenon, but *all and none* of these at once. In effect, it is something imperfect that cannot exist, an idea wherein some parts of several different and *inconsistent* ideas are put together.'[11] It is true the mind in this imperfect state has need of such ideas, and makes all the haste to them it can, for the conveniency of communication and enlargement of knowledge, to both which it is naturally very much inclined. But yet one has reason to suspect such ideas are marks of our imperfection. At least this is enough to shew that the most abstract and general ideas are not those that the mind is first and most easily acquainted with, nor such as its earliest knowledge is conversant about.' B.4. C.7. Sect. 9. If any man has the faculty of framing in his mind such an idea of a triangle as is here described, it is in vain to pretend to dispute him out of it, nor would I go about it. All I desire is, that the reader would fully and certainly inform himself whether he has such an idea or no. And this, methinks, can be no hard task for any one to perform. What more easy than for any one to look a little into his own thoughts, and there try whether he has, or can attain to have, an idea that shall correspond with the description that is here given of the general idea of a triangle, which is, *neither oblique, nor rectangle, equilateral, equicrural, nor scalenon, but all and none of these at once* ?

14   Much is here said of the difficulty that abstract ideas carry with them, and the pains and skill requisite to the forming them. And it is on all hands agreed that there is need of great toil and labour of the mind, to emancipate our thoughts from particular objects, and raise them to those sublime speculations that are conversant about abstract ideas. From all which the natural consequence should seem to be, that so difficult a thing

as the forming abstract ideas was not necessary for *communication*, which is so easy and familiar to all sorts of men. But we are told, if they seem obvious and easy to grown men, *It is only because by constant and familiar use they are made so*. Now I would fain know at what time it is, men are employed in surmounting that difficulty, and furnishing themselves with those necessary helps for discourse. It cannot be when they are grown up, for then it seems they are not conscious of any such pains-taking ; it remains therefore to be the business of their childhood. And surely, the great and multiplied labour of framing abstract notions, will be found a hard task for that tender age. Is it not a hard thing to imagine, that a couple of children cannot prate together, of their sugar-plums and rattles and the rest of their little trinkets, till they have first tacked together numberless inconsistencies, and so framed in their minds *abstract general ideas*, and annexed them to every common name they make use of ?

15 Nor do I think them a whit more needful for the *enlargement of knowledge* than for *communication*. It is I know a point much insisted on, that all knowledge and demonstration are about universal notions,[12] to which I fully agree : but then it doth not appear to me that those notions are formed by *abstraction* in the manner premised ; *universality*, so far as I can comprehend, not consisting in the absolute, positive nature or conception of any thing, but in the relation it bears to the particulars signified or represented by it : by virtue whereof it is that things, names, or notions, being in their own nature *particular*, are rendered *universal*. Thus when I demonstrate any proposition concerning triangles, it is to be supposed that I have in view the universal idea of a triangle ; which ought not to be understood as if I could frame an idea of a triangle which was neither equilateral nor scalenon nor equicrural. But only that the particular triangle I consider, whether of this or that sort it matters not, doth equally stand for and represent all rectilinear triangles whatsoever, and is in that sense *universal*. All which seems very plain and not to include any difficulty in it.

16 But here it will be demanded, how we can know any proposition to be true of all particular triangles, except we have first seen it demonstrated of the abstract idea of a triangle which equally agrees to all ? For because a property may be demonstrated to agree to some one particular triangle, it will not thence follow that it equally belongs to any other triangle, which in all respects is not the same with it. For example, having demonstrated that the three angles of an isosceles rectangular triangle are equal to two right ones, I cannot therefore conclude this affection agrees to all other triangles, which have neither a right angle, nor two equal sides. It seems

therefore that, to be certain this proposition is universally true, we must either make a particular demonstration for every particular triangle, which is impossible, or once for all demonstrate it of the *abstract idea of a triangle*, in which all the particulars do indifferently partake, and by which they are all equally represented. To which I answer, that though the idea I have in view whilst I make the demonstration, be, for instance, that of an isosceles rectangular triangle, whose sides are of a determinate length, I may nevertheless be certain it extends to all other rectilinear triangles, of what sort or bigness soever. And that, because neither the right angle, nor the equality, nor determinate length of the sides, are at all concerned in the demonstration. It is true, the diagram I have in view includes all these particulars, but then there is not the least mention made of them in the proof of the proposition. It is not said, the three angles are equal to two right ones, because one of them is a right angle, or because the sides comprehending it are of the same length. Which sufficiently shews that the right angle might have been oblique, and the sides unequal, and for all that the demonstration have held good. And for this reason it is, that I conclude that to be true of any obliquangular or scalenon, which I had demonstrated of a particular right-angled, equicrural triangle ; and not because I demonstrated the proposition of the abstract idea of a triangle.[13] And here it must be acknowledged that a man may consider a figure merely as triangular, without attending to the particular qualities of the angles, or relations of the sides. So far he may abstract : but this will never prove, that he can frame an abstract general inconsistent idea of a triangle. In like manner we may consider Peter so far forth as man, or so far forth as animal, without framing the forementioned abstract idea, either of man or of animal, in as much as all that is perceived is not considered.[a]

17   It were an endless, as well as an useless thing, to trace the Schoolmen,[14] those great masters of abstraction, through all the manifold inextricable labyrinths of error and dispute, which their doctrine of abstract natures and notions seems to have led them into. What bickerings and controversies, and what a learned dust have been raised about those matters, and what mighty advantage hath been from thence derived to mankind, are things at this day too clearly known to need being insisted on. And it had been well if the ill effects of that doctrine were confined to those only who make the most avowed profession of it. When men consider the great pains, industry and parts, that have for so many ages been laid out on the cultivation and advancement of the sciences, and that

---

[a]   *And here it must be acknowledged . . . not considered.*—added in 1734 edition.

notwithstanding all this, the far greater part of them remain full of darkness and uncertainty, and disputes that are like never to have an end, and even those that are thought to be supported by the most clear and cogent demonstrations, contain in them paradoxes which are perfectly irreconcilable to the understandings of men, and that taking all together, a small portion of them doth supply any real benefit to mankind, otherwise than by being an innocent diversion and amusement. I say, the consideration of all this is apt to throw them into a despondency, and perfect contempt of all study. But this may perhaps cease, upon a view of the false principles that have obtained in the world, amongst all which there is none, methinks, hath a more wide influence over the thoughts of speculative men, than this of abstract general ideas.

18 I come now to consider the source of this prevailing notion, and that seems to me to be language. And surely nothing of less extent than reason it self could have been the source of an opinion so universally received. The truth of this appears as from other reasons, so also from the plain confession of the ablest patrons of abstract ideas, who acknowledge that they are made in order to naming ; from which it is a clear consequence, that if there had been no such thing as speech or universal signs, there never had been any thought of abstraction. See B. 3 C. 6. Sect. 39 *and elsewhere of the Essay on Human Understanding*. Let us therefore examine the manner wherein words have contributed to the origin of that mistake. First then, 'tis thought that every name hath, or ought to have, one only precise and settled signification, which inclines men to think there are certain *abstract, determinate ideas*, which constitute the true and only immediate signification of each general name. And that it is by the mediation of these abstract ideas, that a general name comes to signify any particular thing. Whereas, in truth, there is no such thing as one precise and definite signification annexed to any general name, they all signifying indifferently a great number of particular ideas. All which doth evidently follow from what has been already said, and will clearly appear to any one by a little reflexion. To this it will be objected, that every name that has a definition, is thereby restrained to one certain signification. For example, a *triangle* is defined to be a *plane surface comprehended by three right lines* ;[15] by which that name is limited to denote one certain idea and no other. To which I answer, that in the definition it is not said whether the surface be great or small, black or white, nor whether the sides are long or short, equal or unequal, nor with what angles they are inclined to each other ; in all which there may be great variety, and consequently there is no one settled idea which limits the signification of the word *triangle*. 'Tis one

thing for to keep a name constantly to the same definition, and another to make it stand every where for the same idea : the one is necessary, the other useless and impracticable.

19   But to give a farther account how words came to produce the doctrine of abstract ideas, it must be observed that it is a received opinion, that language has no other end but the communicating our ideas, and that every significant name stands for an idea.[16] This being so, and it being withal certain, that names, which yet are not thought altogether insignificant, do not always mark out particular conceivable ideas, it is straightway concluded that they stand for abstract notions. That there are many names in use amongst speculative men, which do not always suggest to others determinate particular ideas, is what no body will deny. And a little attention will discover, that it is not necessary (even in the strictest reasonings) significant names which stand for ideas should, every time they are used, excite in the understanding the ideas they are made to stand for : in reading and discoursing, names being for the most part used as letters are in *algebra*, in which though a particular quantity be marked by each letter, yet to proceed right it is not requisite that in every step each letter suggest to your thoughts, that particular quantity it was appointed to stand for.

20   Besides, the communicating of ideas marked by words is not the chief and only end of language, as is commonly supposed.[17] There are other ends, as the raising of some passion, the exciting to, or deterring from an action, the putting the mind in some particular disposition ; to which the former is in many cases barely subservient, and sometimes entirely omitted, when these can be obtained without it, as I think doth not infrequently happen in the familiar use of language. I entreat the reader to reflect with himself, and see if it doth not often happen either in hearing or reading a discourse, that the passions of fear, love, hatred, admiration, disdain, and the like arise, immediately in his mind upon the perception of certain words, without any ideas coming between. At first, indeed, the words might have occasioned ideas that were fit to produce those emotions ; but, if I mistake not, it will be found that when language is once grown familiar, the hearing of the sounds or sight of the characters is oft immediately attended with those passions, which at first were wont to be produced by the intervention of ideas, that are now quite omitted. May we not, for example, be affected with the promise of a *good thing*, though we have not an idea of what it is ? Or is not the being threatened with danger sufficient to excite a dread, though we think not of any particular evil likely to befall us, nor yet frame to our selves an idea of danger in abstract ? If any one shall join ever so little reflexion of his own to what

has been said, I believe it will evidently appear to him, that general names are often used in the propriety of language without the speaker's designing them for marks of ideas in his own, which he would have them raise in the mind of the hearer. Even proper names themselves do not seem always spoken, with a design to bring into our view the ideas of those individuals that are supposed to be marked by them. For example, when a Schoolman tells me *Aristotle hath said it*, all I conceive he means by it, is to dispose me to embrace his opinion with the deference and submission which custom has annexed to that name. And this effect may be so instantly produced in the minds of those who are accustomed to resign their judgment to the authority of that philosopher, as it is impossible any idea either of his person, writings, or reputation should go before. Innumerable examples of this kind may be given, but why should I insist on those things, which every one's experience will, I doubt not, plentifully suggest unto him?

21   We have, I think, shewn the impossibility of *abstract ideas*. We have considered what has been said for them by their ablest patrons ; and endeavoured to shew they are of no use for those ends, to which they are thought necessary. And lastly, we have traced them to the source from whence they flow, which appears to be language. It cannot be denied that words are of excellent use, in that by their means all that stock of knowledge which has been purchased by the joint labours of inquisitive men in all ages and nations, may be drawn into the view and made the possession of one single person. But at the same time it must be owned that most parts of knowledge have been strangely perplexed and darkened by the abuse of words, and general ways of speech wherein they are delivered. Since therefore words are so apt to impose on the understanding, whatever ideas I consider, I shall endeavour to take them bare and naked into my view, keeping out of my thoughts, so far as I am able, those names which long and constant use hath so strictly united with them ; from which I may expect to derive the following advantages.

22   First, I shall be sure to get clear of all controversies purely verbal ; the springing up of which weeds in almost all the sciences has been a main hindrance to the growth of true and sound knowledge. Secondly, this seems to be a sure way to extricate my self out of that fine and subtle net of *abstract ideas*, which has so miserably perplexed and entangled the minds of men, and that with this peculiar circumstance, that by how much the finer and more curious was the wit of any man, by so much the deeper was he like to be ensnared, and faster held therein. Thirdly, so long as I confine my thoughts to my own ideas divested of words, I do not see how I can easily be mistaken. The objects I consider, I clearly and adequately know. I

cannot be deceived in thinking I have an idea which I have not. It is not possible for me to imagine, that any of my own ideas are alike or unlike, that are not truly so. To discern the agreements or disagreements there are between my ideas, to see what ideas are included in any compound idea, and what not, there is nothing more requisite, than an attentive perception of what passes in my own understanding.

23   But the attainment of all these advantages doth presuppose an entire deliverance from the deception of words, which I dare hardly promise my self ; so difficult a thing it is to dissolve an union so early begun, and confirmed by so long a habit as that betwixt words and ideas. Which difficulty seems to have been very much increased by the doctrine of *abstraction*. For so long as men thought abstract ideas were annexed to their words, it doth not seem strange that they should use words for ideas : it being found an impracticable thing to lay aside the word, and retain the abstract idea in the mind, which in it self was perfectly inconceivable. This seems to me the principal cause, why those men who have so emphatically recommended to others, the laying aside all use of words in their meditations, and contemplating their bare ideas, have yet failed to perform it themselves.[18] Of late many have been very sensible of the absurd opinions and insignificant disputes, which grow out of the abuse of words. And in order to remedy these evils they advise well, that we attend to the ideas signified, and draw off our attention from the words which signify them. But how good soever this advice may be, they have given others, it is plain they could not have a due regard to it themselves, so long as they thought the only immediate use of words was to signify ideas, and that the immediate signification of every general name was a *determinate, abstract idea*.

24   But these being known to be mistakes, a man may with greater ease prevent his being imposed on by words. He that knows he has no other than particular ideas, will not puzzle himself in vain to find out and conceive the abstract idea, annexed to any name. And he that knows names do not always stand for ideas, will spare himself the labour of looking for ideas, where there are none to be had. It were therefore to be wished that every one would use his utmost endeavours, to obtain a clear view of the ideas he would consider, separating from them all that dress and encumbrance of words which so much contribute to blind the judgment and divide the attention. In vain do we extend our view into the heavens, and pry into the entrails of the earth, in vain do we consult the writings of learned men, and trace the dark footsteps of antiquity ; we need only draw the curtain of words, to behold the fairest tree of knowledge, whose fruit is excellent, and within the reach of our hand.

25 Unless we take care to clear the first principles of knowledge, from the embarras and delusion of words, we may make infinite reasonings upon them to no purpose ; we may draw consequences from consequences, and be never the wiser. The farther we go, we shall only lose our selves the more irrecoverably, and be the deeper entangled in difficulties and mistakes. Whoever therefore designs to read the following sheets, I entreat him to make my words the occasion of his own thinking, and endeavour to attain the same train of thoughts in reading, that I had in writing them. By this means it will be easy for him to discover the truth or falsity of what I say. He will be out of all danger of being deceived by my words, and I do not see how he can be led into an error by considering his own naked, undisguised ideas.

OF THE PRINCIPLES OF
HUMAN KNOWLEDGE
PART I

1 It is evident to any one who takes a survey of the objects of human knowledge, that they are either ideas actually imprinted on the senses, or else such as are perceived by attending to the passions and operations of the mind, or lastly ideas formed by help of memory and imagination, either compounding, dividing, or barely representing those originally perceived in the aforesaid ways.[19] By sight I have the ideas of light and colours with their several degrees and variations. By touch I perceive, for example, hard and soft, heat and cold, motion and resistance, and of all these more and less either as to quantity or degree. Smelling furnishes me with odours ; the palate with tastes, and hearing conveys sounds to the mind in all their variety of tone and composition. And as several of these are observed to accompany each other, they come to be marked by one name, and so to be reputed as one thing. Thus, for example, a certain colour, taste, smell, figure and consistence having been observed to go together, are accounted one distinct thing, signified by the name *apple*.[20] Other collections of ideas constitute a stone, a tree, a book, and the like sensible things ; which, as they are pleasing or disagreeable, excite the passions of love, hatred, joy, grief, and so forth. *collections of ideas = distinct things*

2 But besides all that endless variety of ideas or objects of knowledge, there is likewise something which knows or perceives them, and exercises divers operations, as willing, imagining, remembering about them. This perceiving, active being is what I call *mind*, *spirit*, *soul* or *my self*. By which words I do not denote any one of my ideas, but a thing entirely distinct from them, wherein they exist, or, which is the same thing, whereby they are perceived ; for the existence of an idea consists in being perceived.[21]

3 That neither our thoughts, nor passions, nor ideas formed by the imagination, exist without the mind,[22] is what every body will allow. And it seems no less evident that the various sensations or ideas imprinted on the sense, however blended or combined together (that is, whatever objects they compose) cannot exist otherwise than in a mind perceiving them. I

[handwritten annotation: existence is dependent upon perception]

think an intuitive knowledge[23] may be obtained of this, by any one that shall attend to what is meant by the term *exist* when applied to sensible things. The table I write on, I say, exists, that is, I see and feel it ; and if I were out of my study I should say it existed, meaning thereby that if I was in my study I might perceive it,[24] or that some other spirit actually does perceive it. There was an odour, that is, it was smelled ; there was a sound, that is to say, it was heard ; a colour or figure, and it was perceived by sight or touch. This is all that I can understand by these and the like expressions. For as to what is said of the absolute existence of unthinking things without any relation to their being perceived, that seems perfectly unintelligible. Their *esse* is *percipi*,[25] nor is it possible they should have any existence, out of the minds or thinking things which perceive them.

4   It is indeed an opinion strangely prevailing amongst men, that houses, mountains, rivers, and in a word all sensible objects have an existence natural or real, distinct from their being perceived by the understanding. But with how great an assurance and acquiescence soever this principle may be entertained in the world ; yet whoever shall find in his heart to call it in question, may, if I mistake not, perceive it to involve a manifest contradiction. For what are the forementioned objects but the things we perceive by sense, and what do we perceive besides our own ideas or sensations ; and is it not plainly repugnant that any one of these or any combination of them should exist unperceived ?

5   If we throughly examine this tenet, it will, perhaps, be found at bottom to depend on the doctrine of *abstract ideas*.[26] For can there be a nicer strain of abstraction than to distinguish the existence of sensible objects from their being perceived, so as to conceive them existing unperceived ? Light and colours, heat and cold, extension and figures, in a word the things we see and feel, what are they but so many sensations, notions, ideas or impressions on the sense ; and is it possible to separate, even in thought, any of these from perception ? For my part I might as easily divide a thing from it self. I may indeed divide in my thoughts or conceive apart from each other those things which, perhaps, I never perceived by sense so divided. Thus I imagine the trunk of a human body without the limbs, or conceive the smell of a rose without thinking on the rose it self. So far I will not deny I can abstract, if that may properly be called *abstraction*, which extends only to the conceiving separately such objects, as it is possible may really exist or be actually perceived asunder. But my conceiving or imagining power does not extend beyond the possibility of real existence or perception. Hence as it is impossible for me to see or feel any thing without an actual sensation of that thing, so is it impossible for me to conceive in my

thoughts any sensible thing or object distinct from the sensation or perception of it.[b]

6   Some truths there are so near and obvious to the mind, that a man need only open his eyes to see them. Such I take this important one to be, to wit, that all the choir of heaven and furniture of the earth, in a word all those bodies which compose the mighty frame of the world, have not any subsistence without a mind, that their being is to be perceived or known ; that consequently so long as they are not actually perceived by me, or do not exist in my mind or that of any other created spirit, they must either have no existence at all, or else subsist in the mind of some eternal spirit :[27] it being perfectly unintelligible and involving all the absurdity of abstraction, to attribute to any single part of them an existence independent of a spirit. To be convinced of which, the reader need only reflect and try to separate in his own thoughts the being of a sensible thing from its being perceived.

7   From what has been said, it follows, there is not any other substance than *spirit*, or that which perceives.[28] But for the fuller proof of this point, let it be considered, the sensible qualities are colour, figure, motion, smell, taste, and such like, that is, the ideas perceived by sense. Now for an idea to exist in an unperceiving thing, is a manifest contradiction ; for to have an idea is all one as to perceive : that therefore wherein colour, figure, and the like qualities exist, must perceive them ; hence it is clear there can be no unthinking substance or *substratum*[29] of those ideas.[30]

8   But say you, though the ideas themselves do not exist without the mind, yet there may be things like them whereof they are copies or resemblances, which things exist without the mind, in an unthinking substance. I answer, an idea can be like nothing but an idea ;[31] a colour or figure can be like nothing but another colour or figure. If we look but ever so little into our thoughts, we shall find it impossible for us to conceive a likeness except only between our ideas. Again,[32] I ask whether those supposed originals or external things, of which our ideas are the pictures or representations, be themselves perceivable or no ? If they are, then they are ideas, and we have gained our point ; but if you say they are not, I appeal to any one whether it be sense, to assert a colour is like something which is invisible ; hard or soft, like something which is intangible ; and so of the rest.

9   Some there are who make a distinction betwixt *primary* and *secondary* qualities : by the former, they mean extension, figure, motion, rest,

---

[b]   The 1710 edition continues: *In truth the object and the sensation are the same thing, and cannot therefore be abstracted from each other.*

solidity or impenetrability and number : by the latter they denote all other sensible qualities, as colours, sounds, tastes, and so forth.[33] The ideas we have of these they acknowledge not to be the resemblances of any thing existing without the mind or unperceived ; but they will have our ideas of the primary qualities to be patterns or images of things which exist without the mind, in an unthinking substance which they call *matter*. By matter therefore we are to understand an inert, senseless[34] substance, in which extension, figure, and motion, do actually subsist. But it is evident from what we have already shewn, that extension, figure and motion are only ideas existing in the mind, and that an idea can be like nothing but another idea, and that consequently neither they nor their archetypes can exist in an unperceiving substance.[35] Hence it is plain, that the very notion of what is called *matter* or *corporeal substance*, involves a contradiction in it.

10   They who assert that figure, motion, and the rest of the primary or original qualities do exist without the mind, in unthinking substances, do at the same time acknowledge that colours, sounds, heat, cold, and such like secondary qualities, do not, which they tell us are sensations existing in the mind alone,[36] that depend on and are occasioned by the different size, texture and motion of the minute particles of matter. This they take for an undoubted truth, which they can demonstrate beyond all exception. Now if it be certain, that those original qualities are inseparably united with the other sensible qualities, and not, even in thought, capable of being abstracted from them, it plainly follows that they exist only in the mind. But I desire any one to reflect and try, whether he can by any abstraction of thought, conceive the extension and motion of a body, without all other sensible qualities.[37] For my own part, I see evidently that it is not in my power to frame an idea of a body extended and moved, but I must withal give it some colour or other sensible quality which is acknowledged to exist only in the mind.[38] In short, extension, figure, and motion, abstracted from all other qualities, are inconceivable. Where therefore the other sensible qualities are, there must these be also, to wit, in the mind and no where else.

11   Again, *great* and *small*, *swift* and *slow*, are allowed to exist no where without the mind, being entirely relative, and changing as the frame or position of the organs of sense varies.[39] The extension therefore which exists without the mind, is neither great nor small, the motion neither swift nor slow, that is, they are nothing at all. But say you, they are extension in general, and motion in general :[40] thus we see how much the tenet of extended, moveable substances existing without the mind, depends on

that strange doctrine of *abstract ideas*. And here I cannot but remark, how nearly the vague and indeterminate description of matter or corporeal substance, which the modern philosophers are run into by their own principles, resembles that antiquated and so much ridiculed notion of *materia prima*,[41] to be met with in Aristotle and his followers. Without extension solidity cannot be conceived ; since therefore it has been shewn that extension exists not in an unthinking substance, the same must also be true of solidity.

12   That number is entirely the creature of the mind, even though the other qualities be allowed to exist without, will be evident to whoever considers, that the same thing bears a different denomination of number, as the mind views it with different respects. Thus, the same extension is one or three or thirty six, according as the mind considers it with reference to a yard, a foot, or an inch. Number is so visibly relative, and dependent on men's understanding,[42] that it is strange to think how any one should give it an absolute existence without the mind. We say one book, one page, one line ; all these are equally units, though some contain several of the others. And in each instance it is plain, the unit relates to some particular combination of ideas arbitrarily put together by the mind.

13   Unity I know some will have to be a simple or uncompounded idea, accompanying all other ideas into the mind.[43] That I have any such idea answering the word *unity*, I do not find ; and if I had, methinks I could not miss finding it ; on the contrary it should be the most familiar to my understanding, since it is said to accompany all other ideas, and to be perceived by all the ways of sensation and reflexion. To say no more, it is an *abstract idea*.

14   I shall farther add, that after the same manner, as modern philosophers prove certain sensible qualities to have no existence in matter, or without the mind, the same thing may be likewise proved of all other sensible qualities whatsoever.[44] Thus, for instance, it is said that heat and cold are affections only of the mind, and not at all patterns of real beings, existing in the corporeal substances which excite them, for that the same body which appears cold to one hand, seems warm to another. Now why may we not as well argue that figure and extension are not patterns or resemblances of qualities existing in matter, because to the same eye at different stations, or eyes of a different texture at the same station, they appear various, and cannot therefore be the images of any thing settled and determinate without the mind ? Again, it is proved that sweetness is not really in the sapid thing, because the thing remaining unaltered the sweetness is changed into bitter, as in case of a fever or otherwise vitiated palate. Is it

not as reasonable to say, that motion is not without the mind, since if the succession of ideas in the mind become swifter, the motion, it is acknowledged, shall appear slower without any alteration in any external object.

15 In short, let anyone consider those arguments, which are thought manifestly to prove that colours and tastes exist only in the mind, and he shall find they may with equal force, be brought to prove the same thing of extension, figure, and motion. Though it must be confessed this method of arguing doth not so much prove that there is no extension or colour in an outward object, as that we do not know by sense which is the true extension or colour of the object.[45] But the arguments foregoing plainly shew it to be impossible that any colour or extension at all, or other sensible quality whatsoever, should exist in an unthinking subject without the mind, or in truth, that there should be any such thing as an outward object.

16 But let us examine a little the received opinion. It is said extension is a mode or accident of matter, and that matter is the *substratum* that supports it. Now I desire that you would explain what is meant by matter's *supporting* extension :[46] say you, I have no idea of matter, and therefore cannot explain it. I answer, though you have no positive, yet if you have any meaning at all, you must at least have a relative idea of matter ; though you know not what it is, yet you must be supposed to know what relation it bears to accidents, and what is meant by its supporting them. It is evident *support* cannot here be taken in its usual or literal sense, as when we say that pillars support a building : in what sense therefore must it be taken ?

17 If we inquire into what the most accurate philosophers declare themselves to mean by *material substance* ; we shall find them acknowledge, they have no other meaning annexed to those sounds, but the idea of being in general, together with the relative notion of its supporting accidents. The general idea of being appeareth to me the most abstract and incomprehensible of all other ; and as for its supporting accidents, this, as we have just now observed, cannot be understood in the common sense of those words ; it must therefore be taken in some other sense, but what that is they do not explain. So that when I consider the two parts or branches which make the signification of the words *material substance*, I am convinced there is no distinct meaning annexed to them. But why should we trouble ourselves any farther, in discussing this material *substratum* or support of figure and motion, and other sensible qualities ? Does it not suppose they have an existence without the mind ? And is not this a direct repugnancy, and altogether inconceivable ?

18 But though it were possible that solid, figured, moveable substances may exist without the mind, corresponding to the ideas we have of bodies, yet how is it possible for us to know this ?[47] Either we must know it by sense, or by reason. As for our senses, by them we have the knowledge only of our sensations, ideas, or those things that are immediately perceived by sense, call them what you will : but they do not inform us that things exist without the mind, or unperceived, like to those which are perceived. This the materialists themselves acknowledge. It remains therefore that if we have any knowledge at all of external things, it must be by reason, inferring their existence from what is immediately perceived by sense. But what reason can induce us to believe the existence of bodies without the mind, from what we perceive, since the very patrons of matter themselves do not pretend, there is any necessary connexion betwixt them and our ideas ? I say it is granted on all hands (and what happens in dreams, phrensies, and the like, puts it beyond dispute) that it is possible we might be affected with all the ideas we have now, though no bodies existed without, resembling them. Hence it is evident the supposition of external bodies is not necessary for the producing our ideas : since it is granted they are produced sometimes, and might possibly be produced always in the same order we see them in at present, without their concurrence.

19 But though we might possibly have all our sensations without them, yet perhaps it may be thought easier to conceive and explain the manner of their production, by supposing external bodies in their likeness rather than otherwise ; and so it might be at least probable there are such things as bodies that excite their ideas in our minds. But neither can this be said ; for though we give the materialists their external bodies, they by their own confession are never the nearer knowing how our ideas are produced : since they own themselves unable to comprehend in what manner body can act upon spirit, or how it is possible it should imprint any idea in the mind.[48] Hence it is evident the production of ideas or sensations in our minds, can be no reason why we should suppose matter or corporeal substances, since that is acknowledged to remain equally inexplicable with, or without this supposition. If therefore it were possible for bodies to exist without the mind, yet to hold they do so, must needs be a very precarious opinion ; since it is to suppose, without any reason at all, that God has created innumerable beings that are entirely useless, and serve to no manner of purpose.

20 In short, if there were external bodies, it is impossible we should ever come to know it ; and if there were not, we might have the very same reasons to think there were that we have now. Suppose, what no one can

deny possible, an intelligence, without the help of external bodies, to be affected with the same train of sensations or ideas that you are, imprinted in the same order and with like vividness in his mind. I ask whether that intelligence hath not all the reason to believe the existence of corporeal substances, represented by his ideas, and exciting them in his mind, that you can possibly have for believing the same thing? Of this there can be no question ; which one consideration is enough to make any reasonable person suspect the strength of whatever arguments he may think himself to have, for the existence of bodies without the mind.

21   Were it necessary to add any farther proof against the existence of matter, after what has been said, I could instance several of those errors and difficulties (not to mention impieties) which have sprung from that tenet. It has occasioned numberless controversies and disputes in philosophy, and not a few of far greater moment in religion. But I shall not enter into the detail of them in this place, as well because I think, arguments *a posteriori* are unnecessary for confirming what has been, if I mistake not, sufficiently demonstrated *a priori*, as because I shall hereafter find occasion to say somewhat of them.[49]

22   I am afraid I have given cause to think me needlessly prolix in handling this subject. For to what purpose is it to dilate on that which may be demonstrated with the utmost evidence in a line or two, to any one that is capable of the least reflexion ? It is but looking into your own thoughts, and so trying whether you can conceive it possible for a sound, or figure, or motion, or colour, to exist without the mind, or unperceived. This easy trial may make you see, that what you contend for, is a downright contradiction. Insomuch that I am content to put the whole upon this issue ; if you can but conceive it possible for one extended moveable substance, or in general, for any one idea or any thing like an idea, to exist otherwise than in a mind perceiving it, I shall readily give up the cause : And as for all that *compages* of external bodies which you contend for, I shall grant you its existence, though you cannot either give me any reason why you believe it exists, or assign any use to it when it is supposed to exist.[50] I say, the bare possibility of your opinion's being true, shall pass for an argument that it is so.

23   But say you, surely there is nothing easier than to imagine trees, for instance, in a park, or books existing in a closet, and no body by to perceive them. I answer, you may so, there is no difficulty in it : but what is all this, I beseech you, more than framing in your mind certain ideas which you call *books* and *trees*, and at the same time omitting to frame the idea of any one that may perceive them ? But do not you your self perceive or think of

them all the while ? This therefore is nothing to the purpose : it only shows you have the power of imagining or forming ideas in your mind ; but it doth not shew that you can conceive it possible, the objects of your thought may exist without the mind : to make out this, it is necessary that you conceive them existing unconceived or unthought of, which is a manifest repugnancy. When we do our utmost to conceive the existence of external bodies, we are all the while only contemplating our own ideas.[51] But the mind taking no notice of itself, is deluded to think it can and doth conceive bodies existing unthought of or without the mind ; though at the same time they are apprehended by or exist in it self.[52] A little attention will discover to any one the truth and evidence of what is here said, and make it unnecessary to insist on any other proofs against the existence of material substance.

24   It is very obvious, upon the least inquiry into our own thoughts, to know whether it be possible for us to understand what is meant, by the *absolute existence of sensible objects in themselves, or without the mind*. To me it is evident those words mark out either a direct contradiction, or else nothing at all. And to convince others of this, I know no readier or fairer way, than to entreat they would calmly attend to their own thoughts : and if by this attention, the emptiness or repugnancy of those expressions does appear, surely nothing more is requisite for their conviction. It is on this therefore that I insist, to wit, that the absolute existence of unthinking things are words without a meaning, or which include a contradiction. This is what I repeat and inculcate, and earnestly recommend to the attentive thoughts of the reader.

25   All our ideas, sensations, or the things which we perceive, by whatsoever names they may be distinguished, are visibly inactive, there is nothing of power or agency included in them. So that one idea or object of thought cannot produce, or make any alteration in another. To be satisfied of the truth of this, there is nothing else requisite but a bare observation of our ideas. For since they and every part of them exist only in the mind, it follows that there is nothing in them but what is perceived. But whoever shall attend to his ideas, whether of sense or reflexion, will not perceive in them any power or activity ; there is therefore no such thing contained in them. A little attention will discover to us that the very being of an idea implies passiveness and inertness in it, insomuch that it is impossible for an idea to do any thing, or, strictly speaking, to be the cause of any thing : neither can it be the resemblance or pattern of any active being, as is evident from *Sect*. 8. Whence it plainly follows that extension, figure and motion, cannot be the cause of our sensations. To say therefore, that these

are the effects of powers resulting from the configuration, number, motion, and size of corpuscles, must certainly be false.[53]

26   We perceive a continual succession of ideas, some are anew excited, others are changed or totally disappear. There is therefore some cause of these ideas whereon they depend, and which produces and changes them. That this cause cannot be any quality or idea or combination of ideas, is clear from the preceding section. It must therefore be a substance ; but it has been shewn that there is no corporeal or material substance : it remains therefore that the cause of ideas is an incorporeal active substance or spirit.

27   A spirit is one simple, undivided, active being : as it perceives ideas, it is called the *understanding*, and as it produces or otherwise operates about them, it is called the *will*. Hence there can be no idea formed of a soul or spirit : for all ideas whatever, being passive and inert, *vide Sect.* 25, they cannot represent unto us, by way of image or likeness, that which acts. A little attention will make it plain to any one, that to have an idea which shall be like that active principle of motion and change of ideas, is absolutely impossible. Such is the nature of *spirit* or that which acts, that it cannot be of it self perceived, but only by the effects which it produceth. If any man shall doubt of the truth of what is here delivered, let him but reflect and try if he can frame the idea of any power or active being ; and whether he hath ideas of two principal powers, marked by the names *will* and *understanding*, distinct from each other as well as from a third idea of substance or being in general, with a relative notion of its supporting or being the subject of the aforesaid powers, which is signified by the name *soul* or *spirit*. This is what some hold ; but so far as I can see, the words *will, soul, spirit*,[c] do not stand for different ideas, or in truth, for any idea at all, but for something which is very different from ideas, and which being an agent cannot be like unto, or represented by, any idea whatsoever. Though it must be owned at the same time, that we have some notion of soul, spirit, and the operations of the mind, such as willing, loving, hating, in as much as we know or understand the meaning of those words.[d]

28   I find I can excite ideas in my mind at pleasure, and vary and shift the scene as oft as I think fit. It is no more than willing, and straightway this or that idea arises in my fancy : and by the same power it is obliterated, and makes way for another. This making and unmaking of ideas doth very properly denominate the mind active. Thus much is certain, and grounded

[c] The 1710 edition reads: *will, understanding, mind, soul, spirit.*
[d] *Though . . . those words.*—added in 1734 edition.

on experience : but when we talk of unthinking agents, or of exciting ideas exclusive of volition, we only amuse our selves with words.

29   But whatever power I may have over my own thoughts, I find the ideas actually perceived by sense have not a like dependence on my will. When in broad day-light I open my eyes, it is not in my power to choose whether I shall see or no, or to determine what particular objects shall present themselves to my view ; and so likewise as to the hearing and other senses, the ideas imprinted on them are not creatures of my will. There is therefore some other will or spirit that produces them.

30   The ideas of sense are more strong, lively, and distinct than those of the imagination ; they have likewise a steadiness, order, and coherence, and are not excited at random, as those which are the effects of human wills often are, but in a regular train or series, the admirable connexion whereof sufficiently testifies the wisdom and benevolence of its Author. Now the set rules or established methods, wherein the mind we depend on excites in us the ideas of sense, are called the *Laws of Nature* : and these we learn by experience, which teaches us that such and such ideas are attended with such and such other ideas, in the ordinary course of things.

31   This gives us a sort of foresight, which enables us to regulate our actions for the benefit of life. And without this we should be eternally at a loss : we could not know how to act any thing[54] that might procure us the least pleasure, or remove the least pain of sense. That food nourishes, sleep refreshes, and fire warms us ; that to sow in the seed-time is the way to reap in the harvest, and, in general, that to obtain such or such ends, such or such means are conducive, all this we know, not by discovering any necessary connexion between our ideas, but only by the observation of the settled laws of Nature, without which we should be all in uncertainty and confusion, and a grown man no more know how to manage himself in the affairs of life, than an infant just born.

32   And yet this consistent uniform working, which so evidently displays the goodness and wisdom of that governing spirit whose will constitutes the Laws of Nature, is so far from leading our thoughts to him, that it rather sends them a wandering after second causes.[55] For when we perceive certain ideas of sense constantly followed by other ideas, and we know this is not of our doing, we forthwith attribute power and agency to the ideas themselves, and make one the cause of another, than which nothing can be more absurd and unintelligible. Thus, for example, having observed that when we perceive by sight a certain round luminous figure, we at the same time perceive by touch the idea or sensation called *heat*, we do from thence conclude the sun to be the cause of heat. And in like

manner perceiving the motion and collision of bodies to be attended with sound, we are inclined to think the latter an effect of the former.

33　The ideas imprinted on the senses by the Author of Nature are called *real things* : and those excited in the imagination being less regular, vivid and constant, are more properly termed *ideas*, or *images of things*, which they copy and represent. But then our sensations, be they never so vivid and distinct, are nevertheless *ideas*, that is, they exist in the mind, or are perceived by it, as truly as the ideas of its own framing. The ideas of sense are allowed to have more reality in them, that is, to be more strong, orderly, and coherent than the creatures of the mind ; but this is no argument that they exist without the mind. They are also less dependent on the spirit, or thinking substance which perceives them, in that they are excited by the will of another and more powerful spirit :[56] yet still they are *ideas*, and certainly no *idea*, whether faint or strong, can exist otherwise than in a mind perceiving it.

34　Before we proceed any farther, it is necessary to spend some time in answering objections which may probably be made against the principles hitherto laid down.[57] In doing of which, if I seem too prolix to those of quick apprehensions, I hope it may be pardoned, since all men do not equally apprehend things of this nature ; and I am willing to be understood by every one. First then, it will be objected that by the foregoing principles, all that is real and substantial in Nature is banished out of the world : and instead thereof a chimerical scheme of ideas takes place. All things that exist, exist only in the mind, that is, they are purely notional. What therefore becomes of the sun, moon, and stars ? What must we think of houses, rivers, mountains, trees, stones ; nay, even of our own bodies ?[58] Are all these but so many chimeras and illusions on the fancy ? To all which, and whatever else of the same sort may be objected, I answer, that by the principles premised, we are not deprived of any one thing in Nature. Whatever we see, feel, hear, or any wise conceive or understand, remains as secure as ever, and is as real as ever. There is a *rerum natura*, and the distinction between realities and chimeras retains its full force. This is evident from *Sect.* 29, 30, and 33, where we have shewn what is meant by *real things* in opposition to *chimeras*, or ideas of our own framing ; but then they both equally exist in the mind, and in that sense are alike *ideas*.

35　I do not argue against the existence of any one thing that we can apprehend, either by sense or reflexion. That the things I see with mine eyes and touch with my hands do exist, really exist, I make not the least question. The only thing whose existence we deny, is that which philosophers call matter or corporeal substance. And in doing of this, there is no damage done to the rest of mankind, who, I dare say, will never miss it. The atheist indeed will want the colour of an empty name to support his impiety ;[59] and the philosophers may possibly find, they have lost a great handle for trifling and disputation.

36   If any man thinks this detracts from the existence or reality of things, he is very far from understanding what hath been premised in the plainest terms I could think of. Take here an abstract of what has been said. There are spiritual substances, minds, or human souls, which will or excite ideas in themselves at pleasure : but these are faint, weak, and unsteady in respect of others they perceive by sense, which being impressed upon them according to certain rules or laws of Nature, speak themselves the effects of a mind more powerful and wise than human spirits. These latter are said to have more *reality* in them than the former : by which is meant that they are more affecting, orderly, and distinct, and that they are not fictions of the mind perceiving them. And in this sense, the sun that I see by day is the real sun, and that which I imagine by night is the idea of the former. In the sense here given of *reality*, it is evident that every vegetable, star, mineral, and in general each part of the mundane system, is as much a *real being* by our principles as by any other. Whether others mean any thing by the term *reality* different from what I do, I entreat them to look into their own thoughts and see.

37   It will be urged that thus much at least is true, to wit, that we take away all corporeal substances. To this my answer is, that if the word *substance* be taken in the vulgar sense, for a combination of sensible qualities, such as extension, solidity, weight, and the like ; this we cannot be accused of taking away. But if it be taken in a philosophic sense, for the support of accidents or qualities without the mind : then indeed I acknowledge that we take it away, if one may be said to take away that which never had any existence, not even in the imagination.

38   But, say you, it sounds very harsh to say we eat and drink ideas, and are clothed with ideas. I acknowledge it does so, the word *idea* not being used in common discourse to signify the several combinations of sensible qualities, which are called *things* : and it is certain that any expression which varies from the familiar use of language, will seem harsh and ridiculous. But this doth not concern the truth of the proposition, which in other words is no more than to say, we are fed and clothed with those things which we perceive immediately by our senses.[60] The hardness or softness, the colour, taste, warmth, figure, and such like qualities, which combined together constitute the several sorts of victuals and apparel, have been shewn to exist only in the mind that perceives them ; and this is all that is

meant by calling them *ideas* ; which word, if it was as ordinarily used as *thing*, would sound no harsher nor more ridiculous than it. I am not for disputing about the propriety, but the truth of the expression. If therefore you agree with me that we eat and drink, and are clad with the immediate objects of sense which cannot exist unperceived or without the mind : I shall readily grant it is more proper or conformable to custom, that they should be called things rather than ideas.

39   If it be demanded why I make use of the word *idea*, and do not rather in compliance with custom call them things. I answer, I do it for two reasons : first, because the term *thing*, in contradistinction to *idea*, is generally supposed to denote somewhat existing without the mind : secondly, because *thing* hath a more comprehensive signification than *idea*, including spirits or thinking things as well as ideas. Since therefore the objects of sense exist only in the mind, and are withal thoughtless and inactive, I chose to mark them by the word *idea*, which implies those properties.

40   But say what we can, some one perhaps may be apt to reply, he will still believe his senses, and never suffer any arguments, how plausible soever, to prevail over the certainty of them. Be it so, assert the evidence of sense as high as you please, we are willing to do the same. That what I see, hear and feel doth exist, that is to say, is perceived by me, I no more doubt than I do of my own being. But I do not see how the testimony of sense can be alleged, as a proof for the existence of any thing, which is not perceived by sense. We are not for having any man turn *sceptic*, and disbelieve his senses ; on the contrary we give them all the stress and assurance imaginable ; nor are there any principles more opposite to scepticism, than those we have laid down, as shall be hereafter clearly shewn.

41   Secondly, it will be objected that there is a great difference betwixt real fire, for instance, and the idea of fire, betwixt dreaming or imagining one's self burnt, and actually being so : this and the like may be urged in opposition to our tenets. To all which the answer is evident from what hath been already said, and I shall only add in this place, that if real fire be very different from the idea of fire, so also is the real pain that it occasions, very different from the idea of the same pain : and yet no body will pretend that real pain either is, or can possibly be, in an unperceiving thing or without the mind, any more than its idea.

42   Thirdly, it will be objected that we see things actually without or at a distance from us, and which consequently do not exist in the mind, it being absurd that those things which are seen at the distance of several miles, should be as near to us as our own thoughts. In answer to this, I desire it may be considered, that in a dream we do oft perceive things as

existing at a great distance off, and yet for all that, those things are acknowledged to have their existence only in the mind.[61]

43   But for the fuller clearing of this point, it may be worth while to consider, how it is that we perceive distance and things placed at a distance by sight. For that we should in truth see external space, and bodies actually existing in it, some nearer, others farther off, seems to carry with it some opposition to what hath been said, of their existing no where without the mind. The consideration of this difficulty it was, that gave birth to my *Essay towards a new Theory of Vision*, which was published not long since.[62] Wherein it is shewn that *distance* or outness is neither immediately of it self perceived by sight, nor yet apprehended or judged of by lines and angles, or any thing that hath a necessary connexion with it : but that it is only suggested to our thoughts, by certain visible ideas and sensations attending vision, which in their own nature have no manner of similitude or relation, either with distance, or things placed at a distance.[63] But by a connexion taught us by experience, they come to signify and suggest them to us, after the same manner that words of any language suggest the ideas they are made to stand for.[64] Insomuch that a man born blind, and afterwards made to see, would not, at first sight, think the things he saw, to be without his mind, or at any distance from him.[65] See *Sect.* 41 of the fore-mentioned treatise.

44   The ideas of sight and touch make two species, entirely distinct and heterogeneous. The former are marks and prognostics of the latter. That the proper objects of sight neither exist without the mind, nor are the images of external things, was shewn even in that treatise. Though throughout the same, the contrary be supposed true of tangible objects : not that to suppose that vulgar error, was necessary for establishing the notion therein laid down ; but because it was beside my purpose to examine and refute it in a discourse concerning *vision*. So that in strict truth the ideas of sight, when we apprehend by them distance and things placed at a distance, do not suggest or mark out to us things actually existing at a distance, but only admonish us what ideas of touch will be imprinted in our minds at such and such distances of time, and in consequence of such and such actions. It is, I say, evident from what has been said in the foregoing parts of this treatise, and in *Sect.* 147, and elsewhere of the essay concerning vision, that visible ideas are the language whereby the governing spirit, on whom we depend, informs us what tangible ideas he is about to imprint upon us, in case we excite this or that motion in our own bodies.[66] But for a fuller information in this point, I refer to the essay it self.

45   Fourthly, it will be objected that from the foregoing principles it follows, things are every moment annihilated and created anew. The objects of sense exist only when they are perceived : the trees therefore are in the garden, or the chairs in the parlour, no longer than while there is some body by to perceive them. Upon shutting my eyes all the furniture in the room is reduced to nothing, and barely upon opening them it is again created. In answer to all which, I refer the reader to what has been said in *Sect.* 3, 4, &c. and desire he will consider whether he means any thing by the actual existence of an idea, distinct from its being perceived. For my part, after the nicest inquiry I could make, I am not able to discover that any thing else is meant by those words. And I once more entreat the reader to sound his own thoughts, and not suffer himself to be imposed on by words. If he can conceive it possible either for his ideas or their archetypes[67] to exist without being perceived, then I give up the cause : but if he cannot, he will acknowledge it is unreasonable for him to stand up in defence of he knows not what, and pretend to charge on me as an absurdity, the not assenting to those propositions which at bottom have no meaning in them.

46   It will not be amiss to observe, how far the received principles of philosophy are themselves chargeable with those pretended absurdities. It is thought strangely absurd that upon closing my eyelids, all the visible objects round me should be reduced to nothing ; and yet is not this what philosophers commonly acknowledge, when they agree on all hands,[68] that light and colours, which alone are the proper and immediate objects of sight, are mere sensations that exist no longer than they are perceived ? Again, it may to some perhaps seem very incredible, that things should be every moment creating, yet this very notion is commonly taught in the Schools. For the Schoolmen, though they acknowledge the existence of matter, and that the whole mundane fabrick is framed out of it, are nevertheless of opinion that it cannot subsist without the divine conservation, which by them is expounded to be a continual creation.[69]

47   Farther, a little thought will discover to us, that though we allow the existence of matter or corporeal substance, yet it will unavoidably follow from the principles which are now generally admitted, that the particular bodies of what kind soever, do none of them exist whilst they are not perceived.[70] For it is evident from *Sect.* 11. and the following sections, that the matter philosophers contend for, is an incomprehensible somewhat which hath none of those particular qualities, whereby the bodies falling under our senses are distinguished one from another. But to make this more plain, it must be remarked, that the infinite divisibility of matter

is now universally allowed, at least by the most approved and considerable philosophers, who on the received principles demonstrate it beyond all exception. Hence it follows, that there is an infinite number of parts in each particle of matter, which are not perceived by sense. The reason therefore, that any particular body seems to be of a finite magnitude, or exhibits only a finite number of parts to sense, is, not because it contains no more, since in itself it contains an infinite number of parts, but because the sense is not acute enough to discern them. In proportion therefore as the sense is rendered more acute, it perceives a greater number of parts in the object, that is, the object appears greater, and its figure varies, those parts in its extremities which were before unperceivable, appearing now to bound it in very different lines and angles from those perceived by an obtuser sense. And at length, after various changes of size and shape, when the sense becomes infinitely acute, the body shall seem infinite. During all which there is no alteration in the body, but only in the sense. Each body therefore considered in it self, is infinitely extended, and consequently void of all shape or figure. From which it follows, that though we should grant the existence of matter to be ever so certain, yet it is withal as certain, the materialists themselves are by their own principles forced to acknowledge, that neither the particular bodies perceived by sense, nor any thing like them exists without the mind. Matter, I say, and each particle thereof is according to them infinite and shapeless, and it is the mind that frames all that variety of bodies which compose the visible world, any one whereof does not exist longer than it is perceived.

48   If we consider it, the objection proposed in *Sect.* 45 will not be found reasonably charged on the principles we have premised, so as in truth to make any objection at all against our notions. For though we hold indeed the objects of sense to be nothing else but ideas which cannot exist unperceived ; yet we may not hence conclude they have no existence except only while they are perceived by us, since there may be some other spirit that perceives them, though we do not.[71] Wherever bodies are said to have no existence without the mind, I would not be understood to mean this or that particular mind, but all minds whatsoever. It does not therefore follow from the foregoing principles, that bodies are annihilated and created every moment, or exist not at all during the intervals between our perception of them.

49   Fifthly, it may perhaps be objected, that if extension and figure exist only in the mind, it follows that the mind is extended and figured ; since extension is a mode or attribute, which (to speak with the Schools) is predicated of the subject in which it exists.[72] I answer, those qualities are in

the mind only as they are perceived by it, that is, not by way of *mode* or *attribute*, but only by way of *idea* ; and it no more follows, that the soul or mind is extended because extension exists in it alone, than it does that it is red or blue, because those colours are on all hands acknowledged to exist in it, and no where else.[73] As to what philosophers say of subject and mode, that seems very groundless and unintelligible. For instance, in this proposition, a die is hard, extended and square, they will have it that the word *die* denotes a subject or substance, distinct from the hardness, extension and figure, which are predicated of it, and in which they exist. This I cannot comprehend : to me a die seems to be nothing distinct from those things which are termed its modes or accidents. And to say a die is hard, extended and square, is not to attribute those qualities to a subject distinct from and supporting them, but only an explication of the meaning of the word *die*.[74]

50   Sixthly, you will say there have been a great many things explained by matter and motion : take away these, and you destroy the whole corpuscular philosophy, and undermine those mechanical principles which have been applied with so much success to account for the *phenomena*. In short, whatever advances have been made, either by ancient or modern philosophers, in the study of Nature, do all proceed on the supposition, that corporeal substance or matter doth really exist. To this I answer, that there is not any one *phenomenon* explained on that supposition, which may not as well be explained without it, as might easily be made appear by an induction of particulars. To explain the *phenomena*, is all one as to shew, why upon such and such occasions we are affected with such and such ideas.[75] But how matter should operate on a spirit, or produce any idea in it, is what no philosopher will pretend to explain. It is therefore evident, there can be no use of matter in natural philosophy. Besides, they who attempt to account for things, do it not by corporeal substance, but by figure, motion, and other qualities, which are in truth no more than mere ideas, and therefore cannot be the cause of any thing, as hath been already shewn. See *Sect.* 25.

51   Seventhly, it will upon this be demanded whether it does not seem absurd to take away natural causes, and ascribe every thing to the immediate operation of spirits ? We must no longer say upon these principles that fire heats, or water cools, but that a spirit heats, and so forth. Would not a man be deservedly laughed at, who should talk after this manner ? I answer, he would so ; in such things we ought to *think with the learned, and speak with the vulgar*.[76] They who to demonstration are convinced of the truth of the Copernican system,[77] do nevertheless say the sun rises, the sun

sets, or comes to the meridian : and if they affected a contrary style in common talk, it would without doubt appear very ridiculous. A little reflexion on what is here said will make it manifest, that the common use of language would receive no manner of alteration or disturbance from the admission of our tenets.

52   In the ordinary affairs of life, any phrases may be retained, so long as they excite in us proper sentiments, or dispositions to act in such a manner as is necessary for our well-being, how false soever they may be, if taken in a strict and speculative sense. Nay this is unavoidable, since propriety being regulated by custom, language is suited to the received opinions, which are not always the truest. Hence it is impossible, even in the most rigid philosophic reasonings, so far to alter the bent and genius of the tongue we speak, as never to give a handle for cavillers to pretend difficulties and inconsistencies. But a fair and ingenuous reader will collect the sense, from the scope and tenor and connexion of a discourse, making allowances for those inaccurate modes of speech, which use has made inevitable.

53   As to the opinion that there are no corporeal causes, this has been heretofore maintained by some of the Schoolmen, as it is of late by others among the modern philosophers, who though they allow matter to exist, yet will have God alone to be the immediate efficient cause of all things.[78] These men saw, that amongst all the objects of sense, there was none which had any power or activity included in it, and that by consequence this was likewise true of whatever bodies they supposed to exist without the mind, like unto the immediate objects of sense. But then, that they should suppose an innumerable multitude of created beings, which they acknowledge are not capable of producing any one effect in Nature, and which therefore are made to no manner of purpose, since God might have done every thing as well without them ; this I say, though we should allow it possible, must yet be a very unaccountable and extravagant supposition.[79]

54   In the eighth place, the universal concurrent assent of mankind may be thought by some, an invincible argument in behalf of matter, or the existence of external things. Must we suppose the whole world to be mistaken ? And if so, what cause can be assigned of so widespread and predominant an error ? I answer, first, that upon a narrow inquiry, it will not perhaps be found, so many as is imagined do really believe the existence of matter or things without the mind. Strictly speaking, to believe that which involves a contradiction, or has no meaning in it, is impossible : and whether the foregoing expressions are not of that sort, I refer it to the

impartial examination of the reader. In one sense indeed, men may be said to believe that matter exists, that is, they act as if the immediate cause of their sensations, which affects them every moment and is so nearly present to them, were some senseless unthinking being. But that they should clearly apprehend any meaning marked by those words, and form thereof a settled speculative opinion, is what I am not able to conceive. This is not the only instance wherein men impose upon themselves, by imagining they believe those propositions they have often heard, though at bottom they have no meaning in them.

55   But secondly, though we should grant a notion to be ever so universally and stedfastly adhered to, yet this is but a weak argument of its truth, to whoever considers what a vast number of prejudices and false opinions are every where embraced with the utmost tenaciousness, by the unreflecting (which are the far greater) part of mankind. There was a time when the *Antipodes* and motion of the earth were looked upon as monstrous absurdities, even by men of learning : and if it be considered what a small proportion they bear to the rest of mankind, we shall find that at this day, those notions have gained but a very inconsiderable footing in the world.

56   But it is demanded, that we assign a cause of this prejudice, and account for its obtaining in the world. To this I answer, that men knowing they perceived several ideas, whereof they themselves were not the authors, as not being excited from within, nor depending on the operation of their wills, this made them maintain, those ideas or objects of perception had an existence independent of, and without the mind, without ever dreaming that a contradiction was involved in those words. But philosophers having plainly seen, that the immediate objects of perception do not exist without the mind, they in some degree corrected the mistake of the vulgar, but at the same time run into another which seems no less absurd, to wit, that there are certain objects really existing without the mind, or having a subsistence distinct from being perceived, of which our ideas are only images or resemblances, imprinted by those objects on the mind. And this notion of the philosophers owes its origin to the same cause with the former, namely, their being conscious that they were not the authors of their own sensations, which they evidently knew were imprinted from without, and which therefore must have some cause, distinct from the minds on which they are imprinted.

57   But why they should suppose the ideas of sense to be excited in us by things in their likeness, and not rather have recourse to *spirit* which alone can act, may be accounted for, first, because they were not aware of

the repugnancy there is, as well in supposing things like unto our ideas existing without, as in attributing to them power or activity. Secondly, because the supreme spirit which excites those ideas in our minds, is not marked out and limited to our view by any particular finite collection of sensible ideas, as human agents are by their size, complexion, limbs, and motions. And thirdly, because his operations are regular and uniform. Whenever the course of Nature is interrupted by a miracle, men are ready to own the presence of a superior agent. But when we see things go on in the ordinary course, they do not excite in us any reflexion ; their order and concatenation, though it be an argument of the greatest wisdom, power, and goodness in their Creator, is yet so constant and familiar to us, that we do not think them the immediate effects of a *free spirit* : especially since inconstancy and mutability in acting, though it be an imperfection, is looked on as a mark of *freedom*.

58   Tenthly, it will be objected, that the notions we advance, are inconsistent with several sound truths in philosophy and mathematics. For example, the motion of the earth is now universally admitted by astronomers, as a truth grounded on the clearest and most convincing reasons ; but on the foregoing principles, there can be no such thing. For motion being only an idea, it follows that if it be not perceived, it exists not; but the motion of the earth is not perceived by sense. I answer, that tenet, if rightly understood, will be found to agree with the principles we have premised : for the question, whether the earth moves or no, amounts in reality to no more than this, to wit, whether we have reason to conclude from what hath been observed by astronomers, that if we were placed in such and such circumstances, and such or such a position and distance, both from the earth and sun, we should perceive the former to move among the choir of the planets, and appearing in all respects like one of them :[80] and this, by the established rules of Nature, which we have no reason to mistrust, is reasonably collected from the phenomena.

59   We may, from the experience we have had of the train and succession of ideas in our minds, often make, I will not say uncertain conjectures, but sure and well-grounded predictions, concerning the ideas we shall be affected with, pursuant to a great train of actions, and be enabled to pass a right judgment of what would have appeared to us, in case we were placed in circumstances very different from those we are in at present. Herein consists the knowledge of Nature, which may preserve its use and certainty very consistently with what hath been said. It will be easy to apply this to whatever objections of the like sort may be drawn from the magnitude of the stars, or any other discoveries in astronomy or Nature.

60   In the eleventh place, it will be demanded to what purpose serves that curious organization of plants, and the admirable mechanism in the parts of animals ;[81] might not vegetables grow, and shoot forth leaves and blossoms, and animals perform all their motions, as well without as with all that variety of internal parts so elegantly contrived and put together, which being ideas have nothing powerful or operative in them, nor have any necessary connexion with the effects ascribed to them ? If it be a spirit that immediately produces every effect by a *fiat*, or act of his will, we must think all that is fine and artificial in the works, whether of man or Nature, to be made in vain. By this doctrine, though an artist hath made the spring and wheels, and every movement of a watch, and adjusted them in such a manner as he knew would produce the motions he designed ; yet he must think all this done to no purpose, and that it is an intelligence which directs the index,[82] and points to the hour of the day. If so, why may not the intelligence do it, without his being at the pains of making the movements, and putting them together ? Why does not an empty case serve as well as another ? And how comes it to pass, that whenever there is any fault in the going of a watch, there is some corresponding disorder to be found in the movements, which being mended by a skilful hand, all is right again ? The like may be said of all the clockwork of Nature, great part whereof is so wonderfully fine and subtle, as scarce to be discerned by the best microscope. In short, it will be asked, how upon our principles any tolerable account can be given, or any final cause[83] assigned of an innumerable multitude of bodies and machines framed with the most exquisite art, which in the common philosophy have very apposite uses assigned them, and serve to explain abundance of phenomena.

61   To all which I answer, first, that though there were some difficulties relating to the administration of providence, and the uses by it assigned to the several parts of Nature, which I could not solve by the foregoing principles, yet this objection could be of small weight against the truth and certainty of those things which may be proved *a priori*, with the utmost evidence. Secondly, but neither are the received principles free from the like difficulties ; for it may still be demanded, to what end God should take those round-about methods of effecting things by instruments and machines, which no one can deny might have been effected by the mere command of his will, without all that *apparatus* : nay, if we narrowly consider it, we shall find the objection may be retorted with greater force on those who hold the existence of those machines without the mind ; for it has been made evident, that solidity, bulk, figure, motion and the like, have no *activity* or *efficacy* in them, so as to be capable of producing any one

effect in Nature. See *Sect.* 25. Whoever therefore supposes them to exist (allowing the supposition possible) when they are not perceived, does it manifestly to no purpose ; since the only use that is assigned to them, as they exist unperceived, is that they produce those perceivable effects, which in truth cannot be ascribed to any thing but spirit.

62   But to come nearer the difficulty, it must be observed, that though the fabrication of all those parts and organs be not absolutely necessary to the producing any effect, yet it is necessary to the producing of things in a constant, regular way, according to the Laws of Nature. There are certain general laws that run through the whole chain of natural effects : these are learned by the observation and study of Nature, and are by men applied as well to the framing artificial things for the use and ornament of life, as to the explaining the various *phenomena :* which explication consists only in shewing the conformity any particular phenomenon hath to the general Laws of Nature, or, which is the same thing, in discovering the *uniformity* there is in the production of natural effects ; as will be evident to whoever shall attend to the several instances, wherein philosophers pretend to account for appearances. That there is a great and conspicuous use in these regular constant methods of working observed by the Supreme Agent, hath been shewn in *Sect.* 31. And it is no less visible, that a particular size, figure, motion and disposition of parts are necessary, though not absolutely to the producing any effect, yet to the producing it according to the standing mechanical Laws of Nature. Thus, for instance, it cannot be denied that God, or the intelligence which sustains and rules the ordinary course of things might, if he were minded to produce a miracle, cause all the motions on the dial-plate of a watch, though no body had ever made the movements, and put them in it : but yet if he will act agreeably to the rules of mechanism, by him for wise ends established and maintained in the Creation, it is necessary that those actions of the watchmaker, whereby he makes the movements and rightly adjusts them, precede the production of the aforesaid motions ; as also that any disorder in them be attended with the perception of some corresponding disorder in the movements, which being once corrected all is right again.

63   It may indeed on some occasions be necessary, that the Author of Nature display his overruling power in producing some appearance out of the ordinary series of things. Such exceptions from the general rules of Nature are proper to surprise and awe men into an acknowledgment of the Divine Being : but then they are to be used but seldom, otherwise there is a plain reason why they should fail of that effect. Besides, God seems to choose the convincing our reason of his attributes by the works of Nature,

which discover so much harmony and contrivance in their make, and are such plain indications of wisdom and beneficence in their Author, rather than to astonish us into a belief of his being by anomalous and surprising events.

64   To set this matter in a yet clearer light, I shall observe that what has been objected in *Sect.* 60 amounts in reality to no more than this : ideas are not any how and at random produced, there being a certain order and connexion between them, like to that of cause and effect : there are also several combinations of them, made in a very regular and artificial manner, which seem like so many instruments in the hand of Nature, that being hid as it were behind the scenes, have a secret operation in producing those appearances which are seen on the theatre of the world, being themselves discernible only to the curious eye of the philosopher. But since one idea cannot be the cause of another, to what purpose is that connexion ? And since those instruments, being barely *inefficacious perceptions* in the mind, are not subservient to the production of natural effects ; it is demanded why they are made, or, in other words, what reason can be assigned why God should make us, upon a close inspection into his works, behold so great variety of ideas, so artfully laid together, and so much according to rule ; it not being credible, that he would be at the expense (if one may so speak) of all that art and regularity to no purpose ?

65   To all which my answer is, first, that the connexion of ideas does not imply the relation of *cause* and *effect*, but only of a mark or *sign* with the thing *signified*. The fire which I see is not the cause of the pain I suffer upon my approaching it, but the mark that forewarns me of it. In like manner, the noise that I hear is not the effect of this or that motion or collision of the ambient bodies, but the sign thereof.[84] Secondly, the reason why ideas are formed into machines, that is, artificial and regular combinations, is the same with that for combining letters into words. That a few original ideas may be made to signify a great number of effects and actions, it is necessary they be variously combined together : and to the end their use be permanent and universal, these combinations must be made by *rule*, and with *wise contrivance*. By this means abundance of information is conveyed unto us, concerning what we are to expect from such and such actions, and what methods are proper to be taken, for the exciting such and such ideas : which in effect is all that I conceive to be distinctly meant, when it is said that by discerning the figure, texture, and mechanism of the inward parts of bodies, whether natural or artificial, we may attain to know the several uses and properties depending thereon, or the nature of the thing.[85]

66   Hence it is evident, that those things which under the notion of a cause co-operating or concurring to the production of effects, are altogether inexplicable, and run us into great absurdities, may be very naturally explained, and have a proper and obvious use assigned them, when they are considered only as marks or signs for our information. And it is the searching after, and endeavouring to understand those signs instituted by the Author of Nature,[e] that ought to be the employment of the natural philosopher, and not the pretending to explain things by corporeal causes ; which doctrine seems to have too much estranged the minds of men from that active principle, that supreme and wise spirit, *in whom we live, move, and have our being.*[86]

67   In the twelfth place, it may perhaps be objected, that though it be clear from what has been said, that there can be no such thing as an inert, senseless, extended, solid, figured, moveable substance, existing without the mind, such as philosophers describe matter : yet if any man shall leave out of his idea of *matter*, the positive ideas of extension, figure, solidity and motion, and say that he means only by that word, an inert senseless substance, that exists without the mind, or unperceived, which is the occasion of our ideas, or at the presence whereof God is pleased to excite ideas in us : it doth not appear, but that matter taken in this sense may possibly exist.[87] In answer to which I say, first, that it seems no less absurd to suppose a substance without accidents, than it is to suppose accidents without a substance. But secondly, though we should grant this unknown substance may possibly exist, yet where can it be supposed to be ? That it exists not in the mind is agreed, and that it exists not in place is no less certain ; since all extension exists only in the mind, as hath been already proved. It remains therefore that it exists no where at all.

68   Let us examine a little the description that is here given us of *matter*. It neither acts, nor perceives, nor is perceived : for this is all that is meant by saying it is an inert, senseless, unknown substance ; which is a definition entirely made up of negatives, excepting only the relative notion of its standing under or supporting : but then it must be observed, that it *supports* nothing at all ; and how nearly this comes to the description of a *non-entity*, I desire may be considered. But, say you, it is the *unknown occasion*, at the presence of which, ideas are excited in us by the will of God.[88] Now I would fain know how any thing can be present to us, which is neither perceivable by sense nor reflexion, nor capable of producing any

---

[e] The 1710 edition reads: *to understand this language (if I may so call it) of the Author of Nature . . .*

idea in our minds, nor is at all extended, nor hath any form, nor exists in any place. The words *to be present*, when thus applied, must needs be taken in some abstract and strange meaning, and which I am not able to comprehend.

69   Again, let us examine what is meant by *occasion* : so far as I can gather from the common use of language, that word signifies, either the agent which produces any effect, or else something that is observed to accompany, or go before it, in the ordinary course of things. But when it is applied to matter as above described, it can be taken in neither of those senses. For matter is said to be passive and inert, and so cannot be an agent or efficient cause. It is also unperceivable, as being devoid of all sensible qualities, and so cannot be the occasion of our perceptions in the latter sense : as when the burning my finger is said to be the occasion of the pain that attends it. What therefore can be meant by calling matter an *occasion* ? This term is either used in no sense at all, or else in some sense very distant from its received signification.

70   You will perhaps say that matter, though it be not perceived by us, is nevertheless perceived by God, to whom it is the occasion of exciting ideas in our minds. For, say you, since we observe our sensations to be imprinted in an orderly and constant manner, it is but reasonable to suppose there are certain constant and regular occasions of their being produced. That is to say, that there are certain permanent and distinct parcels of matter, corresponding to our ideas, which, though they do not excite them in our minds, or any ways immediately affect us, as being altogether passive and unperceivable to us, they are nevertheless to God, by whom they are perceived, as it were so many occasions to remind him when and what ideas to imprint on our minds : that so things may go on in a constant uniform manner.

71   In answer to this I observe, that as the notion of matter is here stated, the question is no longer concerning the existence of a thing distinct from *spirit* and *idea*, from perceiving and being perceived : but whether there are not certain ideas, of I know not what sort, in the mind of God, which are so many marks or notes that direct him how to produce sensations in our minds, in a constant and regular method : much after the same manner as a musician is directed by the notes of music to produce that harmonious train and composition of sound, which is called a *tune* ; though they who hear the music do not perceive the notes, and may be entirely ignorant of them. But this notion of matter seems too extravagant to deserve a confutation. Besides, it is in effect no objection against what we have advanced, to wit, that there is no senseless, unperceived *substance*.

72   If we follow the light of reason, we shall, from the constant uniform method of our sensations, collect the goodness and wisdom of the *spirit* who excites them in our minds. But this is all that I can see reasonably concluded from thence. To me, I say, it is evident that the being of a *spirit infinitely wise, good, and powerful* is abundantly sufficient to explain all the appearances of Nature. But as for *inert senseless matter*, nothing that I perceive has any the least connexion with it, or leads to the thoughts of it. And I would fain see any one explain any the meanest[89] phenomenon in Nature by it, or shew any manner of reason, though in the lowest rank of probability,[90] that he can have for its existence ; or even make any tolerable sense or meaning of that supposition. For as to its being an occasion, we have, I think, evidently shewn that with regard to us it is no occasion : it remains therefore that it must be, if at all, the occasion to God of exciting ideas in us ; and what this amounts to, we have just now seen.

73   It is worth while to reflect a little on the motives which induced men to suppose the existence of material substance ; that so having observed the gradual ceasing, and expiration of those motives or reasons, we may proportionably withdraw the assent that was grounded on them. First therefore, it was thought that colour, figure, motion, and the rest of the sensible qualities or accidents, did really exist without the mind ; and for this reason, it seemed needful to suppose some unthinking *substratum* or *substance* wherein they did exist, since they could not be conceived to exist by themselves. Afterwards, in process of time, men being convinced that colours, sounds, and the rest of the sensible secondary qualities had no existence without the mind, they stripped this *substratum* or material substance of those qualities, leaving only the primary ones, figure, motion, and such like, which they still conceived to exist without the mind, and consequently to stand in need of a material support. But it having been shewn, that none, even of these, can possibly exist otherwise than in a spirit or mind which perceives them, it follows that we have no longer any reason to suppose the being of *matter*.[91] Nay, that it is utterly impossible there should be any such thing, so long as that word is taken to denote an *unthinking substratum* of qualities or accidents, wherein they exist without the mind.

74   But though it be allowed by the *materialists* themselves, that matter was thought of only for the sake of supporting accidents ; and the reason entirely ceasing, one might expect the mind should naturally, and without any reluctance at all, quit the belief of what was solely grounded thereon. Yet the prejudice is riveted so deeply in our thoughts, that we can scarce tell how to part with it, and are therefore inclined, since the *thing* it self is

indefensible, at least to retain the *name* ; which we apply to I know not what abstracted and indefinite notions of *being*, or *occasion*, though without any shew of reason, at least so far as I can see. For what is there on our part, or what do we perceive amongst all the ideas, sensations, notions, which are imprinted on our minds, either by sense or reflexion, from whence may be inferred the existence of an inert, thoughtless, unperceived occasion ? and on the other hand, on the part of an *all-sufficient spirit*, what can there be that should make us believe, or even suspect, he is *directed* by an inert occasion to excite ideas in our minds ?

75   It is a very extraordinary instance of the force of prejudice, and much to be lamented, that the mind of man retains so great a fondness against all the evidence of reason, for a stupid thoughtless *somewhat*, by the interposition whereof it would, as it were, screen it self from the providence of God, and remove him farther off from the affairs of the world. But though we do the utmost we can, to secure the belief of *matter*, though when reason forsakes us, we endeavour to support our opinion on the bare possibility of the thing, and though we indulge our selves in the full scope of an imagination not regulated by reason, to make out that poor *possibility*, yet the upshot of all is, that there are certain *unknown ideas* in the mind of God ; for this, if any thing, is all that I conceive to be meant by *occasion* with regard to God. And this, at the bottom, is no longer contending for the *thing*, but for the *name*.

76   Whether therefore there are such ideas in the mind of God, and whether they may be called by the name *matter*, I shall not dispute. But if you stick to the notion of an unthinking substance, or support of extension, motion, and other sensible qualities, then to me it is most evidently impossible there should be any such thing. Since it is a plain repugnancy, that those qualities should exist in or be supported by an unperceiving substance.

77   But say you, though it be granted that there is no thoughtless support of extension, and the other qualities or accidents which we perceive ; yet there may, perhaps, be some inert unperceiving substance, or *substratum* of some other qualities, as incomprehensible to us as colours are to a man born blind, because we have not a sense adapted to them. But if we had a new sense, we should possibly no more doubt of their existence, than a blind man made to see does of the existence of light and colours. I answer, first, if what you mean by the word *matter* be only the unknown support of unknown qualities, it is no matter whether there is such a thing or no, since it no way concerns us : and I do not see the advantage there is in disputing about we know not *what*, and we know not *why*.

78   But secondly, if we had a new sense, it could only furnish us with new ideas or sensations : and then we should have the same reason against their existing in an unperceiving substance, that has been already offered with relation to figure, motion, colour, and the like. Qualities, as hath been shewn,[92] are nothing else but *sensations* or *ideas*, which exist only in a *mind* perceiving them ; and this is true not only of the ideas we are acquainted with at present, but likewise of all possible ideas whatsoever.

79   But you will insist, what if I have no reason to believe the existence of matter, what if I cannot assign any use to it, or explain any thing by it, or even conceive what is meant by that word ? Yet still it is no contradiction to say that matter exists, and that this matter is *in general* a *substance*, or *occasion of ideas* ; though, indeed, to go about to unfold the meaning, or adhere to any particular explication of those words, may be attended with great difficulties. I answer, when words are used without a meaning, you may put them together as you please, without danger of running into a contradiction. You may say, for example, that *twice two* is equal to *seven*, so long as you declare you do not take the words of that proposition in their usual acceptation, but for marks of you know not what. And by the same reason you may say, there is an inert thoughtless substance without accidents, which is the occasion of our ideas. And we shall understand just as much by one proposition, as the other.

80   In the last place, you will say, what if we give up the cause of material substance, and assert, that matter is an unknown *somewhat*, neither substance nor accident, spirit nor idea, inert, thoughtless, indivisible, immoveable, unextended, existing in no place ? For, say you, whatever may be urged against *substance* or *occasion*, or any other positive or relative notion of matter, hath no place at all, so long as this *negative* definition of matter is adhered to. I answer, you may, if so it shall seem good, use the word *matter* in the same sense, that other men use *nothing*, and so make those terms convertible in your style. For after all, this is what appears to me to be the result of that definition, the parts whereof when I consider with attention, either collectively, or separate from each other, I do not find that there is any kind of effect or impression made on my mind, different from what is excited by the term *nothing*.

81   You will reply perhaps, that in the foresaid definition is included, what doth sufficiently distinguish it from nothing, the positive, abstract idea of *quiddity, entity,* or *existence*. I own indeed, that those who pretend to the faculty of framing abstract general ideas, do talk as if they had such an idea, which is, say they, the most abstract and general notion of all, that is to me the most incomprehensible of all others. That there are a great

variety of spirits of different orders and capacities, whose faculties, both in number and extent, are far exceeding those the Author of my being has bestowed on me, I see no reason to deny. And for me to pretend to determine by my own few, stinted, narrow inlets of perception, what ideas the inexhaustible power of the Supreme Spirit may imprint upon them, were certainly the utmost folly and presumption. Since there may be, for aught that I know, innumerable sorts of ideas or sensations, as different from one another, and from all that I have perceived, as colours are from sounds. But how ready soever I may be, to acknowledge the scantiness of my comprehension, with regard to the endless variety of spirits and ideas, that might possibly exist, yet for any one to pretend to a notion of entity or existence, *abstracted* from *spirit* and *idea*, from perceiving and being perceived, is, I suspect, a downright repugnancy and trifling with words. It remains that we consider the objections, which may possibly be made on the part of religion.

82   Some there are who think, that though the arguments for the real existence of bodies, which are drawn from reason, be allowed not to amount to demonstration, yet the Holy Scriptures are so clear in the point, as will sufficiently convince every good Christian, that bodies do really exist, and are something more than mere ideas ; there being in Holy Writ innumerable facts related, which evidently suppose the reality of timber, and stone, mountains, and rivers, and cities, and human bodies.[93] To which I answer, that no sort of writings whatever, sacred or profane, which use those and the like words in the vulgar acceptation, or so as to have a meaning in them, are in danger of having their truth called in question by our doctrine. That all those things do really exist, that there are bodies, even corporeal substances, when taken in the vulgar sense, has been shown to be agreeable to our principles : and the difference betwixt *things* and *ideas*, *realities* and *chimeras*, has been distinctly explained.* And I do not think, that either what philosophers call *matter*, or the existence of objects without the mind, is any where mentioned in Scripture.[94]

83   Again, whether there be, or be not external things, it is agreed on all hands, that the proper use of words, is the marking our conceptions, or things only as they are known and perceived by us ; whence it plainly follows, that in the tenets we have laid down, there is nothing inconsistent with the right use and significancy of *language*, and that discourse of what kind soever, so far as it is intelligible, remains undisturbed. But all this

* Sect. 29, 30, 33, 36, &c.

seems so manifest, from what hath been set forth in the premises, that it is needless to insist any farther on it.

84   But, it will be urged, that miracles do, at least, lose much of their stress and import by our principles. What must we think of Moses's rod, was it not *really* turned into a serpent, or was there only a change of *ideas* in the minds of the spectators ? And can it be supposed, that our Saviour did no more at the marriage-feast in Cana, than impose on the sight, and smell, and taste of the guests, so as to create in them the appearance or idea only of wine ?[95] The same may be said of all other miracles : which, in consequence of the foregoing principles, must be looked upon only as so many cheats, or illusion of fancy. To this I reply, that the rod was changed into a real serpent, and the water into real wine. That this doth not, in the least, contradict what I have elsewhere said, will be evident from *Sect.* 34, and 35. But this business of *real* and *imaginary* hath been already so plainly and fully explained, and so often referred to, and the difficulties about it are so easily answered from what hath gone before, that it were an affront to the reader's understanding, to resume the explication of it in this place. I shall only observe, that if at table all who were present should see, and smell, and taste, and drink wine, and find the effects of it, with me there could be no doubt of its reality. So that, at bottom, the scruple concerning real miracles hath no place at all on ours, but only on the received principles, and consequently maketh rather *for*, than *against* what hath been said.

85   Having done with the objections, which I endeavoured to propose in the clearest light, and gave them all the force and weight I could, we proceed in the next place to take a view of our tenets in their consequences.[96] Some of these appear at first sight, as that several difficult and obscure questions, on which abundance of speculation hath been thrown away, are entirely banished from philosophy. Whether corporeal substance can think ? Whether matter be infinitely divisible ? And how it operates on spirit ?[97] these and the like inquiries have given infinite amusement to philosophers in all ages. But depending on the existence of *matter*, they have no longer any place on our principles. Many other advantages there are, as well with regard to *religion* as the *sciences*, which it is easy for any one to deduce from what hath been premised. But this will appear more plainly in the sequel.[98]

86   From the principles we have laid down, it follows, human knowledge may naturally be reduced to two heads, that of *ideas*, and that of *spirits*. Of each of these I shall treat in order. And first as to ideas or

unthinking things, our knowledge of these hath been very much obscured and confounded, and we have been led into very dangerous errors, by supposing a twofold existence of the objects of sense, the one *intelligible*, or in the mind, the other *real* and without the mind : whereby unthinking things are thought to have a natural subsistence of their own, distinct from being perceived by spirits. This which, if I mistake not, hath been shewn to be a most groundless and absurd notion, is the very root of *scepticism* ; for so long as men thought that real things subsisted without the mind, and that their knowledge was only so far forth *real* as it was conformable to *real things*, it follows, they could not be certain that they had any real knowledge at all. For how can it be known, that the things which are perceived, are conformable to those which are not perceived, or exist without the mind ?

87   Colour, figure, motion, extension and the like, considered only as so many *sensations* in the mind, are perfectly known, there being nothing in them which is not perceived. But if they are looked on as notes or images, referred to *things* or *archetypes* existing without the mind, then are we involved all in *scepticism*. We see only the appearances, and not the real qualities of things. What may be the extension, figure, or motion of any thing really and absolutely, or in it self, it is impossible for us to know, but only the proportion or the relation they bear to our senses. Things remaining the same, our ideas vary, and which of them, or even whether any of them at all represent the true quality really existing in the thing, it is out of our reach to determine. So that, for aught we know, all we see, hear, and feel, may be only phantom and vain chimera, and not at all agree with the real things, existing in *rerum natura*. All this scepticism follows, from our supposing a difference between *things* and *ideas*, and that the former have a subsistence without the mind, or unperceived. It were easy to dilate on this subject, and shew how the arguments urged by *sceptics* in all ages, depend on the supposition of external objects.

88   So long as we attribute a real existence to unthinking things, distinct from their being perceived, it is not only impossible for us to know with evidence the nature of any real unthinking being, but even that it exists. Hence it is, that we see philosophers distrust their senses, and doubt of the existence of heaven and earth, of every thing they see or feel, even of their own bodies. And after all their labour and struggle of thought, they are forced to own, we cannot attain to any self-evident or demonstrative knowledge of the existence of sensible things.[99] But all this doubtfulness, which so bewilders and confounds the mind, and makes *philosophy* ridiculous in the eyes of the world, vanishes, if we annex a meaning to our

words, and do not amuse our selves with the terms *absolute, external, exist*, and such like, signifying we know not what. I can as well doubt of my own being, as of the being of those things which I actually perceive by sense : it being a manifest contradiction, that any sensible object should be immediately perceived by sight or touch, and at the same time have no existence in Nature, since the very existence of an unthinking being consists in *being perceived*.

89 Nothing seems of more importance, towards erecting a firm system of sound and real knowledge, which may be proof against the assaults of *scepticism*, than to lay the beginning in a distinct explication of what is meant by *thing, reality, existence :* for in vain shall we dispute concerning the real existence of things, or pretend to any knowledge thereof, so long as we have not fixed the meaning of those words. *Thing* or *being* is the most general name of all, it comprehends under it two kinds entirely distinct and heterogeneous, and which have nothing common but the name, to wit, *spirits* and *ideas*. The former are *active, indivisible substances :* the latter are *inert, fleeting, dependent beings*, which subsist not by themselves, but are supported by, or exist in minds or spiritual substances.[100] We[f] comprehend our own existence by inward feeling or reflexion, and that of other spirits by reason. We may be said to have some knowledge or notion of our own minds, of spirits and active beings, whereof in a strict sense we have not ideas. In like manner we know and have a notion of relations between things or ideas, which relations are distinct from the ideas or things related, inasmuch as the latter may be perceived by us without our perceiving the former. To me it seems that ideas, spirits and relations are all in their respective kinds, the object of human knowledge and subject of discourse : and that the term *idea* would be improperly extended to signify every thing we know or have any notion of.

90 Ideas imprinted on the senses are real things, or do really exist ; this we do not deny, but we deny they can subsist without the minds which perceive them, or that they are resemblances of any archetypes existing without the mind : since the very being of a sensation or idea consists in being perceived, and an idea can be like nothing but an idea. Again, the things perceived by sense may be termed *external*, with regard to their origin, in that they are not generated from within, by the mind it self, but imprinted by a spirit distinct from that which perceives them. Sensible objects may likewise be said to be without the mind, in another sense,

[f] The remainder of this paragraph was added in the 1734 edition.

namely when they exist in some other mind. Thus when I shut my eyes, the things I saw may still exist, but it must be in another mind.

91   It were a mistake to think, that what is here said derogates in the least from the reality of things. It is acknowledged on the received principles, that extension, motion, and in a word all sensible qualities, have need of a support, as not being able to subsist by themselves. But the objects perceived by sense, are allowed to be nothing but combinations of those qualities, and consequently cannot subsist by themselves. Thus far it is agreed on all hands. So that in denying the things perceived by sense, an existence independent of a substance, or support wherein they may exist, we detract nothing from the received opinion of their *reality*, and are guilty of no innovation in that respect. All the difference is, that according to us the unthinking beings perceived by sense, have no existence distinct from being perceived, and cannot therefore exist in any other substance, than those unextended, indivisible substances, or *spirits*, which act, and think, and perceive them : whereas philosophers vulgarly hold, that the sensible qualities exist in an inert, extended, unperceiving substance, which they call *matter*, to which they attribute a natural subsistence, exterior to all thinking beings, or distinct from being perceived by any mind whatsoever, even the eternal mind of the Creator, wherein they suppose only ideas of the corporeal substances created by him : if indeed they allow them to be at all created.[101]

92   For as we have shewn the doctrine of matter or corporeal substance, to have been the main pillar and support of *scepticism*, so likewise upon the same foundation have been raised all the impious schemes of *atheism* and irreligion. Nay so great a difficulty hath it been thought, to conceive matter produced out of nothing, that the most celebrated among the ancient philosophers, even of these who maintained the being of a God, have thought matter to be uncreated and coeternal with him.[102] How great a friend material substance hath been to *atheists* in all ages, were needless to relate. All their monstrous systems have so visible and necessary a dependence on it, that when this corner-stone is once removed, the whole fabric cannot choose but fall to the ground ; insomuch that it is no longer worth while, to bestow a particular consideration on the absurdities of every wretched sect of *atheists*.

93   That impious and profane persons should readily fall in with those systems which favour their inclinations, by deriding immaterial substance, and supposing the soul to be divisible and subject to corruption as the body ; which exclude all freedom, intelligence, and design from the formation of things, and instead thereof make a self-existent, stupid, unthinking

substance the root and origin of all beings. That they should hearken to those who deny a providence, or inspection of a superior mind over the affairs of the world, attributing the whole series of events either to blind chance or fatal necessity, arising from the impulse of one body on another. All this is very natural. And on the other hand, when men of better principles observe the enemies of religion lay so great a stress on *unthinking matter*, and all of them use so much industry and artifice to reduce every thing to it ; methinks they should rejoice to see them deprived of their grand support, and driven from that only fortress, without which your *Epicureans*, *Hobbists*, and the like,[103] have not even the shadow of a pretence, but become the most cheap and easy triumph in the world.

94   The existence of matter, or bodies unperceived, has not only been the main support of *atheists* and *fatalists*,[104] but on the same principle doth *idolatry* likewise in all its various forms depend. Did men but consider that the sun, moon, and stars, and every other object of the senses, are only so many sensations in their minds, which have no other existence but barely being perceived, doubtless they would never fall down, and worship their own *ideas* ; but rather address their homage to that Eternal Invisible Mind which produces and sustains all things.

95   The same absurd principle, by mingling it self with the articles of our faith, hath occasioned no small difficulties to Christians. For example, about the *resurrection*, how many scruples and objections have been raised by Socinians and others ?[105] But do not the most plausible of them depend on the supposition, that a body is denominated the *same*, with regard not to the form or that which is perceived by sense, but the material substance which remains the same under several forms ? Take away this *material substance*, about the identity whereof all the dispute is, and mean by *body* what every plain ordinary person means by that word, to wit, that which is immediately seen and felt, which is only a combination of sensible qualities, or ideas : and then their most unanswerable objections come to nothing.

96   Matter being once expelled out of Nature, drags with it so many sceptical and impious notions, such an incredible number of disputes and puzzling questions, which have been thorns in the sides of divines, as well as philosophers, and made so much fruitless work for mankind ; that if the arguments we have produced against it, are not found equal to demonstration (as to me they evidently seem) yet I am sure all friends to knowledge, peace, and religion, have reason to wish they were.

97   Beside the external existence of the objects of perception, another great source of errors and difficulties, with regard to ideal knowledge,[106] is

the doctrine of *abstract ideas*, such as it hath been set forth in the Introduction. The plainest things in the world, those we are most intimately acquainted with, and perfectly know, when they are considered in an abstract way, appear strangely difficult and incomprehensible. Time, place, and motion, taken in particular or concrete, are what every body knows ; but having passed through the hands of a metaphysician, they become too abstract and fine, to be apprehended by men of ordinary sense. Bid your servant meet you at such a *time*, in such a *place*, and he shall never stay to deliberate on the meaning of those words : in conceiving that particular time and place, or the motion by which he is to get thither, he finds not the least difficulty. But if *time* be taken, exclusive of all those particular actions and ideas that diversify the day, merely for the continuation of existence, or duration in abstract, then it will perhaps gravel even a philosopher to comprehend it.[107]

98   Whenever I attempt to frame a simple idea of *time*, abstracted from the succession of ideas in my mind, which flows uniformly, and is participated by all beings, I am lost and embrangled in inextricable difficulties. I have no notion of it at all, only I hear others say, it is infinitely divisible, and speak of it in such a manner as leads me to entertain odd thoughts of my existence : since that doctrine lays one under an absolute necessity of thinking, either that he passes away innumerable ages without a thought,[108] or else that he is annihilated every moment of his life :[109] both which seem equally absurd. Time therefore[110] being nothing, abstracted from the succession of ideas in our minds,[111] it follows that the duration of any finite spirit must be estimated by the number of ideas or actions succeeding each other in that same spirit or mind. Hence it is a plain consequence that the soul always thinks:[112] and in truth whoever shall go about to divide in his thoughts, or abstract the *existence* of a spirit from its *cogitation*, will, I believe, find it no easy task.

99   So likewise, when we attempt to abstract extension and motion from all other qualities, and consider them by themselves, we presently lose sight of them, and run into great extravagancies. All which depend on a two-fold abstraction : first, it is supposed that extension, for example, may be abstracted from all other sensible qualities ; and secondly, that the entity of extension may be abstracted from its being perceived.[113] But whoever shall reflect, and take care to understand what he says, will, if I mistake not, acknowledge that all sensible qualities are alike *sensations*, and alike *real* ; that where the extension is, there is the colour too, to wit, in his mind, and that their archetypes can exist only in some other *mind* : and that the objects of sense are nothing but those sensations combined, blended,

or (if one may so speak) concreted together : none of all which can be supposed to exist unperceived.

100   What it is for a man to be happy, or an object good, every one may think he knows. But to frame an abstract idea of *happiness*, prescinded from all particular pleasure, or of *goodness*, from every thing that is good, this is what few can pretend to. So likewise, a man may be just and virtuous, without having precise ideas of *justice* and *virtue*. The opinion that those and the like words stand for general notions abstracted from all particular persons and actions, seems to have rendered morality difficult, and the study thereof of less use to mankind.[g] And in effect, the doctrine of *abstraction* has not a little contributed towards spoiling the most useful parts of knowledge.[114]

101   The two great provinces of speculative science, conversant about ideas received from sense and their relations,[h] are *natural philosophy* and *mathematics* ; with regard to each of these I shall make some observations.[115] And first, I shall say somewhat of natural philosophy. On this subject it is, that the *sceptics* triumph : all that stock of arguments they produce to depreciate our faculties, and make mankind appear ignorant and low, are drawn principally from this head, to wit, that we are under an invincible blindness as to the *true* and *real* nature of things. This they exaggerate, and love to enlarge on. We are miserably bantered, say they, by our senses, and amused only with the outside and shew of things. The real essence,[116] the internal qualities, and constitution of every the meanest object, is hid from our view ; something there is in every drop of water, every grain of sand, which it is beyond the power of human understanding to fathom or comprehend. But it is evident from what has been shown, that all this complaint is groundless, and that we are influenced by false principles to that degree as to mistrust our senses, and think we know nothing of those things which we perfectly comprehend.

102   One great inducement to our pronouncing our selves ignorant of the nature of things, is the current opinion that every thing includes within it self the cause of its properties : or that there is in each object an inward essence, which is the source whence its discernible qualities flow, and whereon they depend. Some have pretended to account for appearances by occult qualities,[117] but of late they are mostly resolved into mechanical

---

[g] The 1710 edition continues here: *And in effect, one may make a great progress in* School-Ethics, *without ever being the wiser or better man for it, or knowing how to behave himself in the affairs of life, more to the advantage of himself, or his neighbours, than he did before. This hint may suffice, to let any one see, the doctrine of* abstraction . . .

[h] *and their relations*—added in 1734 edition.

causes, to wit, the figure, motion, weight, and such like qualities of insensible particles : whereas in truth, there is no other agent or efficient cause than *spirit*, it being evident that motion, as well as all other *ideas*, is perfectly inert. See *Sect.* 25. Hence, to endeavour to explain the production of colours or sounds, by figure, motion, magnitude and the like, must needs be labour in vain. And accordingly, we see the attempts of that kind are not at all satisfactory. Which may be said, in general, of those instances, wherein one idea or quality is assigned for the cause of another. I need not say, how many *hypotheses* and speculations are left out, and how much the study of Nature is abridged by this doctrine.

103 The great mechanical principle now in vogue is *attraction*.[118] That a stone falls to the earth, or the sea swells towards the moon, may to some appear sufficiently explained thereby. But how are we enlightened by being told this is done by attraction ? Is it that that word signifies the manner of the tendency, and that it is by the mutual drawing[119] of bodies, instead of their being impelled or protruded towards each other ? But nothing is determined of the manner of action, and it may as truly (for aught we know) be termed *impulse* or *protrusion* as *attraction*. Again, the parts of steel we see cohere firmly together, and this also is accounted for by attraction ; but in this, as in the other instances, I do not perceive that any thing is signified besides the effect it self : for as to the manner of the action whereby it is produced, or the cause which produces it, these are not so much as aimed at.

104 Indeed, if we take a view of the several *phenomena*, and compare them together, we may observe some likeness and conformity between them. For example, in the falling of a stone to the ground, in the rising of the sea towards the moon, in cohesion and crystallization, there is something alike, namely an union or mutual approach of bodies. So that any one of these or the like *phenomena*, may not seem strange or surprising to a man who hath nicely observed and compared the effects of Nature. For that only is thought so which is uncommon, or a thing by it self, and out of the ordinary course of our observation. That bodies should tend towards the centre of the earth, is not thought strange, because it is what we perceive every moment of our lives. But that they should have a like gravitation towards the centre of the moon, may seem odd and unaccountable to most men, because it is discerned only in the tides. But a philosopher, whose thoughts take in a larger compass of nature, having observed a certain similitude of appearances, as well in the heavens as the earth, that argue innumerable bodies to have a mutual tendency towards each other, which he denotes by the general name *attraction*, whatever can be reduced

to that, he thinks justly accounted for. Thus he explains the tides by the attraction of the terraqueous globe towards the moon, which to him doth not appear odd or anomalous, but only a particular example of a general rule or law of Nature.

105　If therefore we consider the difference there is betwixt natural philosophers and other men, with regard to their knowledge of the *phenomena*, we shall find it consists, not in an exacter knowledge of the efficient cause that produces them, for that can be no other than the *will of a spirit*, but only in a greater largeness of comprehension, whereby analogies, harmonies, and agreements are discovered in the works of Nature, and the particular effects explained, that is, reduced to general rules, see *Sect.* 62, which rules grounded on the analogy, and uniformness observed in the production of natural effects, are most agreeable, and sought after by the mind ; for that they extend our prospect beyond what is present, and near to us, and enable us to make very probable conjectures, touching things that may have happened at very great distances of time and place, as well as to predict things to come ; which sort of endeavour towards omniscience, is much affected by the mind.[120]

106　But we should proceed warily in such things : for we are apt to lay too great a stress on analogies, and to the prejudice of truth, humour that eagerness of the mind, whereby it is carried to extend its knowledge into general theorems. For example, gravitation, or mutual attraction, because it appears in many instances, some are straightway for pronouncing *universal* ; and that to *attract, and be attracted by every other body, is an essential quality inherent in all bodies whatsoever.*[121] Whereas it appears the fixed stars have no such tendency towards each other : and so far is that gravitation, from being *essential* to bodies, that, in some instances a quite contrary principle seems to shew it self : as in the perpendicular[122] growth of plants, and the elasticity of the air. There is nothing necessary or essential in the case, but it depends entirely on the will of the *governing spirit*, who causes certain bodies to cleave together, or tend towards each other, according to various laws, whilst he keeps others at a fixed distance ; and to some he gives a quite contrary tendency to fly asunder, just as he sees convenient.

107　After what has been premised, I think we may lay down the following conclusions. First, it is plain philosophers amuse themselves in vain, when they inquire for any natural efficient cause, distinct from a *mind* or *spirit*. Secondly, considering the whole creation is the workmanship of a *wise and good agent*, it should seem to become[123] philosophers, to employ their thoughts (contrary to what some hold) about the final causes of things : and I must confess, I see no reason, why pointing out the various ends, to which natural things are adapted, and for which they were originally with unspeakable wisdom contrived, should not be thought one good way of accounting for them, and altogether worthy a philosopher.[124] Thirdly, from what hath been premised no reason can be drawn, why the history of Nature should not still be studied, and observations and experiments made, which, that they are of use to mankind, and enable us to draw any general conclusions, is not the result of any immutable habitudes, or relations between things themselves, but only of God's goodness and kindness to men in the administration of the world. See *Sect.* 30 and 31. Fourthly, by a diligent observation of the *phenomena* within our view, we may discover the general laws of Nature, and from them deduce the other *phenomena*, I do not say *demonstrate* ; for all deductions of that kind depend on a supposition that the Author of Nature always operates uniformly, and in a constant observance of those rules we take for principles : which we cannot evidently know.

108[i] Those men who frame general rules from the *phenomena*, and afterwards derive the *phenomena* from those rules, seem to consider signs rather than causes. A man may well understand natural signs without knowing their analogy,[j] or being able to say by what rule a thing is so or so. And as it is very possible to write improperly, through too strict an observance of general grammar-rules : so in arguing from general rules of Nature, it is not impossible we may extend the analogy too far, and by that means run into mistakes.[125]

109 As in reading other books, a wise man will choose to fix his thoughts on the sense and apply it to use, rather than lay them out in grammatical remarks on the language ; so in perusing the volume of Nature, it seems beneath the dignity of the mind to affect an exactness in reducing each particular phenomenon to general rules, or shewing how it follows from them. We should propose to our selves nobler views, such as to recreate and exalt the mind, with a prospect of the beauty, order, extent, and variety of natural things : hence, by proper inferences, to enlarge our notions of the grandeur, wisdom, and beneficence of the Creator : and

---

[i] In the 1710 edition, this paragraph begins: *It appears from Sect. 66, etc. that the steady, consistent methods of Nature, may not unfitly be stiled the* language *of its* Author, *whereby He discovers His* attributes *to our view, and directs us how to act for the convenience and felicity of life. And to me, those* men . . .

[j] *seem to consider signs rather than causes . . . analogy*—the 1710 edition reads: *seem to be grammarians, and their art the grammar of Nature. Two ways there are of learning a language, either by rule or by practice : a man may be well read in the language of Nature, without understanding the grammar of it, or being able* . . .

lastly, to make the several parts of the Creation, so far as in us lies, subservient to the ends they were designed for, God's glory, and the sustentation and comfort of our selves and fellow-creatures.

110[k]   The best key for the aforesaid analogy, or natural science, will be easily acknowledged to be a certain celebrated treatise of *mechanics* :[126] in the entrance of which justly admired treatise, time, space and motion, are distinguished into *absolute* and *relative*, *true* and *apparent*, *mathematical* and *vulgar* : which distinction, as it is at large explained by the author, doth suppose those quantities to have an existence without the mind : and that they are ordinarily conceived with relation to sensible things, to which nevertheless in their own nature, they bear no relation at all.

111   As for *time*, as it is there taken in an absolute or abstracted sense, for the duration or perseverance[127] of the existence of things, I have nothing more to add concerning it, after what hath been already said on that subject, *Sect.* 97 and 98. For the rest,[128] this celebrated author holds there is an *absolute space*, which, being unperceivable to sense, remains in it self similar and immoveable : and relative space to be the measure thereof, which being moveable, and defined by its situation in respect of sensible bodies, is vulgarly taken for immoveable space. *Place* he defines to be that part of space which is occupied by any body. And according as the space is absolute or relative, so also is the place. *Absolute motion* is said to be the translation of a body from absolute place to absolute place, as relative motion is from one relative place to another. And because the parts of absolute space, do not fall under our senses, instead of them we are obliged to use their sensible measures : and so define both place and motion with respect to bodies, which we regard as immoveable. But it is said, in philosophical matters we must abstract from our senses, since it may be, that none of those bodies which seem to be quiescent, are truly so : and the same thing which is moved relatively, may be really at rest. As likewise one and the same body may be in relative rest and motion, or even moved with contrary relative motions at the same time, according as its place is variously defined. All which ambiguity[129] is to be found in the apparent motions, but not at all in the true or absolute, which should therefore be alone regarded in philosophy. And the true, we are told, are

---

[k] In the 1710 edition, this paragraph begins: *The best grammar of the kind we are speaking of, will be easily acknowledg'd to be a treatise of mechanics, demonstrated and applied to Nature, by a philosopher of a neighbouring nation whom all the world admire. I shall not take upon me to make remarks, on the performance of that extraordinary person : only some things he has advanced, so directly opposite to the doctrine we have hitherto laid down, that we shou'd be wanting, in the regard due to the authority of so great a man, did we not take some notice of them. In the entrance of that justly admired treatise . . .*

distinguished from apparent or relative motions by the following proper-ties. First, in true or absolute motion, all parts which preserve the same position with respect to the whole, partake of the motions of the whole. Secondly, the place being moved, that which is placed therein is also moved : so that a body moving in a place which is in motion, doth partici-pate the motion of its place. Thirdly, true motion is never generated or changed, otherwise than by force impressed on the body it self. Fourthly, true motion is always changed by force impressed on the body moved. Fifthly, in circular motion barely relative, there is no centrifugal force, which nevertheless in that which is true or absolute, is proportional to the quantity of motion.

112　But notwithstanding what hath been said, it doth not appear to me, that there can be any motion other than *relative :* so that to conceive motion, there must be at least conceived two bodies, whereof the distance or position in regard to each other is varied. Hence if there was one only body in being, it could not possibly be moved. This seems evident, in that the idea I have of motion doth necessarily include relation.

113　But though in every motion it be necessary to conceive more bodies than one, yet it may be that one only is moved, namely that on which the force causing the change of distance is impressed, or in other words, that to which the action is applied. For however some may define relative motion, so as to term that body *moved*, which changes its distance from some other body, whether the force or action causing that change were applied to it, or no : yet as relative motion is that which is perceived by sense, and regarded in the ordinary affairs of life, it should seem that every man of common sense knows what it is, as well as the best philosopher : now I ask any one, whether in his sense of motion as he walks along the streets, the stones he passes over may be said to *move*, because they change distance with his feet ? To me it seems, that though motion includes a rela-tion of one thing to another, yet it is not necessary that each term of the relation be denominated from it.[130] As a man may think of somewhat which doth not think, so a body may be moved to or from another body, which is not therefore itself in motion.[1]

114　As the place happens to be variously defined, the motion which is related to it varies. A man in a ship may be said to be quiescent, with rela-tion to the sides of the vessel, and yet move with relation to the land. Or he may move eastward in respect of the one, and westward in respect of the

---

[1] In the 1710 edition, this paragraph ends : . . . *in motion, I mean* relative *motion, for other I am not able to conceive.*

other. In the common affairs of life, men never go beyond the earth to define the place of any body : and what is quiescent in respect of that, is accounted *absolutely* to be so. But philosophers, who have a greater extent of thought, and juster notions of the system of things, discover even the earth it self to be moved. In order therefore to fix their notions, they seem to conceive the corporeal world as finite, and the utmost unmoved walls or shell thereof to be the place, whereby they estimate true motions. If we sound our own conceptions, I believe we may find all the absolute motion we can frame an idea of, to be at bottom no other than relative motion thus defined. For as hath been already observed, absolute motion exclusive of all external relation is incomprehensible : and to this kind of relative motion, all the above-mentioned properties, causes, and effects ascribed to absolute motion,[131] will, if I mistake not, be found to agree. As to what is said of the centrifugal force, that it doth not at all belong to circular relative motion : I do not see how this follows from the experiment which is brought to prove it. See *Philosophiae Naturalis Principia Mathematica, in Schol. Def.* VIII. For the water in the vessel, at that time wherein it is said to have the greatest relative circular motion, hath, I think, no motion at all : as is plain from the foregoing section.[132]

115   For to denominate a body *moved*, it is requisite, first, that it change its distance or situation with regard to some other body : and secondly, that the force or action occasioning that change be applied to it. If either of these be wanting, I do not think that agreeably to the sense of mankind, or the propriety of language, a body can be said to be in motion. I grant indeed, that it is possible for us to think a body, which we see change its distance from some other, to be moved, though it have no force applied to it (in which sense there may be apparent motion), but then it is, because the force causing the change of distance, is imagined by us to be applied or impressed on that body thought to move. Which indeed shews we are capable of mistaking a thing to be in motion which is not,[m] and that is all.

---

[m] In the 1710 edition this sentence ends: *which is not, but does not prove that, in the common acceptation of motion, a body is moved meerly because it changes distance from another ; since as soon as we are undeceiv'd, and find that the moving force was not communicated to it, we no longer hold it to be moved. So on the other hand, when one only body (the parts whereof preserve a given position between themselves) is imagin'd to exist ; some there are who think that it can be moved all manner of ways, tho' without any change of distance or situation to any other bodies ; which we shou'd not deny, if they meant only that it might have an impressed force, which, upon the bare creation of other bodies, wou'd produce a motion of some certain quantity and determination. But that an actual motion (distinct from the impressed force, or power productive of change of place in case there were bodies present whereby to define it) can exist in such a single body, I must confess I am not able to comprehend.*

116   From what hath been said, it follows that the philosophic consideration of motion doth not imply the being of an *absolute space*, distinct from that which is perceived by sense, and related to bodies : which that it cannot exist without the mind, is clear upon the same principles, that demonstrate the like of all other objects of sense. And perhaps, if we inquire narrowly, we shall find we cannot even frame an idea of *pure space*, exclusive of all body. This I must confess seems impossible, as being a most abstract idea. When I excite a motion in some part of my body, if it be free or without resistance, I say there is *space :* but if I find a resistance, then I say there is *body :* and in proportion as the resistance to motion is lesser or greater, I say the space is more or less *pure*. So that when I speak of pure or empty space, it is not to be supposed, that the word *space* stands for an idea distinct from, or conceivable without body and motion. Though indeed we are apt to think every noun substantive stands for a distinct idea, that may be separated from all others : which hath occasioned infinite mistakes.[133] When therefore supposing all the world to be annihilated besides my own body, I say there still remains *pure space :* thereby nothing else is meant, but only that I conceive it possible, for the limbs of my body to be moved on all sides without the least resistance : but if that too were annihilated, then there could be no motion, and consequently no space. Some perhaps may think the sense of seeing doth furnish them with the idea of pure space ;[134] but it is plain from what we have elsewhere shewn, that the ideas of space and distance are not obtained by that sense. See the *Essay concerning Vision*.[135]

117   What is here laid down, seems to put an end to all those disputes and difficulties, which have sprung up amongst the learned concerning the nature of *pure space*. But the chief advantage arising from it, is, that we are freed from that dangerous *dilemma*, to which several who have employed their thoughts on this subject, imagine themselves reduced, to wit, of thinking either that real space is God, or else that there is something beside God which is eternal, uncreated, infinite, indivisible, immutable.[136] Both which may justly be thought pernicious and absurd notions. It is certain that not a few divines, as well as philosophers of great note, have, from the difficulty they found in conceiving either limits or annihilation of space, concluded it must be *divine*. And some of late have set themselves particularly to shew, that the incommunicable attributes of God agree to it.[137] Which doctrine, how unworthy soever it may seem of the Divine Nature, yet I do not see how we can get clear of it, so long as we adhere to the received opinions.

118   Hitherto of natural philosophy : we come now to make some

inquiry concerning that other great branch of speculative knowledge, to wit, *mathematics*. These, how celebrated soever they may be, for their clearness and certainty of demonstration, which is hardly any where else to be found, cannot nevertheless be supposed altogether free from mistakes ; if in their principles there lurks some secret error, which is common to the professors of those sciences with the rest of mankind. Mathematicians, though they deduce their theorems from a great height of evidence, yet their first principles are limited by the consideration of quantity : and they do not ascend into any inquiry concerning those transcendental maxims, which influence all the particular sciences, each part whereof, mathematics not excepted, doth consequently participate of the errors involved in them. That the principles laid down by mathematicians are true, and their way of deduction from those principles clear and incontestable, we do not deny. But we hold, there may be certain erroneous maxims of greater extent than the object of mathematics, and for that reason not expressly mentioned, though tacitly supposed throughout the whole progress of that science ; and that the ill effects of those secret unexamined errors are diffused through all the branches thereof. To be plain, we suspect the mathematicians are, as well as other men, concerned in the errors arising from the doctrine of abstract general ideas, and the existence of objects without the mind.

119   *Arithmetic* hath been thought to have for its object abstract ideas of *number*. Of which to understand the properties and mutual habitudes is supposed no mean part of speculative knowledge. The opinion of the pure and intellectual nature of numbers in abstract, hath made them in esteem with those philosophers, who seem to have affected an uncommon fineness and elevation of thought. It hath set a price on the most trifling numerical speculations which in practice are of no use, but serve only for amusement : and hath therefore so far infected the minds of some, that they have dreamt of mighty *mysteries* involved in numbers, and attempted the explication of natural things by them. But if we inquire into our own thoughts, and consider what hath been premised, we may perhaps entertain a low opinion of those high flights and abstractions, and look on all inquiries about numbers, only as so many *difficiles nugae*, so far as they are not subservient to practice, and promote the benefit of life.

120   Unity in abstract we have before considered in *Sect.* 13, from which and what hath been said in the Introduction, it plainly follows there is not any such idea. But number being defined a *collection of units*, we may conclude that, if there be no such thing as unity or unit in abstract, there are no ideas of number in abstract denoted by the numerical names and

figures. The theories therefore in arithmetic, if they are abstracted from the names and figures, as likewise from all use and practice, as well as from the particular things numbered, can be supposed to have nothing at all for their object. Hence we may see, how entirely the science of numbers is subordinate to practice, and how jejune and trifling it becomes, when considered as a matter of mere speculation.

121 However since there may be some, who, deluded by the specious shew of discovering abstracted verities, waste their time in arithmetical theorems and problems, which have not any use : it will not be amiss, if we more fully consider, and expose the vanity of that pretence ; and this will plainly appear, by taking a view of arithmetic in its infancy, and observing what it was that originally put men on the study of that science, and to what scope they directed it. It is natural to think that at first, men, for ease of memory and help of computation, made use of counters, or in writing of single strokes, points or the like, each whereof was made to signify an unit, that is, some one thing of whatever kind they had occasion to reckon. Afterwards they found out the more compendious ways, of making one character stand in place of several strokes, or points. And lastly, the notation of the Arabians or Indians[138] came into use, wherein by the repetition of a few characters or figures, and varying the signification of each figure according to the place it obtains, all numbers may be most aptly expressed : which seems to have been done in imitation of language, so that an exact analogy is observed betwixt the notation by figures and names, the nine simple figures answering the nine first numeral names and places in the former, corresponding to denominations in the latter. And agreeably to those conditions of the simple and local value of figures, were contrived methods of finding from the given figures or marks of the parts, what figures and how placed, are proper to denote the whole or *vice versa*. And having found the sought figures, the same rule or analogy being observed throughout, it is easy to read them into words ; and so the number becomes perfectly known. For then the number of any particular things is said to be known, when we know the name or figures (with their due arrangement) that according to the standing analogy belong to them. For these signs being known, we can by the operations of arithmetic, know the signs of any part of the particular sums signified by them ; and thus computing in signs (because of the connexion established betwixt them and the distinct multitudes[139] of things, whereof one is taken for a unit), we may be able rightly to sum up, divide, and proportion the things themselves that we intend to number.

122   In *arithmetic* therefore we regard not the *things* but the *signs*, which nevertheless are not regarded for their own sake, but because they direct us how to act with relation to things, and dispose rightly of them. Now agreeably to what we have before observed, of words in general (*Sect.* 19. *Introd.*) it happens here likewise, that abstract ideas are thought to be signified by numeral names or characters, while they do not suggest ideas of particular things to our minds. I shall not at present enter into a more particular dissertation on this subject ; but only observe that it is evident from what hath been said, those things which pass for abstract truths and theorems concerning numbers, are, in reality, conversant about no object distinct from particular numerable things, except only names and characters ; which originally came to be considered, on no other account but their being *signs*, or capable to represent aptly, whatever particular things men had need to compute. Whence it follows, that to study them for their own sake would be just as wise, and to as good purpose, as if a man, neglecting the true use or original intention and subserviency of language, should spend his time in impertinent criticisms upon words, or reasonings and controversies purely verbal.

123   From numbers we proceed to speak of *extension*, which considered as relative, is the object of geometry. The *infinite* divisibility of *finite* extension, though it is not expressly laid down, either as an axiom or theorem in the elements of that science, yet is throughout the same every where supposed, and thought to have so inseparable and essential a connexion with the principles and demonstrations in geometry, that mathematicians never admit it into doubt, or make the least question of it. And as this notion is the source from whence do spring all those amusing geometrical paradoxes,[140] which have such a direct repugnancy to the plain common sense of mankind, and are admitted with so much reluctance into a mind not yet debauched by learning : so is it the principal occasion of all that nice and extreme subtelty, which renders the study of *mathematics* so difficult and tedious. Hence if we can make it appear, that no finite extension contains innumerable parts, or is infinitely divisible, it follows that we shall at once clear the science of geometry from a great number of difficulties and contradictions, which have ever been esteemed a reproach to human reason, and withal make the attainment thereof a business of much less time and pains, than it hitherto hath been.

124   Every particular finite extension, which may possibly be the object of our thought, is an *idea* existing only in the mind, and consequently each part thereof must be perceived. If therefore I cannot perceive innumerable parts in any finite extension that I consider, it is certain they

149

are not contained in it : but it is evident, that I cannot distinguish innumerable parts in any particular line, surface, or solid, which I either perceive by sense, or figure to my self in my mind : wherefore I conclude they are not contained in it. Nothing can be plainer to me, than that the extensions I have in view are no other than my own ideas, and it is no less plain, that I cannot resolve any one of my ideas into an infinite number of other ideas, that is, that they are not infinitely divisible. If by *finite extension* be meant something distinct from a finite idea, I declare I do not know what that is, and so cannot affirm or deny any thing of it. But if the terms *extension*, *parts*, and the like, are taken in any sense conceivable, that is, for ideas ; then to say a finite quantity or extension consists of parts infinite in number, is so manifest a contradiction, that every one at first sight acknowledges it to be so. And it is impossible it should ever gain the assent of any reasonable creature, who is not brought to it by gentle and slow degrees, as a converted Gentile to the belief of *transubstantiation*.[141] Ancient and rooted prejudices do often pass into principles : and those propositions which once obtain the force and credit of a *principle*, are not only themselves, but likewise whatever is deducible from them, thought privileged from all examination. And there is no absurdity so gross, which by this means the mind of man may not be prepared to swallow.

125   He whose understanding is prepossessed with the doctrine of abstract general ideas, may be persuaded, that (whatever be thought of the ideas of sense), extension in *abstract* is infinitely divisible. And one who thinks the objects of sense exist without the mind, will perhaps in virtue thereof be brought to admit, that a line but an inch long may contain innumerable parts really existing, though too small to be discerned. These errors are grafted as well in the minds of *geometricians*, as of other men, and have a like influence on their reasonings ; and it were no difficult thing, to shew how the arguments from geometry made use of to support the infinite divisibility of extension, are bottomed on them. At present we shall only observe in general, whence it is that the mathematicians are all so fond and tenacious of this doctrine.

126   It hath been observed in another place, that the theorems and demonstrations in geometry are conversant about universal ideas. *Sect.* 15. *Introd.* Where it is explained in what sense this ought to be understood, to wit, that the particular lines and figures included in the diagram, are supposed to stand for innumerable others of different sizes : or in other words, the geometer considers them abstracting from their magnitude : which doth not imply that he forms an abstract idea, but only that he cares not what the particular magnitude is, whether great or small, but looks on that

as a thing indifferent to the demonstration : hence it follows, that a line in the scheme,[142] but an inch long, must be spoken of, as though it contained ten thousand parts, since it is regarded not in it self, but as it is universal ; and it is universal only in its signification, whereby it represents innumerable lines greater than it self, in which may be distinguished ten thousand parts or more, though there may not be above an inch in it. After this manner the properties of the lines signified are (by a very usual figure) transferred to the sign, and thence through mistake thought to appertain to it considered in its own nature.[143]

127 Because there is no number of parts so great, but it is possible there may be a line containing more, the inch-line is said to contain parts more than any assignable number ; which is true, not of the inch taken absolutely, but only for the things signified by it. But men not retaining that distinction in their thoughts, slide into a belief that the small particular line described on paper contains in it self parts innumerable. There is no such thing as the ten-thousandth part of an *inch* ; but there is of a *mile* or *diameter of the earth*, which may be signified by that inch. When therefore I delineate a triangle on paper, and take one side not above an inch, for example, in length to be the *radius* : this I consider as divided into ten thousand or an hundred thousand parts, or more. For though the ten-thousandth part of that line considered in it self, is nothing at all, and consequently may be neglected without any error or inconveniency ; yet these described lines being only marks standing for greater quantities, whereof it may be the ten-thousandth part is very considerable, it follows, that to prevent notable errors in practice, the *radius* must be taken of ten thousand parts, or more.[144]

128 From what hath been said the reason is plain why, to the end any theorem may become universal in its use, it is necessary we speak of the lines described on paper, as though they contained parts which really they do not. In doing of which, if we examine the matter throughly, we shall perhaps discover that we cannot conceive an inch it self as consisting of, or being divisible into a thousand parts, but only some other line which is far greater than an inch, and represented by it. And that when we say a line is *infinitely divisible*, we must mean a line which is *infinitely great*. What we have here observed seems to be the chief cause, why to suppose the infinite divisibility of finite extension hath been thought necessary in geometry.

129 The several absurdities and contradictions which flowed from this false principle might, one would think, have been esteemed so many demonstrations against it. But by I know not what *logic*, it is held that

proofs *a posteriori* are not to be admitted against propositions relating to infinity.[145] As though it were not impossible even for an infinite mind to reconcile contradictions. Or as if any thing absurd and repugnant could have a necessary connexion with truth, or flow from it. But whoever considers the weakness of this pretence, will think it was contrived on purpose to humour the laziness of the mind, which had rather acquiesce in an indolent scepticism, than be at the pains to go through with a severe examination of those principles it hath ever embraced for true.

130   Of late the speculations about infinites have run so high, and grown to such strange notions, as have occasioned no small scruples and disputes among the geometers of the present age. Some there are of great note, who not content with holding that finite lines may be divided into an infinite number of parts, do yet farther maintain, that each of those infinitesimals is it self subdivisible into an infinity of other parts, or infinitesimals of a second order, and so on *ad infinitum*. These, I say, assert there are infinitesimals of infinitesimals of infinitesimals, without ever coming to an end. So that according to them an inch doth not barely contain an infinite number of parts, but an infinity of an infinity of an infinity *ad infinitum* of parts. Others there be who hold all orders of infinitesimals below the first to be nothing at all, thinking it with good reason absurd, to imagine there is any positive quantity or part of extension, which though multiplied infinitely, can never equal the smallest given extension. And yet on the other hand it seems no less absurd, to think the square, cube, or other power of a positive real root,[146] should it self be nothing at all ; which they who hold infinitesimals of the first order, denying all of the subsequent orders, are obliged to maintain.

131   Have we not therefore reason to conclude, that they are *both* in the wrong, and that there is in effect no such thing as parts infinitely small, or an infinite number of parts contained in any finite quantity ? But you will say, that if this doctrine obtains, it will follow the very foundations of geometry are destroyed : and those great men who have raised that science to so astonishing an height, have been all the while building a castle in the air. To this it may be replied, that whatever is useful in geometry and promotes the benefit of human life, doth still remain firm and unshaken on our principles. That science considered as practical, will rather receive advantage than any prejudice from what hath been said. But to set this in a due light, may be the subject of a distinct inquiry. For the rest, though it should follow that some of the more intricate and subtle parts of *speculative mathematics* may be pared off without any prejudice to truth ; yet I do not see what damage will be thence derived to mankind. On the contrary,

it were highly to be wished, that men of great abilities and obstinate application would draw off their thoughts from those amusements, and
employ them in the study of such things as lie nearer the concerns of life,
or have a more direct influence on the manners.

132   If it be said that several theorems undoubtedly true, are discovered by methods in which infinitesimals are made use of, which could
never have been, if their existence included a contradiction in it. I answer,
that upon a thorough examination it will not be found, that in any instance
it is necessary to make use of or conceive infinitesimal parts of finite lines,
or even quantities less than the *minimum sensibile :*[147] nay, it will be evident
this is never done, it being impossible.[n]

133   By what we have premised, it is plain that very numerous and
important errors have taken their rise from those false principles, which
were impugned in the foregoing parts of this treatise. And the opposites of
those erroneous tenets at the same time appear to be most fruitful principles, from whence do flow innumerable consequences highly advanta-
geous to true philosophy as well as to religion. Particularly, *matter* or *the
absolute existence of corporeal objects*, hath been shewn to be that wherein
the most avowed and pernicious enemies of all knowledge, whether
human or divine, have ever placed their chief strength and confidence.
And surely, if by distinguishing the real existence of unthinking things
from their being perceived, and allowing them a subsistence of their own
out of the minds of spirits, no one thing is explained in Nature ; but on the
contrary a great many inexplicable difficulties arise : if the supposition of
matter is barely precarious, as not being grounded on so much as one
single reason : if its consequences cannot endure the light of examination
and free inquiry, but screen themselves under the dark and general pretence of *infinites being incomprehensible :*[148] if withal the removal of this
matter be not attended with the least evil consequence, if it be not even
missed in the world, but every thing as well, nay much easier conceived
without it : if lastly, both *sceptics* and *atheists* are for ever silenced upon supposing only spirits and ideas, and this scheme of things is perfectly agreeable both to *reason* and *religion :* methinks we may expect it should
be admitted and firmly embraced, though it were proposed only as an

---

[n] The 1710 edition continues: *And whatever mathematicians may think of fluxions or the differen-
tial calculus and the like, a little reflexion will shew them, that in working by those methods, they do not
conceive or imagine lines or surfaces less than what are perceivable to sense. They may, indeed, call those
little and almost insensible quantities infinitesimals or infinitesimals of infinitesimals, if they please :
but at bottom this is all, they being in truth finite, nor does the solution of problems require the supposing
any other. But this will be more clearly made out hereafter.*

hypothesis, and the existence of matter had been allowed possible, which yet I think we have evidently demonstrated that it is not.

134   True it is, that in consequence of the foregoing principles, several disputes and speculations, which are esteemed no mean parts of learning, are rejected as useless. But how great a prejudice soever against our notions, this may give to those who have already been deeply engaged, and made large advances in studies of that nature : yet by others, we hope it will not be thought any just ground of dislike to the principles and tenets herein laid down, that they abridge the labour of study, and make human sciences more clear, compendious, and attainable, than they were before.

135   Having dispatched what we intended to say concerning the knowledge of *ideas*, the method we proposed leads us, in the next place, to treat of *spirits* : with regard to which, perhaps human knowledge is not so deficient as is vulgarly imagined. The great reason that is assigned for our being thought ignorant of the nature of spirits, is, our not having an idea of it. But surely it ought not to be looked on as a defect in a human understanding, that it does not perceive the idea of *spirit*, if it is manifestly impossible there should be any such *idea*.[149] And this, if I mistake not, has been demonstrated in *Sect.* 27 : to which I shall here add that a spirit has been shown to be the only substance or support, wherein the unthinking beings or ideas can exist : but that this *substance* which supports or perceives ideas should it self be an *idea* or like an *idea*, is evidently absurd.

136   It will perhaps be said, that we want a sense (as some have imagined) proper to know substances withal, which if we had, we might know our own soul, as we do a triangle. To this I answer, that in case we had a new sense bestowed upon us, we could only receive thereby some new sensations or ideas of sense. But I believe no body will say, that what he means by the terms *soul* and *substance*, is only some particular sort of idea or sensation. We may therefore infer, that all things duly considered, it is not more reasonable to think our faculties defective, in that they do not furnish us with an idea of spirit or active thinking substance, than it would be if we should blame them for not being able to comprehend a *round square*.

137   From the opinion that spirits are to be known after the manner of an idea or sensation, have risen many absurd and heterodox tenets, and much scepticism about the nature of the soul. It is even probable, that this opinion may have produced a doubt in some, whether they had any soul at all distinct from their body, since upon inquiry they could not find they had an idea of it. That an *idea* which is inactive, and the existence whereof consists in being perceived, should be the image or likeness of an agent sub-

sisting by it self, seems to need no other refutation, than barely attending to what is meant by those words. But perhaps you will say, that though an *idea* cannot resemble a *spirit*, in its thinking, acting, or subsisting by it self, yet it may in some other respects : and it is not necessary that an idea or image be in all respects like the original.

138   I answer, if it does not in those mentioned, it is impossible it should represent it in any other thing. Do but leave out the power of willing, thinking, and perceiving ideas, and there remains nothing else wherein the idea can be like a spirit. For by the word *spirit* we mean only that which thinks, wills, and perceives ; this, and this alone, constitutes the signification of that term. If therefore it is impossible that any degree of those powers should be represented in an idea, it is evident there can be no idea° of a spirit.[150]

139   But it will be objected, that if there is no idea signified by the terms *soul*, *spirit*, and *substance*, they are wholly insignificant, or have no meaning in them. I answer, those words do mean or signify a real thing, which is neither an idea nor like an idea, but that which perceives ideas, and wills, and reasons about them. What I am my self, that which I denote by the term I, is the same with what is meant by *soul* or *spiritual substance*. If it be said that this is only quarrelling at a word, and that since the immediate significations of other names are by common consent called *ideas*, no reason can be assigned, why that which is signified by the name *spirit* or *soul* may not partake in the same appellation. I answer, all the unthinking objects of the mind agree, in that they are entirely passive, and their existence consists only in being perceived : whereas a soul or spirit is an active being, whose existence consists not in being perceived, but in perceiving ideas and thinking. It is therefore necessary, in order to prevent equivocation and confounding natures perfectly disagreeing and unlike, that we distinguish between *spirit* and *idea*. See *Sect.* 27.

140   In a large sense indeed, we may be said to have an idea, or rather a notion^p of *spirit*, that is, we understand the meaning of the word, otherwise we could not affirm or deny any thing of it. Moreover, as we conceive the ideas that are in the minds of other spirits by means of our own, which we suppose to be resemblances of them : so we know other spirits by means of our own soul, which in that sense is the image or idea of them, it having a like respect to other spirits, that blueness or heat by me perceived hath to those ideas perceived by another.[151]

° In this sentence, where the 1734 edition reads *idea*, the 1710 edition reads *idea or notion*.

^p *or rather a notion*—added in 1734 edition.

141 It must not be supposed, that they who assert the natural immortality of the soul are of opinion, that it is absolutely incapable of annihilation even by the infinite power of the Creator who first gave it being : but only that it is not liable to be broken or dissolved by the ordinary Laws of Nature or motion. They indeed, who hold the soul of man to be only a thin vital flame, or system of animal spirits, make it perishing and corruptible as the body, since there is nothing more easily dissipated than such a being, which it is naturally impossible should survive the ruin of the tabernacle, wherein it is enclosed. And this notion hath been greedily embraced and cherished by the worst part of mankind, as the most effectual antidote against all impressions of virtue and religion. But it hath been made evident, that bodies of what frame or texture soever, are barely passive ideas in the mind, which is more distant and heterogeneous from them, than light is from darkness. We have shewn that the soul is indivisible, incorporeal, unextended, and it is consequently incorruptible. Nothing can be plainer, than that the motions, changes, decays, and dissolutions which we hourly see befall natural bodies (and which is what we mean by the *course of Nature*) cannot possibly affect an active, simple, uncompounded substance : such a being therefore is indissoluble by the force of Nature, that is to say, *the soul of man is naturally immortal*.

142 After what hath been said, it is I suppose plain, that our souls are not to be known in the same manner as senseless inactive objects, or by way of *idea*. *Spirits* and *ideas* are things so wholly different, that when we say, *they exist, they are known*, or the like, these words must not be thought to signify any thing common to both natures. There is nothing alike or common in them : and to expect that by any multiplication or enlargement of our faculties, we may be enabled to know a spirit as we do a triangle, seems as absurd as if we should hope to *see a sound*. This is inculcated because I imagine it may be of moment towards clearing several important questions, and preventing some very dangerous errors concerning the nature of the soul.[152] We[q] may not I think strictly be said to have an idea of an active being, or of an action, although we may be said to have a notion of them. I have some knowledge or notion of my mind, and its acts about ideas, inasmuch as I know or understand what is meant by those words. What I know, that I have some notion of. I will not say, that the terms *idea* and *notion* may not be used convertibly, if the world will have it so. But yet it conduceth to clearness and propriety, that we distinguish things very different by different names. It is also to be remarked, that all relations

---

q The remainder of this paragraph was added in the 1734 edition.

including an act of the mind,[153] we cannot so properly be said to have an idea, but rather a notion of the relations or habitudes between things. But if in the modern way the word *idea* is extended to spirits, and relations and acts ; this is after all an affair of verbal concern.

143   It will not be amiss to add, that the doctrine of *abstract ideas* hath had no small share in rendering those sciences intricate and obscure, which are particularly conversant about spiritual things. Men have imagined they could frame abstract notions of the powers and acts of the mind, and consider them prescinded, as well from the mind or spirit it self, as from their respective objects and effects. Hence a great number of dark and ambiguous terms presumed to stand for abstract notions, have been introduced into metaphysics and morality, and from these have grown infinite distractions and disputes amongst the learned.

144   But nothing seems more to have contributed towards engaging men in controversies and mistakes, with regard to the nature and operations of the mind, than the being used to speak of those things, in terms borrowed from sensible ideas. For example, the will is termed the *motion* of the soul :[154] this infuses a belief, that the mind of man is as a ball in motion, impelled and determined by the objects of sense, as necessarily as that is by the stroke of a racket. Hence arise endless scruples and errors of dangerous consequence in morality. All which I doubt not may be cleared, and truth appear plain, uniform, and consistent, could but philosophers be prevailed on to retire into themselves, and attentively consider their own meaning.[r]

145   From what hath been said, it is plain that we cannot know the existence of other spirits, otherwise than by their operations, or the ideas by them excited in us. I perceive several motions, changes, and combinations of ideas, that inform me there are certain particular agents like my self, which accompany them, and concur in their production. Hence the knowledge I have of other spirits is not immediate, as is the knowledge of my ideas ; but depending on the intervention of ideas, by me referred to agents or spirits distinct from myself, as effects or concomitant signs.

146   But though there be some things which convince us, human agents are concerned in producing them ; yet it is evident to every one, that those things which are called the works of Nature, that is, the far greater part of the ideas or sensations perceived by us, are not produced by, or

---

[r]   In the 1710 edition, this paragraph ends: *be prevailed on to depart from some receiv'd prejudices and modes of speech, and retiring into themselves attentively consider their own meaning. But the difficulties arising on this head, demand a more particular disquisition, than suits with the design of this treatise.*

dependent on the wills of men. There is therefore some other spirit that causes them, since it is repugnant that they should subsist by themselves. See *Sect.* 29. But if we attentively consider the constant regularity, order, and concatenation of natural things, the surprising magnificence, beauty, and perfection of the larger, and the exquisite contrivance of the smaller parts of the creation, together with the exact harmony and correspondence of the whole, but above all, the never enough admired laws of pain and pleasure, and the instincts or natural inclinations, appetites, and passions of animals ; I say if we consider all these things, and at the same time attend to the meaning and import of the attributes, one, eternal, infinitely wise, good, and perfect, we shall clearly perceive that they belong to the aforesaid spirit, *who works all in all*, and *by whom all things consist*.[155]

147   Hence it is evident, that God is known as certainly and immediately as any other mind or spirit whatsoever, distinct from our selves.[156] We may even assert, that the existence of God is far more evidently perceived than the existence of men ; because the effects of Nature are infinitely more numerous and considerable, than those ascribed to human agents. There is not any one mark that denotes a man, or effect produced by him, which doth not more strongly evince the being of that spirit who is the *Author of Nature*. For it is evident that in affecting other persons, the will of man hath no other object, than barely the motion of the limbs of his body ;[157] but that such a motion should be attended by, or excite any idea in the mind of another, depends wholly on the will of the Creator. He alone it is who *upholding all things by the Word of his Power*,[158] maintains that intercourse between spirits, whereby they are able to perceive the existence of each other. And yet this pure and clear light which enlightens every one, is it self invisible.

148   It seems to be a general pretence of the unthinking herd, that they cannot see God. Could we but see him, say they, as we see a man, we should believe that he is, and believing obey his commands. But alas we need only open our eyes to see the sovereign Lord of all things with a more full and clear view, than we do any one of our fellow-creatures. Not that I imagine we see God (as some will have it) by a direct and immediate view, or see corporeal things, not by themselves, but by seeing that which represents them in the essence of God, which doctrine is I must confess to me incomprehensible.[159] But I shall explain my meaning. A human spirit or person is not perceived by sense, as not being an idea ; when therefore we see the colour, size, figure, and motions of a man, we perceive only certain sensations or ideas excited in our own minds : and these being exhibited to our view in sundry distinct collections, serve to mark out unto us the exis-

tence of finite and created spirits like our selves. Hence it is plain, we do not see a man, if by *man* is meant that which lives, moves, perceives, and thinks as we do : but only such a certain collection of ideas, as directs us to think there is a distinct principle of thought and motion like to our selves, accompanying and represented by it. And after the same manner we see God ; all the difference is, that whereas some one finite and narrow assemblage of ideas denotes a particular human mind, whithersoever we direct our view, we do at all times and in all places perceive manifest tokens of the divinity : every thing we see, hear, feel, or any wise perceive by sense, being a sign or effect of the power of God ; as is our perception of those very motions, which are produced by men.

149   It is therefore plain, that nothing can be more evident to any one that is capable of the least reflexion, than the existence of God, or a spirit who is intimately present to our minds, producing in them all that variety of ideas or sensations, which continually affect us, on whom we have an absolute and entire dependence, in short, *in whom we live, and move, and have our being.*[160] That the discovery of this great truth which lies so near and obvious to the mind, should be attained to by the reason of so very few, is a sad instance of the stupidity and inattention of men, who, though they are surrounded with such clear manifestations of the Deity, are yet so little affected by them, that they seem as it were blinded with excess of light.

150   But you will say, hath Nature no share in the production of natural things, and must they be all ascribed to the immediate and sole operation of God ? I answer, if by *Nature* is meant only the visible *series* of effects, or sensations imprinted on our minds according to certain fixed and general laws : then it is plain, that Nature taken in this sense cannot produce any thing at all. But if by *Nature* is meant some being distinct from God, as well as from the laws of Nature, and things perceived by sense, I must confess that word is to me an empty sound, without any intelligible meaning annexed to it. Nature in this acceptation is a vain *chimera* introduced by those heathens, who had not just notions of the omnipresence and infinite perfection of God. But it is more unaccountable, that it should be received among Christians professing belief in the Holy Scriptures, which constantly ascribe those effects to the immediate hand of God, that heathen philosophers are wont to impute to *Nature. The Lord, he causeth the vapours to ascend ; he maketh lightnings with rain ; he bringeth forth the wind out of his treasures,* Jerem. Chap. 10. ver. 13. *He turneth the shadow of death into the morning, and maketh the day dark with night,* Amos Chap. 5. ver. 8. *He visiteth the earth, and maketh it soft with showers : he blesseth the springing thereof, and*

crowneth the year with his goodness ; so that the pastures are clothed with flocks, and the valleys are covered over with corn. See *Psalm* 65. But notwithstanding that this is the constant language of Scripture ; yet we have I know not what aversion from believing, that God concerns himself so nearly in our affairs. Fain would we suppose him at a great distance off, and substitute some blind unthinking deputy in his stead, though (if we may believe Saint Paul) *he be not far from every one of us.*[161]

151 It will I doubt not be objected, that the slow and gradual methods observed in the production of natural things, do not seem to have for their cause the immediate hand of an *almighty Agent.* Besides, monsters, untimely births, fruits blasted in the blossom, rains falling in desert places, miseries incident to human life, are so many arguments that the whole frame of Nature is not immediately actuated and superintended by a spirit of infinite wisdom and goodness. But the answer to this objection is in a good measure plain from *Sect.* 62, it being visible, that the aforesaid methods of Nature are absolutely necessary, in order to working by the most simple and general rules, and after a steady and consistent manner ; which argues both the *wisdom* and *goodness* of God. Such is the artificial contrivance of this mighty machine of Nature, that whilst its motions and various phenomena strike on our senses, the hand which actuates the whole is it self unperceivable to men of flesh and blood. *Verily* (saith the prophet) *thou art a God that hidest thy self,* Isaiah Chap. 45. ver. 15. But though God conceal himself from the eyes of the *sensual* and *lazy,* who will not be at the least expence of thought ; yet to an unbiassed and attentive mind, nothing can be more plainly legible,[162] than the intimate presence of an *all-wise Spirit,* who fashions, regulates, and sustains the whole system of being. It is clear from what we have elsewhere observed, that the operating according to general and stated laws, is so necessary for our guidance in the affairs of life, and letting us into the secret of Nature, that without it, all reach and compass of thought, all human sagacity and design could serve to no manner of purpose : it were even impossible there should be any such faculties or powers in the mind. See *Sect.* 31. Which one consideration abundantly out-balances whatever particular inconveniences may thence arise.

152 We should further consider, that the very blemishes and defects of Nature are not without their use, in that they make an agreeable sort of variety, and augment the beauty of the rest of the creation, as shades in a picture serve to set off the brighter and more enlightened parts. We would likewise do well to examine, whether our taxing the waste of seeds and embryos, and accidental destruction of plants and animals, before they

come to full maturity, as an imprudence in the Author of Nature, be not the effect of prejudice contracted by our familiarity with impotent and saving mortals. In *man* indeed a thrifty management of those things, which he cannot procure without much pains and industry, may be esteemed *wisdom*. But we must not imagine, that the inexplicably fine machine[163] of an animal or vegetable, costs the great Creator any more pains or trouble in its production than a pebble doth : nothing being more evident, than that an omnipotent spirit can indifferently produce every thing by a mere *fiat* or act of his will. Hence it is plain, that the splendid profusion of natural things should not be interpreted, weakness or prodigality in the agent who produces them, but rather be looked on as an argument of the riches of his power.

153　As for the mixture of pain or uneasiness which is in the world, pursuant to the general laws of Nature, and the actions of finite imperfect spirits : this, in the state we are in at present is indispensably necessary to our well-being. But our prospects are too narrow : we take, for instance, the idea of some one particular pain into our thoughts, and account it *evil* ; whereas if we enlarge our view, so as to comprehend the various ends, connexions, and dependencies of things, on what occasions and in what proportions we are affected with pain and pleasure, the nature of human freedom, and the design with which we are put into the world ; we shall be forced to acknowledge that those particular things, which considered in themselves appear to be *evil*, have the nature of *good*, when considered as linked with the whole system of beings.[164]

154　From what hath been said it will be manifest to any considering person, that it is merely for want of attention and comprehensiveness of mind, that there are any favourers of *atheism* or the *Manichean heresy* to be found.[165] Little and unreflecting souls may indeed burlesque the works of Providence, the beauty and order whereof they have not capacity, or will not be at the pains to comprehend. But those who are masters of any justness and extent of thought, and are withal used to reflect, can never sufficiently admire the divine traces of wisdom and goodness that shine throughout the economy of Nature. But what truth is there which shineth so strongly on the mind, that by an aversion of thought, a wilful shutting of the eyes, we may not escape seeing it ? Is it therefore to be wondered at, if the generality of men, who are ever intent on business or pleasure, and little used to fix or open the eye of their mind, should not have all that conviction and evidence of the being of God, which might be expected in reasonable creatures ?

155　We should rather wonder, that men can be found so stupid as to neglect, than that neglecting they should be unconvinced of such an evident and momentous truth. And yet it is to be feared that too many of parts and leisure, who live in Christian countries, are merely through a supine and dreadful negligence sunk into a sort of *atheism*. Since it is downright impossible, that a soul pierced and enlightened with a thorough sense of the omnipresence, holiness, and justice of that *Almighty Spirit*, should persist in a remorseless violation of his laws. We ought therefore earnestly to meditate and dwell on those important points ; that so we may attain conviction without all scruple, *that the eyes of the Lord are in every place beholding the evil and the good ;*[166] *that he is with us and keepeth us in all places whither we go, and giveth us bread to eat, and raiment to put on ;* that he is present and conscious to our innermost thoughts ; and that we have a most absolute and immediate dependence on him. A clear view of which great truths cannot choose but fill our hearts with an awful circumspection and holy fear, which is the strongest incentive to *virtue*, and the best guard against *vice*.

156   For after all, what deserves the first place in our studies, is the consideration of *God*, and our *duty* ; which to promote, as it was the main drift and design of my labours, so shall I esteem them altogether useless and ineffectual, if by what I have said I cannot inspire my readers with a pious sense of the presence of God : and having shewn the falseness or vanity of those barren speculations, which make the chief employment of learned men, the better dispose them to reverence and embrace the salutary truths of the Gospel, which to know and to practise is the highest perfection of human nature.

THE BERKELEY–JOHNSON
CORRESPONDENCE

JOHNSON TO BERKELEY

Stratford, Sept. 10, 1729

Rev'd Sir :   [271]

The kind invitation you gave me to lay before you any difficulties that should occur to me in reading those excellent books which you was pleased to order into my hands, is all the apology I shall offer for the trouble I now presume to give you. But nothing could encourage me to expose to your view my low and mean way of thinking and writing, but my hopes of an interest in that candor and tenderness which are so conspicuous both in your writings and conversation.

These books (for which I stand humbly obliged to you) contain speculations the most surprisingly ingenious I have ever met with ; and I must confess that the reading of them has almost convinced me that matter as it has been commonly defined for an unknown Quiddity is but a mere nonentity. That it is a strong presumption against the existence of it, that there never could be conceived any manner of connection between it and our ideas. That the *esse* of things is only their *percipi* ; and that the rescuing us from the absurdities of abstract ideas and the gross notion of matter that have so much obtained, deserves well of the learned world, in that it clears away very many difficulties and perplexities in the sciences.

And I am of opinion that this way of thinking can't fail of prevailing in the world, because it is likely to prevail very much among us in these parts, several ingenious men having entirely come in to it. But there are many others on the other hand that cannot be reconciled to it ; tho' of these there are some who have a very good opinion of it and plainly see many happy consequences attending it, on account of which they are well inclined to embrace it, but think they find some difficulties in their way which they can't get over, and some objections not sufficiently answered to their satisfaction. And since you have condescended to give me leave to do so, I will make bold to lay before you sundry things, which yet remain in the dark either to myself or to others, and which I can't account for either to my own, or at least to their satisfaction.

1   The great prejudice that lies against it with some is its repugnancy to   [272] and subversion of Sir I. Newton's philosophy in sundry points ; to which they have been so much attached that they can't suffer themselves in the least to call it in question in any instance, but indeed it does not appear to me so inconsistent therewith as at first blush it did, for the laws of nature

which he so happily explains are the same whether matter be supposed or not. However, let Sir Isaac Newton, or any other man, be heard only so far as his opinion is supported by reason :—but after all I confess I have so great a regard for the philosophy of that great man, that I would gladly see as much of it as may be, to obtain in this ideal scheme.[1]

2   The objection, that it takes away all subordinate natural causes,[2] and accounts for all appearances merely by the immediate will of the supreme spirit, does not seem to many to be answered to their satisfaction. It is readily granted that our ideas are inert, and can't cause one another, and are truly only signs one of another. For instance my idea of fire is not the cause of my idea of burning and of ashes. But inasmuch as these ideas are so connected as that they seem necessarily to point out to us the relations of cause and effect, we can't help thinking that our ideas are pictures of things without our minds at least, tho' not without the Great Mind, and which are their archetypes, between which these relations do obtain. I kindle a fire and leave it, no created mind beholds it ; I return again and find a great alteration in the fuel ; has there not been in my absence all the while that gradual alteration making in the archetype of my idea of wood which I should have had the idea of if I had been present ? And is there not some archetype of my idea of the fire, which under the agency of the Divine Will has gradually caused this alteration ?[3] And so in all other instances, our ideas are so connected, that they seem necessarily to refer our minds to some originals which are properly (tho' subordinate) causes and effects one of another ; insomuch that unless they be so, we can't help thinking ourselves under a perpetual delusion.[4]

3   That all the phenomena of nature, must ultimately be referred to the will of the Infinite Spirit, is what must be allowed ; but to suppose his immediate energy in the production of every effect, does not seem to impress so lively and great a sense of his power and wisdom upon our minds, as to suppose a subordination of causes and effects among the archetypes of our ideas, as he that should make a watch or clock of ever so beautiful an appearance and that should measure the time ever so exactly yet if he should be obliged to stand by it and influence and direct all its motions, he would seem but very deficient in both his ability and skill in comparison with him who should be able to make one that would regularly keep on its motion and measure the time for a considerable while without the intervention of any immediate force of its author or any one else impressed upon it.[5]

4   And as this tenet seems thus to abate our sense of the wisdom and power of God, so there are some that cannot be persuaded that it is suffi-

[273]

166

ciently cleared from bearing hard on his holiness ; those who suppose that the corrupt affections of our souls and evil practices consequent to them, are occasioned by certain irregular mechanical motions of our bodies, and that these motions come to have an habitual irregular bias and tendency by means of our own voluntary indulgence to them, which we might have governed to better purpose, do in this way of thinking, sufficiently bring the guilt of those ill habits and actions upon ourselves ; but if in an habitual sinner, every object and motion be but an idea, and every wicked appetite the effect of such a set of ideas, and these ideas, the immediate effect of the Almighty upon his mind ; it seems to follow, that the immediate cause of such ideas must be the cause of those immoral appetites and actions ; because he is borne down before them seemingly, even in spite of himself. At first indeed they were only occasions, which might be withstood, and so, proper means of trial, but now they become causes of his immoralities.[6] When therefore a person is under the power of a vicious habit, and it can't but be foreseen that the suggestion of such and such ideas will unavoidably produce those immoralities, how can it consist with the holiness of God to suggest them ?[7]

5   It is, after all that has been said on that head, still something shocking to many to think that there should be nothing but a mere show in all the art and contrivance appearing in the structure (for instance) of a human body, particularly of the organs of sense. The curious structure of the eye, what can it be more than merely a fine show, if there be no connection more than you admit of, between that and vision ? It seems from the make of it to be designed for an instrument or means of conveying the images of external things to the perceptive faculty within ; and if it be not so, if it be really of no use in conveying visible objects to our minds, and if our visible ideas are immediately created in them by the will of the Almighty, why should it be made to seem to be an instrument or medium as much as if indeed it really were so ?[8] It is evident, from the conveying of images into a dark room thro' a lens, that the eye is a lens, and that the images of things are painted on the bottom of it. But to what purpose is all this, if there be no connection between this fine apparatus and the act of vision ; can it be thought a sufficient argument that there is no connection between them because we can't discover it, or conceive how it should be ?   [274]

6   There are some who say, that if our sensations don't depend on any bodily organs—they don't see how death can be supposed to make any alteration in the manner of our perception, or indeed how there should be (properly speaking) any separate state of the soul at all. For if our bodies

are nothing but ideas, and if our having ideas in this present state does not depend on what are thought to be the organs of sense, and lastly, if we are supposed (as doubtless we must) to have ideas in that state ; it should seem that immediately upon our remove from our present situation, we should still be attended with the same ideas of bodies as we have now, and consequently with the same bodies or at least with bodies however different, and if so, what room is there left for any resurrection, properly so-called ? So that while this tenet delivers us from the embarrassments that attend the doctrine of a material resurrection, it seems to have no place for any resurrection at all, at least in the sense that word seems to bear in St. John 5; 28, 29.[9]

7   Some of us are at a loss to understand your meaning when you speak of archetypes. You say the being of things consists in their being perceived. And that things are nothing but ideas, that our ideas have no unperceived archetypes, but yet you allow archetypes to our ideas when things are not perceived by our minds ; they exist in, *i.e.* are perceived by, some other mind. Now I understand you, that there is a two-fold existence of things or ideas, one in the divine mind, and the other in created minds ; the one archetypal, and the other ectypal ; that, therefore, the real original and permanent existence of things is archetypal, being ideas in *mente Divinâ*, and that our ideas are copies of them,[10] and so far forth real things as they are correspondent to their archetypes and exhibited to us, or begotten in us by the will of the Almighty, in such measure and degrees and by such stated laws and rules as He is pleased to observe ; that, therefore, there is no unperceived substance intervening between the divine ideas and ours as a medium, occasion or instrument by which He begets our ideas in us, but that which was thought to be [275] the material existence of things is in truth only ideal in the divine mind. Do I understand you right ? Is it not therefore your meaning, that the existence of our ideas (*i.e.* the ectypal things) depends upon our perceiving them, yet there are external to any created mind, in the all-comprehending Spirit, real and permanent archetypes (as stable and permanent as ever matter was thought to be), to which these ideas of ours are correspondent, and so that (tho' our visible and tangible ideas are *toto coelo* different[11] and distinct things, yet) there may be said to be external to my mind, in the divine mind, an archetype (for instance of the candle that is before me) in which the originals of both my visible and tangible ideas, light, heat, whiteness, softness, etc., under such a particular cylindrical figure, are united, so that it may be properly said to be the same thing that I both see and feel ?[12]

8   If this, or something like it might be understood to be your meaning, it would seem less shocking to say that we don't see and feel the same thing,[13] because we can't dispossess our minds of the notion of an external world, and would be allowed to conceive that, tho' there were no intelligent creature before Adam to be a spectator of it, yet the world was really six days in *archetypo*, gradually proceeding from an informal chaotic state into that beautiful show wherein it first appeared to his mind, and that the comet that appeared in 1680[14] (for instance) has now, tho' no created mind beholds it, a real existence in the all-comprehending spirit, and is making its prodigious tour through the vast fields of ether, and lastly that the whole vast congeries of heaven and earth, the mighty systems of worlds with all their furniture, have a real being in the eternal mind antecedent to and independent on the perception of created spirit,[15] and that when we see and feel, etc., that that almighty mind, by his immediate *fiat*, begets in our minds (*pro nostro modulo*)[16] ideas correspondent to them, and which may be imagined in some degree resemblances of them.

9   But if there be archetypes to our ideas, will it not follow that there is external space, extention, figure and motion, as being archetypes of our ideas, to which we give these names. And indeed for my part I cannot disengage my mind from the persuasion that there is external space ; when I have been trying ever so much to conceive of space as being nothing but an idea in my mind, it will return upon me even in spite of my utmost efforts, certainly there must be, there can't but be, external space. The length, breadth, and thickness of any idea, it's true, are but ideas ; the distance between two trees in my mind is but an idea, but if there are archetypes to [276] the ideas of the trees, there must be an archetype to the idea of the distance between them.[17] Nor can I see how it follows[18] that there is no external absolute height, bigness, or distance of things, because they appear greater or less to us according as we are nearer or remote from them, or see them with our naked eyes, or with glasses ; any more than it follows that a man, for instance, is not really absolutely six foot high measured by a two foot rule applied to his body, because divers pictures of him may be drawn some six, some four, some two foot long according to the same measure. Nobody ever imagined that the idea of distance is without the mind, but does it therefore follow that there is no external distance to which the idea is correspondent, for instance, between Rhode Island and Stratford ? Truly I wish it were not so great, that I might be so happy as to have a more easy access to you, and more nearly enjoy the advantages of your instructions.

10   You allow spirits to have a real existence external to one another. Methinks, if so, there must be distance between them, and space wherein they exist, or else they must all exist in one individual spot or point, and as it were coincide one with another.[19] I can't see how external space and duration are any more abstract ideas than spirits. As we have (properly speaking) no ideas of spirits, so, indeed, neither have we of external space and duration. But it seems to me that the existence of these must unavoidably follow from the existence of those, insomuch that I can no more conceive of their not being, than I can conceive of the non-existence of the infinite and eternal mind. They seem as necessarily existent independent of any created mind as the Deity Himself. Or must we say there is nothing in Dr. Clarke's argument *a priori*, in his demonstration of the being and attributes of God, or in what Sir Isaac Newton says about the infinity and eternity of God in his *Scholium Generale* to his *Principia*?[20] I should be glad to know your sense of what those two authors say upon this subject.

11   You will forgive the confusedness of my thoughts and not wonder at my writing like a man something bewildered, since I am, as it were, got into a new world amazed at everything about me. These ideas of ours, what are they? Is the substance of the mind the *substratum* to its ideas? Is it proper to call them modifications of our minds? Or impressions upon them? Or what?[21] Truly I can't tell what to make of them, any more than of matter itself. What is the *esse* of spirits?—you seem to think it impossible to abstract their existence from their thinking. *Princ.* p. 143. sec. 98.[22] Is then the *esse* of minds nothing else but *percipere*, as the *esse* of ideas is *percipi*? Certainly, methinks there must be an unknown somewhat that thinks and acts, as difficult to be conceived of as matter, and the creation of which, as much beyond us as the creation of matter. Can actions be the *esse* of anything? Can they exist or be exerted without some being who is the agent? And may not that being be easily imagined to exist without acting, *e.g.* without thinking? And consequently (for you are there speaking of duration) may he not be said *durare, etsi non cogitet*,[23] to persist in being, tho' thinking were intermitted for a while? And is not this sometimes fact? The duration of the eternal mind, must certainly imply some thing besides an eternal succession of ideas. May I not then conceive that, tho' I get my idea of duration by observing the succession of ideas in my mind, yet there is a *perseverare in existendo*,[24] a duration of my being, and of the being of other spirits distinct from, and independent of, this succession of ideas.

But, Sir, I doubt I have more than tired your patience with so many (and I fear you will think them impertinent) questions; for tho' they are difficulties with me, or at least with some in my neighbourhood, for whose sake, in part, I write, yet I don't imagine they can appear such to you, who have so perfectly digested your thoughts upon this subject. And perhaps they may vanish before me upon a more mature consideration of it. However, I should be very thankful for your assistance, if it were not a pity you should waste your time (which would be employed to much better purposes) in writing to a person so obscure and so unworthy of such a favor as I am. But I shall live with some impatience till I see the second part of your design accomplished, wherein I hope to see these (if they can be thought such) or any other objections, that may have occurred to you since your writing the first part, obviated ; and the usefulness of this doctrine more particularly displayed in the further application of it to the arts and sciences. May we not hope to see logic, mathematics, and natural philosophy, pneumatology, theology and morality, all in their order, appearing with a new lustre under the advantages they may receive from it ? You have at least given us to hope for a geometry cleared of many perplexities that render that sort of study troublesome, which I shall be very glad of, who have found that science more irksome to me than any other, tho', indeed, I am but very little versed in any of them. But I will not trespass any further upon your patience. My very humble service to Mr. James [278] and Mr. Dalton,[25] and I am with the greatest veneration,

Rev'd Sir,
your most obliged
and most obedient
humble servant
Samuel Johnson

BERKELEY TO JOHNSON

[Nov. 25, 1729]

[279]   Reverend Sir,

The ingenious letter you favoured me with found me very much indis-
posed with a gathering or imposthumation in my head, which confined
me several weeks, and is now, I thank God, relieved. The objections of a
candid thinking man to what I have written will always be welcome, and I
shall not fail to give all the satisfaction I am able, not without hopes of convincing or being convinced. It is a common fault for men to hate opposition, and be too much wedded to their own opinions. I am so sensible of
this in others that I could not pardon it to myself if I considered mine any
further than they seem to me to be true ; which I shall the better be able to
judge of when they have passed the scrutiny of persons so well qualified to
examine them as you and your friends appear to be, to whom my illness
must be an apology for not sending this answer sooner.

1   The true use and end of Natural Philosophy is to explain the phenomena of nature ; which is done by discovering the laws of nature, and
reducing particular appearances to them. This is Sir Isaac Newton's
method ; and such method or design is not in the least inconsistent with
the principles I lay down. This mechanical philosophy doth not assign or
suppose any one natural efficient cause in the strict and proper sense ; nor
is it, as to its use, concerned about matter ; nor is matter connected therewith ; nor doth it infer the being of matter. It must be owned, indeed, that
the mechanical philosophers do suppose (though unnecessarily) the being
of matter.[26] They do even pretend to demonstrate that matter is proportional to gravity, which, if they could, this indeed would furnish an unanswerable objection. But let us examine their demonstration. It is laid down
in the first place, that the momentum of any body is the product of its
quantity by its velocity, *moles in celeritatem ducta.*[27] If, therefore, the velocity
is given, the momentum will be as its quantity. But it is observed that
bodies of all kinds descend in vacuo with the same velocity ; therefore the
momentum of descending bodies is as the quantity or moles, *i.e.* gravity is
[280]   as matter. But this argument concludes nothing, and is a mere circle. For, I
ask, when it is premised that the momentum is equal to the *moles in celeritatem ducta,* how the moles or quantity of matter is estimated ? If you say,
by extent, the proposition is not true ; if by weight, then you suppose that
the quantity of matter is proportional to matter ; *i.e.* the conclusion is

taken for granted in one of the premises. As for absolute space and motion, which are also supposed without any necessity or use, I refer you to what I have already published ;[28] particularly in a Latin treatise, *De Motu*, which I shall take care to send to you.

2   Cause is taken in different senses. A proper active efficient cause I can conceive none but Spirit ; nor any action, strictly speaking, but where there is Will. But this doth not hinder the allowing occasional causes (which are in truth but signs) ; and more is not requisite in the best physics, *i.e.* the mechanical philosophy. Neither doth it hinder the admitting other causes besides God ; such as spirits of different orders, which may be termed active causes, as acting indeed, though by limited and derivative powers. But as for an unthinking agent, no point of physics is explained by it, nor is it conceivable.

3   Those who have all along contended for a material world have yet acknowledged that *natura naturans* (to use the language of the Schoolmen) is God ;[29] and that the divine conservation[30] of things is equipollent to, and in fact the same thing with, a continued repeated creation : in a word, that conservation and creation differ only in the *terminus a quo*. These are the common opinions of the Schoolmen ; and Durandus,[31] who held the world to be a machine like a clock, made and put in motion by God, but afterwards continuing to go of itself, was therein particular, and had few followers. The very poets teach a doctrine not unlike the schools—*Mens agitat molem* (Virg. *Aeneid* VI).[32] The Stoics and Platonists are everywhere full of the same notion. I am not therefore singular in this point itself, so much as in my way of proving it. Further, it seems to me that the power and wisdom of God are as worthily set forth by supposing Him to act immediately as an omnipresent infinitely active Spirit, as by supposing Him to act by the mediation of subordinate causes, in preserving and governing the natural world. A clock may indeed go independent of its maker or artificer, inasmuch   [281] as the gravitation of its pendulum proceeds from another cause, and that the artificer is not the adequate cause of the clock ; so that the analogy would not be just to suppose a clock is in respect of its artist what the world is in respect of its Creator. For aught I can see, it is no disparagement to the perfections of God to say that all things necessarily depend on Him as their Conservator as well as Creator, and that all nature would shrink to nothing, if not upheld and preserved in being by the same force that first created it. This I am sure is agreeable to Holy Scripture, as well as to the writings of the most esteemed philosophers ; and if it is to be considered that men make use of tools and machines to supply defect

of power in themselves, we shall think it no honour to the Divinity to attribute such things to Him.

4   As to guilt, it is the same thing whether I kill a man with my hands or an instrument ; whether I do it myself or make use of a ruffian. The imputation therefore upon the sanctity of God is equal, whether we suppose our sensations to be produced immediately by God, or by the mediation of instruments and subordinate causes, all which are His creatures, and moved by His laws.[33] This theological consideration, therefore, may be waved, as leading beside the question ; for such I hold all points to be which bear equally hard on both sides of it. Difficulties about the principle of moral actions will cease, if we consider that all guilt is in the will, and that our ideas, from whatever cause they are produced, are alike inert.[34]

5   As to the art and contrivance in the parts of animals, &c., I have considered that matter in the *Principles of Human Knowledge*,[35] and, if I mistake not, sufficiently shewn the wisdom and use thereof, considered as signs and means of information. I do not indeed wonder that on first reading what I have written, men are not thoroughly convinced. On the contrary, I should very much wonder if prejudices, which have been many years taking root, should be extirpated in a few hours' reading. I had no inclination to trouble the world with large volumes. What I have done was rather with a view of giving hints to thinking men, who have leisure and curiosity to go to the bottom of things, and pursue them in their own minds. Two or three times reading these small tracts, and making what is read the occasion of thinking, would, I believe, render the whole familiar and easy to the mind, and take off that shocking appearance which hath often been observed to attend speculative truths.

[282]

6   I see no difficulty in conceiving a change of state, such as is vulgarly called Death, as well without as with material substance. It is sufficient for that purpose that we allow sensible bodies, *i.e.* such as are immediately perceived by sight and touch ; the existence of which I am so far from questioning (as philosophers are used to do), that I establish it, I think, upon evident principles. Now, it seems very easy to conceive the soul to exist in a separate state (*i.e.* divested from those limits and laws of motion and perception with which she is embarrassed here), and to exercise herself on new ideas, without the intervention of these tangible things we call bodies. It is even very possible to apprehend how the soul may have ideas of colour without an eye, or of sounds without an ear.

And now, Sir, I submit these hints (which I have hastily thrown together as soon as my illness gave me leave) to your own maturer thoughts, which after all you will find the best instructors. What you have seen of mine was published when I was very young, and without doubt hath many defects. For though the notions should be true (as I verily think they are), yet it is difficult to express them clearly and consistently, language being framed to common use and received prejudices. I do not therefore pretend that my books can teach truth. All I hope for is, that they may be an occasion to inquisitive men of discovering truth, by consulting their own minds, and looking into their own thoughts. As to the Second Part of my treatise concerning the *Principles of Human Knowledge*, the fact is that I had made a considerable progress in it ; but the manuscript was lost about fourteen years ago, during my travels in Italy, and I never had leisure since to do so disagreeable a thing as writing twice on the same subject.

Objections passing through your hands have their full force and clearness. I like them the better. This intercourse with a man of parts and philosophic genius is very agreeable. I sincerely wish we were nearer neighbours. In the meantime, whenever either you or your friends favour me with their thoughts, you may be sure of a punctual correspondence on my part. Before I have done I will venture to recommend these points : (1) To consider well the answers I have already given in my books to several objections. (2) To consider whether any new objection that shall occur doth not suppose the doctrine of abstract general ideas. (3) Whether the [283] difficulties proposed in objection to my scheme can be solved by the contrary ; for if they cannot, it is plain they can be no objections to mine.

I know not whether you have got my treatise concerning the *Principles of Human Knowledge*. I intend to send it to you with my tract *De Motu*. My humble service to your friends, to whom I understand I am indebted for some part of your letter.

I am your faithful humble servant,
George Berkeley.

JOHNSON TO BERKELEY

[284] Rev'd Sir :—

Yours of November 25th, I received not till January 17th, and this being the first convenient opportunity I now return you my humblest thanks for it.

I am very sorry to understand that you have labored under the illness you mention, but am exceeding glad and thankful for your recovery ; I pray God preserve your life and health, that you may have opportunity to perfect these great and good designs for the advancement of learning and religion wherewith your mind labours.

I am very much obliged to you for the favorable opinion you are pleased to express at what I made bold to write to you and that you have so kindly vouchsafed so large and particular an answer to it. But you have done me too great an honor in putting any value on my judgment ; for it is impossible my thoughts on this subject should be of any consequence, who have been bred up under the greatest disadvantages, and have had so little ability and opportunity to be instructed in things of this nature. And therefore I should be very vain [to] pretend any thing else but to be a learner ; 'tis merely with this view that I give you this trouble.

I am sensible that the greatest part of what I wrote was owing to not sufficiently attending to those three important considerations you suggest at the end of your letter : and I hope a little more time and a more careful attention to and application of them, will clear up what difficulties yet lie in the way of our entirely coming into your sentiments. Indeed I had not had opportunity sufficiently to digest your books ; for no sooner had I just read them over, but they were greedily demanded by my friends, who live much scattered up and down, and who expected I would bring them home with me, because I had told them before that if the books were to be had in Boston, I intended to purchase a set of them ; and indeed they have not yet quite finished their tour. The *Theory of Vision* is still at New York and the *Dialogues* just gone to Long Island. But I am the better content to want them because I know they are doing good.

[285] For my part I am content to give up the cause of matter, glad to get rid of the absurdities thereon depending if it be defensible, I am sure, at least, it is not in my power to defend it. And being spoiled of that sandy foundation, I only want now to be thoroughly taught how and where to set down my foot again and make out a clear and consistent scheme without it. And

of all the particulars I troubled you with before, there remain only these that I have any difficulty about, *viz.*, archetypes, space and duration, and the *esse* of spirits. And indeed these were the chief of my difficulties before.[36] Most of the rest were such objections as I found by conversation among my acquaintance, did not appear to them sufficiently answered. But I believe upon a more mature consideration of the matter, and especially of this kind reply, they will see reason to be better satisfied. They that have seen it (especially my friend Mr. Wetmore) join with me in thankfully acknowledging your kindness, and return their very humble service to you.

1   As to those difficulties that yet remain with me, I believe all my hesitation about the first of them (and very likely the rest) is owing to my dulness and want of attention so as not rightly to apprehend your meaning. I believe I expressed myself uncouthly about archetypes in my 7th and 8th articles, but upon looking back upon your *Dialogues*, and comparing again three or four passages, I can't think I meant any thing different from what you intended.

You allow, *Dial.* p. 74, 'That things have an existence distinct from being perceived by us' (*i.e.*, any created spirits), 'and that they exist in, *i.e.* are perceived by, the infinite and omnipresent mind who contains and supports this sensible world as being perceived by him.' And p. 109, 'That things have an existence exterior to our minds, and that during the intervals of their being perceived by us, they exist in another (*i.e.* the infinite) mind' ; from whence you justly and excellently infer the certainty of his existence, 'who knows and comprehends all things and exhibits them to our view in such manner and according to such rules as he himself has ordained.' And p. 113, 'That, *e.g.* a tree, when we don't perceive it, exists without our minds in the infinite mind of God.' And this exterior existence of things (if I understand you right) is what you call the archetypal state of things, p. 150.[37]

From those and the like expressions, I gathered what I said about the archetypes of our ideas, and thence inferred that there is exterior to us, in the divine mind, a system of universal nature, whereof the ideas we have are in such a degree resemblances as the Almighty is pleased to communicate to us. And I cannot yet see but my inference was just ; because according to you, the ideas we see are not in the divine mind, but in our own.[38] When, therefore, you say sensible things exist in, as being perceived by, the infinite mind I humbly conceive you must be understood that the originals or archetypes of our sensible things or ideas exist independent of us in the infinite mind, or that sensible things exist *in archetypo* in the divine mind.

[286]

The divine idea, therefore, of a tree I suppose (or a tree in the divine mind), must be the original or archetype of ours, and ours a copy or image of His (our ideas images of His, in the same sense as our souls are images of Him) of which there may be several, in several created minds, like so many several pictures of the same original to which they are all to be referred.

When therefore, several people are said to see the same tree or star, etc., whether at the same or at so many several distances from it, it is (if I understand you) *unum et idem in archetypo,* tho' *multiplex et diversum in ectypo,*[39] for it is as evident that your idea is not mine nor mine yours when we say we both look on the same tree, as that you are not I, nor I you. But in having each our idea, we being dependent upon and impressed upon by the same almighty mind, wherein you say this tree exists, while we shut our eyes (and doubtless you mean the same also, while they are open), our several trees must, I think be so many pictures (if I may so call them) of the one original, the tree in the infinite mind, and so of all other things. Thus I understand you—not indeed that our ideas are in any measure adequate resemblances of the system in the divine mind, but however that they are just and true resemblances or copies of it, so far as He is pleased to communicate His mind to us.[40]

2   As to space and duration, I do not pretend to have any other notion of their exterior existence than what is necessarily implied in the notion we have of God ;[41] I do not suppose they are any thing distinct from, or exterior to, the infinite and eternal mind ; for I conclude with you that there is nothing exterior to my mind but God and other spirits with the attributes or properties belonging to them and ideas contained in them.

External space and duration therefore I take to be those properties or attributes in God, to which our ideas, which we signify by those names, are correspondent, and of which they are the faint shadows. This I take to be Sir Isaac Newton's meaning when he says, *Schol. General. Deus—durat semper et adest ubique et existendo semper et ubique, durationem et spacium, æternitatem et infinitatem constituit.*[42] And in his *Optics* calls space *as it were God's boundless sensorium,*[43] nor can I think you have a different notion of these attributes from that great philosopher, tho' you may differ in your ways of expressing or explaining yourselves. However it be, when you call the Deity infinite and eternal, and in that most beautiful and charming description, *Dial.* p. 71, etc., when you speak of the *abyss of space and boundless extent* beyond thought and imagination,[44] I don't know how to understand you any otherwise than I understood Sir Isaac, when he uses the like expressions. The truth is we have no proper ideas of God or His attributes, and conceive of them only by analogy from what we find in ourselves ; and

[287]

so, I think we conceive His immensity and eternity to be what in Him are correspondent to our space and duration.

As for the *punctum stans* of the Schools, and the τὸ νῦν of the Platonists, they are notions too fine for my gross thoughts ;[45] I can't tell what to make of those words, they don't seem to convey any ideas or notions to my mind, and whatever the matter is, the longer I think of them, the more they disappear, and seem to dwindle away into nothing. Indeed they seem to me very much like abstract ideas, but I doubt the reason is because I never rightly understood them. I don't see why the term *punctum stans* may not as well, at least, be applied to the immensity as the eternity of God ; for the word *punctum* is more commonly used in relation to extension or space than duration ; and to say that a being is immense, and yet that it is but a point, and that its duration is perpetual without beginning or end, and yet that it is but a τὸ νῦν, looks to me like a contradiction.

I can't therefore understand the term τὸ νῦν unless it be designed to adumbrate the divine omnisciency or the perfection of the divine knowledge, by the more perfect notion we have of things present than of things past ; and in this sense it would imply that all things past, present and to come are always at every point of duration equally perfectly known or present to God's mind (tho' in a manner infinitely more perfect), as the things that are known to us are present to our minds at any point of our duration which we call *now*. So that with respect to His equally perfect knowledge of things past, present or to come, it is in effect always now with Him. To this purpose it seems well applied and intelligible enough, but His duration I take to be a different thing from this, as that point of our duration which we call *now*, is a different thing from our actual knowledge [288] of things, as distinguished from our remembrance. And it may as well be said that God's immensity consists in His knowing at once what is, and is transacted in all places (*e.g.* China, Jupiter, Saturn, all the systems of the fixed stars, etc.) everywhere, however so remote from us (tho' in a manner infinitely more perfect), as we know what is, and is transacted in us and about us just at hand ; as that His eternity consists in this τὸ νῦν as above explained, *i.e.* in His knowing things present, past and to come, however so remote, all at once or equally perfectly, as we know the things that are present to us *now*.

In short our ideas expressed by the terms immensity and eternity are only space and duration considered as boundless or with the negation of any limits, and I can't help thinking there is something analogous to them without us, being in and belonging to, or attributes of, that glorious mind, whom for that reason we call immense and eternal, in whom we and all other spirits, *live, move and have our being*, not all in a point, but in so many different points places or *alicubis*, and variously situated with respect one to another, or else as I said before, it seems as if we should all coincide one with another.

I conclude, if I am wrong in my notion of external space, and duration, it is owing to the rivetted prejudices of abstract ideas ; but really when I have thought it over and over again in my feeble way of thinking, I can't see any connection between them (as I understand them) and that doctrine.[46] They don't seem to be any more abstract ideas than spirits, for, as I said, I take them to be attributes of the necessarily existing spirit ; and consequently the same reasons that convince me of his existence, bring with them the existence of these attributes. So that of the ways of coming to the knowledge of things that you mention, it is that of inference or deduction by which I seem to know that there is external infinite space and duration because there is without me a mind infinite and eternal.

3   As to the *esse* of spirits, I know Descartes held the soul always thinks, but I thought Mr. Locke had sufficiently confuted this notion, which he seems to have entertained only to serve an hypothesis. The Schoolmen, it is true, call the soul *actus* and God *Actus purus* ;[47] but I confess I never could well understand their meaning, perhaps because I never had opportunity to be much versed in their writings. I should have thought the Schoolmen to be of all sorts of writers the most unlikely to have had recourse to for the understanding of your sentiments, because they of all others, deal the most in abstract ideas ; tho' to place the very being of spirits in the mere act of thinking, seems to me very much like making abstract ideas of them.

[289]

There is certainly something passive in our souls, we are purely passive in the reception of our ideas ; and reasoning and willing are actions of something that reasons and wills, and therefore must be only modalities of that something. Nor does it seem to me that when I say (something)[48] I mean an abstract idea. It is true I have no idea of it, but I feel it ; I feel that it is, because I feel or am conscious of the exertions of it ; but the exertions of it are not the thing but the modalities of it, distinguished from it as actions from an agent, which seem to me distinguishable without having recourse to abstract ideas.

And therefore when I suppose the existence of a spirit while it does not actually think, it does not appear to me that I do it by supposing an abstract idea of existence, and another of absolute time.[49] The existence of John asleep by me, without so much as a dream is not an abstract idea, nor is the time passing the while an abstract idea, they are only partial considerations of him. *Perseverare in existendo*[50] in general, without reflecting on any particular thing existing, I take to be what is called an abstract idea of time or duration ; but the *perseverare in existendo* of John is, if I mistake not, a partial consideration of him. And I think it is as easy to conceive of him as continuing to exist without thinking as without seeing.

Has a child no soul till it actually perceives ? And is there not such a thing as sleeping without dreaming, or being in a *deliquium* without a thought ? If there be, and yet at the same time the *esse* of a spirit be nothing else but its actual thinking, the soul must be dead during those intervals ; and if ceasing or intermitting to think be the ceasing to be, or death of the soul, it is many times and easily put to death. According to this tenet, it seems to me the soul may sleep on to the resurrection, or rather may wake up in the resurrection state, the next moment after death. Nay I don't see upon what we can build any natural argument for the soul's immortality. I think I once heard you allow a principle of perception and spontaneous motion in beasts. Now if their *esse* as well as ours consists in perceiving, upon what is the natural immortality of our souls founded that will not equally conclude in favour of them ? I mention this last consideration because I am at [290] a loss to understand how you state the argument for the soul's natural immortality ;[51] for the argument from thinking to immaterial and from thence to indiscerpible, and from thence to immortal don't seem to obtain in your way of thinking.

If *esse* be only *percipere*, upon what is our consciousness founded ? I perceived yesterday, and I perceive now, but last night between my yesterday's and today's perception there has been an intermission when I perceived nothing. It seems to me there must be some principle common to these perceptions,[52] whose *esse* don't depend upon them, but in which they are, as it were, connected, and on which they depend, whereby I am and continue conscious of them.

Lastly, Mr. Locke's argument (B. 2. Ch. 19. Sec. 4.) from the intention and remission of thought, appears to me very considerable ;[53] according to which, upon this supposition, the soul must exist more or have a greater degree of being at one time than at another, according as it thinks more intensely or more remissly.

I own I said very wrong when I said I did not know what to make of ideas more than of matter. My meaning was, in effect, the same as I expressed afterwards about the substance of the soul's being a somewhat as unknown as matter. And what I intended by those questions was whether our ideas are not the substance of the soul itself, under so many various modifications, according to that saying (if I understand it right) *Intellectus intelligendo fit omnia* ?[54] It is true, those expressions (modifications, impressions, etc.) are metaphorical, and it seems to me to be no less so, to say that ideas exist in the mind, and I am under some doubt whether this last way of speaking don't carry us further from the thing, than to say ideas are the mind variously modified ;[55] but as you observe, it is scarce possible to speak of the mind without a metaphor.

Thus Sir, your goodness has tempted me to presume again to trouble you once more ; and I submit the whole to your correction ; but I can't conclude without saying that I am so much persuaded that your books teach truth, indeed the most excellent truths, and that in the most excellent manner, that I can't but express myself again very solicitously desirous that the noble design you have begun may be yet further pursued in the second part. And everybody that has seen the first is earnestly with me in this request. In hopes of which I will not desire you to waste your time in writing to me (tho' otherwise I should esteem it the greatest favor), at least till I have endeavoured further to gain satisfaction by another perusal of the books I have, with the other pieces you are so kind as to offer, which I will thankfully accept, for I had not *The Principles* of my own, it was a borrowed one I used.

[291]

The bearer hereof, Capt. Gorham, is a coaster bound now to Boston, which trade he constantly uses (except that it has been now long interrupted by the winter). But he always touches at Newport, and will wait on the Rev'd Mr. Honyman both going and returning, by whom you will have opportunity to send those books.

I am, Rev'd Sir,
with the greatest gratitude,
your most devoted humble servant,
S. Johnson

Stratford, Feb. 5, 1729/30 [*i.e.* 1730]

BERKELEY TO JOHNSON

Reverend Sir, [292]

Yours of Feb. 5th came not to my hands before yesterday ; and this after-
noon, being informed that a sloop is ready to sail towards your town, I
would not let slip the opportunity of returning you an answer, though
wrote in a hurry.

1   I have no objection against calling the ideas in the mind of God
archetypes of ours.[56] But I object against those archetypes by philosophers
supposed to be real things, and to have an absolute rational existence distinct from their being perceived by any mind whatsoever ; it being the
opinion of all materialists that an ideal existence in the Divine Mind is one
thing, and the real existence of material things another.

2   As to Space. I have no notion of any but that which is relative.[57] I
know some late philosophers have attributed extension to God, particularly mathematicians, one of whom, in a treatise, *De Spatio Reali*, pretends
to find out fifteen of the incommunicable attributes of God in Space.[58] But
it seems to me that, they being all negative, he might as well have found
them in Nothing ;[59] and that it would have been as justly inferred from
Space being impassive, increated, indivisible, etc., that it was Nothing as
that it was God.

Sir Isaac Newton supposeth an absolute Space, different from relative,
and consequent thereto ; absolute Motion different from relative motion ;
and with all other mathematicians he supposeth the infinite divisibility of
the finite parts of this absolute space ; he also supposeth material bodies to
drift therein. Now, though I do acknowledge Sir Isaac to have been an
extraordinary man, and most profound mathematician, yet I cannot agree
with him in these particulars. I make no scruple to use the word Space, as
well as all other words in common use ; but I do not thereby mean a distinct absolute being. For my meaning I refer you to what I have published.

By the τὸ νῦν I suppose to be implied that all things, past and to come, [293]
are actually present to the mind of God, and that there is in Him no
change, variation, or succession. A succession of ideas I take to *constitute*
Time, and not to be only the sensible measure thereof, as Mr. Locke and
others think.[60] But in these matters every man is to think for himself, and
speak as he finds. One of my earliest inquiries was about Time, which led
me into several paradoxes that I did not think fit or necessary to publish ;
particularly the notion that the Resurrection follows the next moment to

death. We are confounded and perplexed about time. (1) Supposing a succession in God. (2) Conceiving that we have an *abstract idea* of Time. (3) Supposing that the Time in one mind is to be measured by the succession of ideas in another. (4) Not considering the true use and end of words, which as often terminate in the will as in the understanding, being employed rather to excite, influence, and direct action, than to produce clear and distinct ideas.

3   That the soul of man is passive as well as active, I make no doubt. Abstract general ideas was a notion that Mr. Locke held in common with the Schoolmen, and I think all other philosophers ; it runs through his whole book of Human Understanding. He holds an abstract idea of existence ; exclusive of perceiving and being perceived. I cannot find I have any such idea, and this is my reason against it.[61] Des Cartes proceeds upon other principles. One square foot of snow is as white as a thousand yards ; one single perception is as truly a perception as one hundred. Now, any degree of perception being sufficient to Existence, it will not follow that we should say one *existed more* at one time than another, any more than we should say a thousand yards of snow are whiter than one yard.[62] But, after all, this comes to a verbal dispute. I think it might prevent a good deal of obscurity and dispute to examine well what I have said about abstraction, and about the true sense and significance of words, in several parts of these things that I have published, though much remains to be said on that subject.

You say you agree with me that there is nothing within your mind[63] but God and other spirits, with the attributes or properties belonging to them, and the ideas contained in them.

This is a principle or main point, from which, and from what I had laid down about abstract ideas, much may be deduced. But if in every inference we should not agree, so long as the main points are settled and well understood, I should be less solicitous about particular conjectures. I could wish that all the things I have published on these philosophical subjects were read in the order wherein I published them ; once, to take in the design and connexion of them, and a second time with a critical eye, adding your own thought and observation upon every part as you went along.

I send you herewith the bound books and one unbound. You will take yourself what you have not already. You will give the *Principles*, the *Theory*, and the *Dialogues*, one of each, with my service, to the gentleman who is Fellow of Newhaven College, whose compliments you brought to me. What remains you will give as you please.

If at any time your affairs should draw you into these parts, you shall be very welcome to pass as many days as you can spend at my house. Four or five days' conversation would set several things in a fuller and clearer light than writing could do in as many months. In the meantime, I shall be glad to hear from you or your friends, whenever you please to favour,

Reverend Sir,
Your very humble servant,
George Berkeley.

Pray let me know whether they would admit the writings of Hooker and Chillingworth into the library of the College in Newhaven.[64]

Rhode Island, March 24, 1730.

PART 3
Glossary, Notes, and Index

Glossary

acceptation: standard meaning
accidents: non-essential qualities
affect (§109): lay claim to, pretend to, assume
affection: quality or attribute caused in its bearer by something external
aforesaid: mentioned previously
agreeably to: in accordance with
alicubi: elsewhere
ambient: surrounding
analogy: a process of reasoning from parallel cases; hence (§108) classification
anomalous: strange, unfamiliar
antipodes: people or places on the opposite side of the globe
apparel: clothing
appellation: name
appertain: belong to
apposite: suited, fit
apprehend, apprehension: understand, understanding, comprehension
archetype: original pattern or model
artifice: skill
artificial: created by skill
asunder: apart
aught: anything
avowed: declared
awful: full of awe

bantered: made fools of
barely: only
bent: natural tendency
betwixt: between
blasted: withered, shriveled
bulk: volume, size
burlesque: ridicule

cavil: raise frivolous objections
cheap: easily got
chimera: a creature of the imagination
chimerical: imaginary, unreal
choir: organized group
circumspection: wariness
clear: make clear, clarify

cleave together: stick together
compages: collection, mass
compass: extent
compendious: inclusive, wide-ranging
comprehend: understand, include
comprehensive: all-inclusive
concatenation: interconnectedness (as of a chain)
concomitant: attendant
conformity: similarity, accordance
confutation: refutation
considerable: reputable
consistence: consistency
contrivance: ingenuity and skill
conversant about: concerning
convertibly: interchangeably
corporeal: material, physical
corpuscle: particle, atom
countenance: encouragement, support
credit: credence, believability
curvilinear: curved

delineate: draw
deliquium: eclipse (of the sun), swoon, fainting-fit
denominate: name, call
derogate: take away from, detract
difficiles nugae: trivial difficulties
dilate: expand, enlarge on
divers: various, different
divine: priest, theologian

economy of Nature (§154): the way the natural system is managed
embarras: obstruction
embrangled: embroiled, entangled
entrails: insides
equicrural: with equal legs, isosceles
equipollent to: equivalent to
excite: cause
essence: intrinsic nature
esteem: judge
explication: explanation
extension or *extention*: size

fabric: building, construction
faculty: power
fain: willingly

Glossary

fancy: imagination
fiat: command (literally, let it happen)
figure: shape
fine: subtle, accurate
fleeting: short-lived
forthwith: immediately
frame: make
furniture: that which furnishes, contents

genius: style, character
gravel (verb): floor, defeat
gross: blatant, obvious

habitude: relation, respect
hearken: listen
heterodox: not in accordance with established religious doctrine (the opposite of orthodox)
heterogeneous: of different types
hitherto: up to now, so far

immutable: unchangeable
impertinent: irrelevant
imposthumation: swelling
incommunicable: unshareable
inculcated: stressed
indiscerpible: indissoluble, indestructible
infinitesimal (noun): infinitely small quantity or part
ingenuous: frank, open
inherent: belonging to, existing in
interposition: placing between

jejune: thin, unsatisfying
just: fair, true

manners: customs, way of life, character
meridian: midday, noon—the highest point of the sun's travels in the day
minimum sensibile: the smallest thing we can sense
mode: quality
monster: a congenitally malformed creature
mundane: of the world

narrow: restricted
nice, nicely: accurate, fine
notwithstanding that: although

obliquangular: not right-angled
oblique: not right-angled

Glossary

occult quality: hidden quality from which the sensible qualities flow
omnipresence: presence everywhere
ornament: adorning

parts: talents
passion: emotion
peruse: read
phrensy: frenzy, madness
prate: talk childishly, prattle
prepossessed: prejudiced
prescind: cut off
prodigality: wastefulness
professor: one who professes, i.e. claims competence in
prognostics: a sign of the future
prolix: long-winded
proportionably: in proportion
propriety: fitness
prospect: view, perspective
protrude: push out
pursuant: following

quiddity: the essence of a thing, what makes it what it is
quiescent: at rest, dormant, unmoving

recreate: relax (cf. modern 'recreation')
rectangular triangle: right-angled triangle
rectilinear: with straight sides
rerum natura: the nature of things

sagacity: wisdom
sapid: having taste
scalenon: having unequal sides
scruple: (verb) to doubt, question, hesitate; (noun) doubt, hesitation
significancy: meaning
since (§43): ago
somewhat: something
sound: investigate
speculative: theoretical
stature: height
stay: wait, delay
stress: emphasis, importance, point
subserviency: purpose
subsist, subsistence: exist, existence
substance: object that exists independently
substantive noun: noun denoting a substance

Glossary

substratum: substance, bearer of properties
sundry: various, different
supine: idle
sustentation: sustenance

tabernacle: a temporary house
tax (verb): accuse
tenet: belief, doctrine
terraqueous: made of earth and water
texture: arrangement of particles on the surface of an object
throughly: thoroughly
thus much: so much
to wit: i.e.
translation: movement

vain, vanity: empty, emptiness
verities: truths
victuals: food
vide: see, refer to (an instruction)
volition: will
vulgar: common, ordinary

want: need, lack
whilst: while
withal: with, as well, likewise
without: outside (as in 'without the mind')
wont to: accustomed to, used to
wonted: customary, usual

Notes

1. Such remarks occur repeatedly in Locke's *Essay*; see 2. 21. 73, 2. 23. 32, 4. 3. 6, 4. 3. 16, 4. 3. 23, 4. 12. 11. Newton wrote: 'what the real substance of anything is we know not' (General Scholium added to book 3 of the 2nd edition of Newton's *Principia*, in *Newton's Philosophy of Nature*, 44). The 'inward essence' of things is their molecular structure—the arrangement of their microscopic parts that explains and causes their observable properties.

2. For such remarks on infinity, see §133 and Locke's *Essay* 2. 17. 17 and 21.

3. e.g. Aristotle, *Metaphysics* 11. 3, 1061a29–b4; Aquinas, *Summa Theologica* 1a, q. 85, 1 *ad* 1; Arnauld, *The Art of Thinking*, 48–50. Descartes claimed that 'it is possible to understand extension without shape or movement (*Principles of Philosophy* 1. 53; *Philosophical Writings*, i. 211). See, in general, on the historical context of Berkeley's discussion of abstraction, Flage, *Berkeley's Doctrine of Notions*, ch. 1.

4. For the following sections on abstraction, see the Editor's Introduction, Sect. 7. In §§7–9 Berkeley lays out the account of abstraction that he wants to reject. First, we are supposed to be able to consider separately each of the properties of an object: its extension apart from its colour or its motion, for instance (§7). Then we can consider the extensions of different objects, and make a 'most abstract idea of extension' as that which is common to all particular extensions (§8). Finally, we can consider abstract ideas of 'compounded beings', i.e. of *man* and of *horse*, by considering together the qualities common to all men, and leaving out any respects in which one man differs from another (§9). In §10 Berkeley gives his reasons for rejecting these claims about abstraction. We can do none of these things, because we cannot separate in the mind (i.e. abstract from each other) qualities that cannot exist separately. In §11 Berkeley considers the main reason offered by Locke for supposing us able to abstract in these ways, which is that we cannot otherwise explain the existence of general words or concepts. In §12 Berkeley offers an alternative explanation of general words, one which involves no appeal to or use of abstraction.

5. 'Common' here means 'shared'; 'agreements' here means 'similarities'.

6. The pressing question is: why is Berkeley so sure that we cannot do these things? The reason must be both simple and direct, since he clearly thinks that it is obvious. The most tempting explanation is that to abstract is to take as separate qualities that cannot exist separately; if they cannot exist separately, they cannot exist separately in (or be separated by) the mind. Every-

one admits that the qualities we are supposed to abstract are incapable of separate existence; nothing can be extended without being both coloured and figured (shaped), for instance. So these qualities cannot be abstracted from each other in the mind. An alternative suggestion, however, is that Berkeley is influenced here by thinking of our mental powers of abstraction in terms of our ability to form mental images. Since there cannot *be* an image of an object that has extension but no shape, or of an object that has extension but no colour, we cannot *form* such an image, and so cannot conceive these qualities separately in the mind. My own view is that the first explanation is more probable, and does not need the second as support. This is perhaps just as well, since Berkeley never explicitly commits himself to the view that ideas are mental images. If he did think of ideas in this way, he would think of conceiving as imagining. See the note to *Principles* §10.

Both of these explanations would make sense of the points that Berkeley makes earlier in this paragraph, that we cannot conceive of shape in general (in the way outlined in §8), since to do so would be to conceive of something that is shaped but has no particular shape. Nor can we conceive of a man who has height and colour but no particular height or colour (in the way required by the story of §9). If we really cannot do these things, the question is why not. The two rival explanations are: nothing could be like that; or, no image could be formed of such a thing.

7. Berkeley now turns to the main reason for holding that we must be capable of these supposed feats of abstraction. This is that otherwise we will not be able to explain the possibility of *general* terms, those capable of being true of more than one object. The term 'man', for instance, is capable of standing for more than one thing; indeed, it stands for any man, or all men equally. (Unlike the term 'Abraham Lincoln', which stands for one man alone.) Any meaningful word or term stands for some idea. The term 'Abraham Lincoln' stands for the idea of Lincoln. What idea does the term 'man' stand for? It must be a special idea, formed for the purpose; it must somehow pick out all men equally, saying nothing about any respect in which one man can differ from another. To create such an idea, we must start from the ideas given us in experience, the ideas of this man and that, and subtract (abstract) from them those respects in which they differ, leaving an artifically shorn idea, the abstract general idea of *man*. This idea is the meaning of the word 'man'.

8. i.e. John Locke; the following quotation is from his *Essay*.

9. Berkeley is about to offer his alternative account of the possibility of general terms or ideas. Hume called this account 'one of the greatest and most valuable discoveries that has been made of late years in the republic of letters' (*Treatise* 1. 1. 7, p. 17). We should note that this remark does not endorse Berkeley's attack on our supposed powers of abstraction. Hume is agreeing

with Berkeley that general terms do not need to be abstract. Berkeley could be right about that, and wrong about the impossibility of abstraction. If abstraction is unnecessary, it does not so much matter whether it is impossible, for present purposes. But Berkeley would certainly want to stick to his view that it is impossible. This is because he will be saying later that various mistaken claims about space, time, and matter depend on mistakes about abstraction. For him, any abstract idea is automatically suspect. See *Principles* §§13, 116, 121.

10. This sentence is important. Berkeley has shown that a particular and unabstracted *object* (the line drawn by the geometrician) can be used to stand for more than one thing. Given this, he can easily claim that a particular and unabstracted *idea* can be used to stand for more than one thing. And if so, a name or term that is general may stand for an idea of that sort, and does not need to stand for a special sort of idea formed for the purpose by abstraction. So: general ideas do not need to be abstract ideas. An idea is a general idea if we use it to stand for 'all other particular ideas of a certain sort'. We can perfectly well use an ordinary idea for this purpose, just as we can use an ordinary line to stand for all lines; we do not need to make a special one for the purpose.

11. The stress on 'all and none' and 'inconsistent' is not in Locke's text; it is added by Berkeley.

12. A universal notion is a notion of *all* objects of a certain sort, e.g. of all triangles. (There is no significant difference, as far as this goes, between being universal and being general.) Berkeley's point is that we do not need a special universal notion of triangle in order to speak or think of all triangles, or to achieve a universal proof that all triangles have angles summing to 180°. For him, a notion is universal if we can use it to stand for all objects of the sort ('in the relation it bears to the particulars . . .'); it is not required somehow to be universal itself. So if we start with particular notions of this or that particular triangle, we do not need to make a *new* one of a special and different sort if we want a notion of all triangles whatever; one of the old ones will do, so long as it can be used to stand for all triangles.

13. The remainder of this paragraph was added in the 1734 edition; Berkeley is stressing the possibility of selective attention to aspects of an idea. He allows that we can concentrate on this or that aspect of a complex idea, but not that we can carve ideas up into parts and then make each part into a separate idea. See the Editor's Introduction, Sects. 7–8.

14. The Schoolmen are philosophers and theologians who taught in medieval universities called 'Schools'. Some of them were of enormous distinction, such as St Thomas Aquinas. But Berkeley regularly uses the terms 'Schools' and 'Schoolmen' as terms of abuse—which they are close to being in Locke (see *Essay* 3. 3. 9 and 15, 3. 4. 8–10, 3. 10. 6 and 8, etc.). For at least two centuries

the Schoolmen had been accused of disputatiousness, irrelevance, and impracticality—in general of making things worse rather than better.

15. i.e. a plane surface bounded by three straight lines.

16. See e.g. Locke, *Essay* 3. 1. 2: 'Besides articulate sounds, therefore, it was further necessary that [man] should be *able to use these sounds as signs of internal conceptions*, and to make them stand as marks for the *ideas* within his own mind, whereby they might be made known to others, and the thoughts of other men's minds be conveyed from one to another.' Ibid. 3. 2. 2: 'That then which words are the marks of are the *ideas* of the speaker.'

17. It is one thing to deny that the communication of ideas is the only end or aim of language, and another to deny that it is the chief aim. Berkeley has not really disputed Locke's account of communication. Now he seems only to argue that speech has other purposes than that of communicating ideas. He says nothing to unsettle the view that the communication of ideas is somehow primary. But what he does say has been held to be a significant precursor of twentieth-century views that language is essentially practical in a way that does not need to focus on causing beliefs in our hearers. J. L. Austin (1911–60) suggested that we use language to do things (e.g. to make promises, to warn, to marry) in ways that do not essentially or primarily depend on the creation of ideas like ours in the minds of our audience. When I shout, 'Look out!', the desired effect might be an action of yours *rather than* the creation of an idea in your mind. See his *How to Do Things with Words* (Oxford: Oxford University Press, 1962). The *Philosophical Investigations* (Oxford: Blackwell, 1953) of Ludwig Wittgenstein (1889–1951) starts with consideration of a simple language whose purpose is practical; one person calls out, 'Slab!' or 'Brick!' and the other brings a slab or a brick. He writes (§6): 'We could imagine that [this] language was the *whole* language . . . of a tribe. The children are brought up to perform *these* actions . . . to react in *this* way to the words of others.' When they have learnt the meanings of these words, they have established 'an association between the word and the thing. But what does this mean? Well, it can mean various things; but one very likely thinks first of all that a picture of the object comes before the child's mind when it hears the word. But now, if this does happen——is it the purpose of the word?—Yes, it *can* be the purpose.——I can imagine such a use of words . . . But in the language [described above] it is *not* the purpose of the words to evoke images.' If this is right, there could be a whole language whose central purpose was not to create images or ideas in the minds of our hearers, but rather to get them do something.

18. Here again Berkeley is probably thinking primarily of Locke; see e.g. *Essay* 4. 3. 30, 4. 4. 17.

19. There is a problem in the very first sentence of the *Principles*. What gives Berkeley the right to assert that every object of the mind is an idea or a collection of ideas? Should we not also consider the possibility that some

physical things are objects of the mind? Common sense would have it that we can think about and perceive physical things. Berkeley's view will be that, since physical things are ideas, it comes to the same thing. But he should not assume this at the outset.

20. Berkeley means that the thing itself, the apple, is a collection of ideas; he is not here expressing the view that the meaning of the word 'apple' is a collection of ideas. But see §49.

21. After this initial catalogue of the objects of knowledge and the things that know them, Berkeley offers us two arguments that the things that we can sense (sensible things) have no existence outside the mind. The first argument runs from §§3–6, and the second is in §7.

22. 'without the mind': this does not mean 'in the absence of the mind' so much as 'outside the mind'; i.e. 'without' is here the opposite of 'within' rather than of 'with'.

23. We know something intuitively if we know it directly or immediately. Intuitive knowledge is to be contrasted with demonstrative knowledge, knowledge reached by inference (reasoning and argument). All you have to do is to concentrate on what you mean by 'exist', Berkeley claims, and you will recognize the truth of what he is saying straight off. The argument in §7, by contrast, reaches the same conclusion by inference. By the end of §7, then, we know both intuitively and demonstratively that the existence of a sensible thing is its being perceived.

Berkeley does not seem to tell us quite why the claim that sensible things can have an existence out of the mind is 'perfectly unintelligible'. I suggest that we should concentrate on what is presented to our senses—the view from our window for example. Could *that thing* exist unperceived? Berkeley's claim is that the thing we sense is something to which sensibility (the ability to be sensed) is essential; it is made to be sensed. But could something that is made to be sensed exist unsensed? Surely not: it would be lacking something that it needs, if it is to exist as it does.

24. The suggestion that the table exists if someone might perceive it, just as much as if someone actually does perceive it, has caused great difficulties in understanding Berkeley's account of sensible things and their existence. The question is whether it is enough for the existence of a sensible thing that some mind *might* perceive it, or whether it is required that it *actually* be perceived. Berkeley sometimes speaks as if actual perception is required (§§1, 6); sometimes it appears that possible perception is enough (§§3, 58). Matters come to a head in the Third Dialogue, where Berkeley writes, 'when things before imperceptible to creatures, are by a decree of God, made perceptible to them, then are they said to begin a relative existence, with respect to created minds' (p. 252). See the Editor's Introduction, Sect. 10.

25. *esse*, to be, exist; *percipi*, to be perceived; the best translation of this phrase is

'For them, to exist is to be perceived'. As we will learn in §98, the opposite is true for minds; for them, to exist is to perceive.

26. This tantalizing claim is never really made good by Berkeley. There are two things it might mean. The first is that since the doctrine of abstract ideas is false, so is the claim that sensible things can exist unperceived. The second is that mistaken views about what one can abstract from what explain why people come falsely to think that sensible things can exist unperceived, but do not show that doctrine to be false. My own view is that Berkeley intends the second of these. Either way, he supposes that if one does not make mistakes about abstraction, one will not be a materialist. See the Editor's Introduction, Sect. 8.

27. See n. 24. Here Berkeley does not allow that the mere possibility of perception is enough for the existence of sensible things; he argues that if they are not actually perceived they do not exist.

28. With this sentence, Berkeley's first argument comes to an end. The second argument occupies the remainder of the paragraph. It is that if sensible qualities are ideas, then to have a quality must be to have an idea. But only minds can have ideas, and to have an idea is to be aware of it; so the sensible qualities must 'belong to' minds that are aware of them rather than to mindless material things. For the flow of the argument in §§1–24, and more comments on the arguments of §§3–7, see the Editor's Introduction, Sect. 6.

29. A substratum is literally a 'layer beneath'. This clause is easier to grasp if one replaces 'ideas' by 'qualities'. A substratum for the qualities of an object is something lying underneath them, that holds them together. The notions of substratum and substance are discussed in greater detail in the first of the *Three Dialogues* pp. 197–9.

30. These first seven paragraphs constitute Berkeley's main positive arguments against materialism and in favour of immaterialism, though support comes in §§22–4.

31. This is Berkeley's 'Likeness Principle'; it is the main weapon in his attack on the view that ideas can represent material things. Those who maintained, with Locke, that the mind is primarily acquainted with its own ideas had to say how it was possible for it *also* to be acquainted (secondarily, presumably) with things of quite another sort, material objects. The normal account was that the ideas *represented* the material things to the mind, or stood proxy for them. But if one says this one has to give some story about what it is for an idea to represent a material thing—a story which tells us something about which ideas represent which things. The story that was normally given appealed to two concepts: resemblance and causation. It was held that an idea represented an object if it was caused by it and sufficiently resembled it. So, for instance, though my own brain is part of the cause of my ideas, none of my ideas of sense represents my brain, since none of them resembles it at all. So I cannot perceive my own brain. Berkeley's Likeness Principle, if sound, undermines all this talk of ideas representing material objects by

resembling them. For if ideas can only resemble ideas, they cannot resemble material things.

32. The 'Again' here seems to show that Berkeley is offering two arguments for the Likeness Principle, not just one. If so, what is the first one? The claim seems to have been that we cannot conceive a resemblance or likeness without conceiving the things that are supposed to be alike; but if the only things we can conceive are ideas, the only likeness we can conceive is between ideas.

33. For the primary–secondary distinction, see the Editor's Introduction, Sects. 3, 4, and 14. By the time that Berkeley was writing, the primary–secondary distinction was effectively received wisdom (in some form or other). The crucial point at the moment is that according to proponents of the distinction, our ideas of the secondary qualities do not resemble any qualities in the object; but things are different with the primary qualities. The idea of squareness resembles squareness as it is in the object; or, things that are square are like the way things look when they look square; or, the way things look when they look square is a good guide to what being square is. The same is not true of the secondary qualities. Since Berkeley's point in the previous paragraph was made largely in terms of colour, a secondary quality, he has to do something more if he is to defeat the restricted claim that our ideas of primary qualities represent to us the real qualities of material things, while those of secondary qualities do not.

34. 'Senseless' here means 'having no senses', 'devoid of sense and feeling'.

35. An archetype is a pattern or model; Berkeley is alluding here to the possible claim that though our ideas of extension etc. exist only in the mind, their archetypes exist 'in reality'. For the phrase 'they or their archetypes', see §45 and n.

36. This claim is only partly true, at best. Locke held nothing of the sort; his view was that colour is not a sensation, existing in the mind alone, but a power existing in the object—a power to cause certain ideas in the mind of a perceiver. As a sensation, it would cease to exist when unperceived; as a power, it can continue in the absence of a perceiver, since things can retain their powers when they are not exercising them. See also n. 53 and, for the historical details, the Editor's Introduction, Sect. 14.

37. Here, as often elsewhere, Berkeley appeals directly to introspection. He offers no argument that this sort of conception is impossible. Commentators have often supposed that Berkeley's position here depends on taking ideas to be mental images, pictures in the mind, so that all conception is imagination. It would be comparatively easy to show that one cannot *form a mental image of* an object existing without colour; colour seems essential to an image, even if it be only black and white. It is much harder to show that one cannot *conceive of* something extended but uncoloured, if conceiving is

different from imagining. The same point is relevant to Berkeley's denial of abstract general ideas. See the note to Intro. §10.

38. This is the place in the *Principles* where Berkeley distinguishes most clearly between the sorts of abstraction that he allows and those he does not allow. He allows selective attention to shape and size rather than colour. He does not allow conceiving of shape and size without conceiving of colour. If we want to know why not, we should expect to find the answer in Intro. §10. See Editor's Introduction, Sect. 8.

39. In §§11–13, Berkeley runs through the primary qualities, arguing of each that it is incapable of existing in an unthinking substance. His arguments are interestingly different in different cases. In the present case, that of extension, he argues that it is relative. But the mere introduction of the term 'relative' will not do all the work that Berkeley wants. Great and small may be relative to each other without being relative to the mind.

40. This move is the one first mentioned in Intro. §8: the 'most abstract idea of extension' described there is what Berkeley here calls 'extension in general', i.e. what remains in common to all extensions, once we have abstracted away all possible differences between them. He appeals here to what he argued there: that when we have done that, nothing is left.

41. '*materia prima*', or primary matter: Aristotle was thought to have believed that everything is made out of the four primary elements, earth, air, fire, and water, and that these elements were somehow the first determinations of an even less determinate but determinable substratum. See Aristotle's *Physics* 1. 6–9. Berkeley is suggesting that this totally indeterminate substratum is rather like 'extension in general, and motion in general'. The interpretation of Aristotle's remarks here is of course contested.

42. Here Berkeley seems to slide from the view that the same thing can be one, three, or thirty-six to the conclusion that number is 'dependent on men's understanding'. He does this by taking himself to have shown that number is relative. But we might reply that the length is objectively or really one yard, three feet, and thirty-six inches. Its number is indeed relative to something, but not to men's understanding. As in §11, the mere introduction of the term 'relative' will not do all the work that Berkeley wants.

43. This view is in Locke's *Essay* 2. 16. 1.

44. Here Berkeley is echoing Bayle; see the Editor's Introduction, Sect. 14.

45. This comparatively low-key conclusion is one that Berkeley abandoned almost immediately. In the first of the *Three Dialogues* he takes these arguments much more seriously, tackling each of the sensible qualities one by one, and arguing that each is no more than a sensation in the mind. In the case of extension, for instance, he concludes that every apparent extension is equally real, and so that no apparent extension can be *the* real extension; the same is true of apparent colour etc. This long series of arguments eventually gives him the result that all sensible qualities are 'ideas or sensations'—a claim that he makes, but hardly establishes, in *Principles* §§1–7. See the

Editor's Introduction, Sects. 6 and 11. In that sense the First Dialogue provides necessary support for the *Principles*.

46. Berkeley here echoes doubts voiced by Locke; see *Essay* 2. 23. 1–2.

47. Up until now Berkeley has been arguing that the notion of material substance is incomprehensible. For three paragraphs he suspends those arguments, and argues instead that even if it were comprehensible, we could have no reason at all for believing there to be any such thing. He returns to his main theme in §22.

48. Berkeley is making use of the famous difficulty of how to suppose the material capable of affecting the mental or vice versa—the problem of mind–body interaction. (See the Editor's Introduction, Sect. 14.) But materialists can make more than one use of the claim that the existence of the material world is the best explanation of some observed phenomenon. We appeal to the real existence of material things not only to explain the occurrence of ideas in the mind, but also to explain the course of nature. We think that natural events are best explained by conceiving of the world as a large physical system, operating on broadly mechanical principles. So even if materialism can offer no explanation of the occurrence of ideas in minds, it may still be required as an explanatory hypothesis. But Berkeley has already set things up in such a way that he can disallow this move. The only possible objects of knowledge are minds and ideas (§§1–2). The only things to be explained, therefore, other than the existence and operations of minds, are the occurrences of ideas. See §51 and the Editor's Introduction, Sect. 11.

49. The distinction between a posteriori and a priori that Berkeley is using here is not quite the one we are now accustomed to. A posteriori arguments against a doctrine are arguments that it has unfortunate or problematic consequences; Berkeley mentions such things in the first two sentences of this paragraph. An a priori argument against a doctrine would, on the distinction so understood, be a direct argument that it is false, or, worse, unintelligible; all the arguments we have seen so far have been of this sort. Berkeley turns to the a posteriori arguments in §§85–156.

50. This shows how much weight Berkeley attaches to the argument he is about to produce, which is sometimes called his Master Argument for that reason. Sadly, it is generally thought to be far from successful; see the Editor's Introduction, Sect. 6.

51. Berkeley's thought here might be that since anything the mind can conceive is an idea, there is no hope of conceiving the existence of material bodies. This claim should remind us of §8: 'If we look but ever so little into our thoughts, we shall find it impossible for us to conceive a likeness except only between our ideas'; see n. 32.

52. Here Berkeley accuses the materialists of asserting a contradiction. He takes it that the materialist claim 'I conceive an unconceived object' implies 'The object that I conceive is both conceived (since I conceive it) and uncon-

ceived'. In the First Dialogue (p. 200), he draws an analogy with the claim 'I see an unseen object', which is certainly contradictory. In the Editor's Introduction, Sect. 6, I suggest that the materialist claim does not imply a contradiction, and that Berkeley's analogy is unsound; the relevant passage from the First Dialogue is quoted there.

53. This is where Berkeley argues against Locke's view that secondary qualities are powers in the objects to cause sensations in perceiving minds—a view that he did not mention in his original attack on the primary–secondary distinction in §§9–10.

54. 'act any thing': this peculiar phrase just means 'do anything'.

55. Second causes are intermediate causes; someone who goes 'a wandering after second causes' holds that God causes physical events, which impinge on our minds and cause ideas in us. The physical events are intermediate links in the causal chain that starts with God and ends with us.

56. Note that Berkeley is careful to say that ideas of sense are *less* dependent on the mind that perceives them, rather than totally independent. He knows that the will of the perceiver is partly involved in the occurrence of ideas of sense, since we can partly determine what we see by deciding to walk away, look the other way, or just shut our eyes. It is important for Berkeley to continue to think of the mind as active in all its operations, even the comparatively passive operation of perception, for the main distinction between mind and idea is the distinction between active and passive.

57. These objections, numbered by Berkeley as 1–12, take us to §82. Berkeley has by now given us everything he needed to establish his metaphysical system, in just thirty-three paragraphs.

58. In the reference to stones, Berkeley shows foresight. In his *Life of Johnson*, Boswell writes: 'After we came out of the church, we stood talking for some time together of Bishop Berkeley's ingenious sophistry to prove the non-existence of matter, and that every thing in the universe is merely ideal. I observed, that though we are satisfied his doctrine is not true, it is impossible to refute it. I never shall forget the alacrity with which Johnson answered, striking his foot with mighty force against a large stone, till he rebounded from it, "I refute it *thus*".' Johnson's 'refutation' is of course completely irrelevant; whatever his other qualities, Johnson was no philosopher. Berkeley's views were constantly mangled in this way. His friend Swift is reported to have told his servant not to bother to open the door when Berkeley knocked, on the grounds that on his own principles Berkeley should be able to walk straight through it. But Fraser, in his *Life and Letters of George Berkeley*, calls this an 'Irish story' (p. 368 n.), implying presumably that we should not believe it.

59. For further comments on the way in which materialism leads to atheism, see §§66, 92.

60. Here we come across Berkeley's ambivalence towards common sense and

common language. In general Berkeley wants to represent himself as defending common sense against the peculiar views of philosophers. Where the word 'vulgar' appears (meaning common, ordinary) it is normally a term of praise, opposed to 'philosophical', a term of abuse. But Berkeley does not find it easy to represent his denial of the existence of matter as an instance of siding with the vulgar. In private correspondence he admits readily enough that his views are a 'paradox' (Letter to Percival, 6 Sept. 1710, *Works*, viii. 36), meaning that they contradict received opinion and for that reason seem absurd. Officially, however, he tries to maintain that most ordinary people already believe what he says. This paragraph represents him trying to get round an obvious difficulty, by saying for once that we should think with the learned. ('Learned' is another term of abuse in the *Principles*; see 'common sense', 'vulgar', and 'learned' in the Index.) Does this involve admitting that his doctrines are in breach of common sense? He seems to be allowing that his views are in breach of ordinary language, since they are not what we would ordinarily say. But he hopes thereby to retain his view that they are not in breach of common sense, meaning by this (1) that no person of common sense would find any reason to reject them, and (2) that they do not require us to abandon or alter the ordinary meanings of words.

61. Whether this is a good argument or not depends on what the current objection is supposed to be. If the objection is that we know for certain that things exist 'out there' because our experience reveals this to us, Berkeley's reply is sound. It is that dreams have all the relevant properties of waking experiences, and are compatible with the complete absence of objects 'out there'; so our experience is no proof of the existence of things out there. But the objection might be that Berkeley's views are at least at odds with our experience, since even if false, our experience clearly represents surrounding objects as existing at a distance from us. If so, the fact that our dreams falsely represent things as existing at a distance from us is irrelevant; it gives us no reason whatever to think that our waking experience does not represent our objects as existing at a distance.

62. The *Essay towards a New Theory of Vision* was published the year before, in 1709. The next sentence recapitulates the arguments of §§1–28 of that work.

63. Berkeley is here rejecting two views, that we *see* distance or outness, and that we *infer* the outward existence of objects from the nature of our ideas, in a way that in no way depends on experience. He argues instead that our visual experience *suggests* to us thoughts of distance, in the sense that the way things look causes us to expect certain other experiences to occur if we act in certain ways; e.g. we expect that if we take a certain number of paces in a certain direction, we will experience a pain in the nose because we will have bumped into a tree. But we are enabled to draw this inference only because our experience has enabled us to correlate visual experiences with tactual

ones. The notion of suggestion (q.v. in Index) is almost a technical term in Berkeley.

64. The point here is that the ideas of sight have no more intrinsic or necessary connection with ideas of distance than words have with the ideas they stand for, though of course long familiarity often leads us to slide from one to the other without noticing that we are doing so. Berkeley expresses this by saying that words suggest ideas to us; see Intro. §19. Cf. *New Theory of Vision* §§143, 147.

65. William Molyneux (1655–98), author of a respected work on optics, asked his friend Locke the following question, reported in Locke's *Essay* 2. 9. 8: 'Suppose a man born blind, and now adult, and taught by his touch to distinguish between a cube and a sphere of the same metal, and nighly of the same bigness [i.e. roughly of the same size], so as to tell, when he felt one and the other, which is the cube, which the sphere. Suppose then the cube and the sphere placed on a table, and the blind man to be made to see: *quaere*, whether by his sight, before he touched them, he could now distinguish and tell which is the globe, which the cube?' Molyneux, Locke, and Berkeley all agreed that the answer was no. If there were a necessary connection between the ideas of vision and those of touch, the answer should have been yes, for the newly sighted person would not have needed further experience to draw the relevant inference.

66. There is more on this point in §65 and §§108–9. The thought that the ideas of sight constitute a language in which God is speaking (as it were) to us is one first suggested in the *New Theory of Vision* §147: 'the proper objects of vision constitute an universal language of the Author of Nature'. The same claim is made in the full title of the *Theory of Vision Vindicated* (1733), which is *The Theory of Vision or Visual Language shewing the immediate Presence and Providence of a Deity, Vindicated and Explained*. In *Principles* §65 Berkeley enlarges his claim: not only visual ideas, but all ideas of sense are part of the language of God.

67. See n. 35. Berkeley is here, as in §9, trying to avoid saying whether our ideas of sense are copies of ideas in the mind of God, or whether they are identical with those ideas. He never comes clean on the point, either in the *Principles*, or in the *Three Dialogues* (see pp. 215–16, 240), or even when explicitly asked about the matter by the American philosopher Samuel Johnson; see Johnson's letter of 10 Sept. 1729 (§§7–8, pp. 168–9), and Berkeley's reply of 25 Nov., which simply ignores Johnson's direct question. Johnson repeated the question in his second letter §1, pp. 177–8, but even to this Berkeley's reply (§1, p. 183) is not really explicit. The matter is important, mainly because it affects Berkeley's conception of the presence of God's mind to ours, and his account of the existence of physical things. See the Editor's Introduction, Sects. 9 and 10.

68. 'Agree on all hands': this is an exaggeration; see nn. 36 and 53.

69. Berkeley here refers to the belief that it was not enough for God to have

created the world in the beginning; he maintains it in existence, or conserves it, by an act of 'continual creation'. See the Berkeley–Johnson letters, pp. 173–4 and nn. 30–1.

70. The argument of this paragraph is obscure. It seems to be that if matter is, as the materialists claim, infinitely divisible, all physical things have an infinite size, and so none has any shape. First, something infinitely divisible would be infinitely large because a view which discerns the infinite parts of the object would be one for which the object had infinite size, i.e. was infinitely large. To put it another way, infinity inwards is the same as infinity outwards. Second, a thing with infinite size would have no shape, because to have a shape is to be limited in some direction, and an object of infinite size would be unlimited.

71. This sentence contains Berkeley's real reply to the fourth objection.

72. The thought here is that if extension and figure are qualities and exist in the mind, they must belong to the mind—but this would mean that the mind has a size and shape. 'Predicated of' means 'said of' or 'attributed to'.

73. Malebranche discusses the possibility that the soul is actually green or red when we see greenness or redness at *Elucidations* 11, pp. 634–5.

74. 'Die' is the singular of 'dice'. The view that Berkeley is rejecting here is the one expressed with some scepticism by Locke in *Essay* 2. 23. 3: 'our complex *ideas* of substances, besides all these simple *ideas* they are made up of, have always the confused *idea* of *something* to which they belong, and in which they subsist; and therefore when we speak of any sort of substance, we say it is a *thing* having such and such qualities: as a body is a *thing* that is extended, figured, and capable of motion; a spirit, a *thing* capable of thinking ... These ... fashions of speaking intimate that the substance is supposed always *something* besides the extension, figure, solidity, motion, thinking or other observable *ideas*, though we know not what it is.' See also *Essay* 2. 23. 4. Despite his scepticism, Locke seems to take the way of speaking he reports seriously; even if the thought is unclear, we have somehow to distinguish between the thing and its qualities. Berkeley suggests that instead of revealing a metaphysical distinction between the qualities and the thing that has them, that way of speaking is only a way of explaining the meaning of a word.

75. See n. 48.

76. See §38 and n.

77. Copernicus held that the earth circles the sun rather than vice versa, as in the Ptolemaic system. This sentence means 'Those who think of Copernicus' view as completely proved, still speak as if it were false.'

78. The 'modern philosopher' concerned is Malebranche; see e.g. his *Recherche* 6. 2. 3. For Malebranche's views in general, and this view in particular, see the Editor's Introduction, Sect. 14. Part of what led Malebranche to this view was a belief that 'a true cause as I understand it is one such that the mind per-

ceives a necessary connection between it and its effect. Now the mind perceives a necessary connection only between the will of an infinitely perfect being and its effects' (ibid., p. 450). This conception of a cause was largely shared by Berkeley, and even by Thomas Hobbes (1588–1679), who defined a cause as follows: 'a cause simply, or an entire cause, is the aggregate of all the accidents both of the agents how many soever they may be, and of the patient, put together; which when they are all supposed to be present, it cannot be understood but that the effect is produced at the same instant; and if any one of them be wanting, it cannot be understood but that the effect is not produced'. This is at pp. 121–2 of Hobbes's *Elements of Philosophy*, in *The English Works of Thomas Hobbes*, ed. Sir W. Molesworth (London: Bohn, 1819), vol. i. It is to be contrasted with that of Locke, who thought we must allow the existence of causal relations that we cannot understand: 'to have the *idea* of *cause* and *effect*, it suffices to consider any simple *idea* or substance as beginning to exist by the operation of some other, without knowing the manner of that operation' (*Essay* 2. 26. 2). For a good discussion of these issues, see Winkler *Berkeley: An Interpretation*, ch. 5, and his introduction to his edition of the *Principles*, 27–9. An 'efficient cause' is the source of the relevant change; as we might put it, it is what *makes* the event happen. See the Editor's Introduction, n. 18.

79. This is Berkeley's favourite objection to Malebranche. He elaborates in §§67–75, and repeats it in the second of the *Three Dialogues* at p. 220. See also Sect. 14 of the Editor's Introduction above.

80. Here Berkeley seems to allow that the possibility of being perceived is sufficient for the existence of sensible things. See §§3, 6, and 48 and the notes to them.

81. The eleventh objection asks how Berkeley's immaterialism can be reconciled with contemporary science; in particular, how he can explain the intricacy of the world that science was revealing by the use of microscopes. The obvious explanation of that intricacy, that the complex inner natures of things are an important part of the explanation of their external and visible nature and behaviour, just as the insides of the watch explain the movement of the hands, is not available to Berkeley. For he has announced (§25) that no physical thing can be a cause; the only cause is spirit or mind. So why is the world the way it is? Why did God bother to put in all the extra detail?

Berkeley's reply is complex. First he argues that the question why God bothered with the extra detail is no easier for the mechanists to answer than it is for him (§61). Then he observes that the inner natures of things, though not absolutely necessary for the production of observable effects, are an important part of the regularity of the natural world; events that would otherwise seem to be unusual are able to be explained as ordinary examples of the operation of the laws of nature, once we know the inner natures of the objects involved (§62). Finally, he offers a reason why God should seek to make the world run in regular and predictable ways, i.e. according to natural laws, which is that this is of great use to us in helping us to order our lives (§65). Increasing scientific knowledge leads to improvements in the human condition, e.g. in medicine, and this is all part of God's plan.

In general, on Berkeley's answer to the eleventh objection, see the Editor's Introduction, Sect. 12.

82. The index is the hour hand of the watch.

83. A final cause is the purpose for which something exists, to be contrasted with an efficient cause.

84. For Berkeley, there is no necessary connection between one natural event and another; natural events are not efficient causes. But a knowledge and understanding of the course of nature is still as useful as it ever was, because with sufficient experience one can tell what to expect next. For the claim that natural events are signs rather than causes, see §108.

85. This paragraph contains one central strand of Berkeley's account of science and scientific knowledge. (For the rest, see §§104–5.) The main point is an analogy between language and nature. Berkeley does not say here that nature is language—that a natural event is an utterance of God's. But this thought is clearly at the back of his mind. (Note the phrase 'abundance of information'.) It emerges more explicitly in *The Theory of Vision Vindicated* §40: 'A great number of arbitrary signs, various and apposite, do constitute a language. If such arbitrary connexion be instituted by men, it is an artificial language; if by the Author of Nature, it is a natural language.' See also *Alciphron* 4. 7:

> EUPHRANOR. But if it shall appear plainly that God speaks to men by the intervention and use of arbitrary, outward, sensible signs, having no resemblance or necessary connexion with the things they stand for and suggest; if it shall appear that, by innumerable combinations of these signs, an endless variety of things is discovered and made known to us; and that we are thereby instructed or informed in their different natures; that we are taught and admonished what to shun, and what to pursue; and are directed how to regulate our motions . . . will this content you?
>
> ALCIPHRON. It is the very thing I would have you make out; for therein consists the force, and use, and nature of language.

The conception of the world as text was not at all unfamiliar to Berkeley's readers. Raymond Sebond, for instance (a 15th-century Spanish theologian), contrasted the Book of Nature with the Holy Scriptures, holding that the basic elements in the Book of Nature are the natural kinds, or natures such as human nature, which can be combined into words and sentences: 'God has given us two books: the Book of the Universal Order of Things (or, of Nature) and the Book of the Bible. The former was given to us first, from the origin of the world: for each creature is like a letter traced by the hand of

God: this Book had to be composed of a great multitude of creatures (which are as so many 'letters'); within them is found Man. He is the main, the capital letter. Now, just as letters and words composed from letters constitute a science by amply marshalling different sentences and meanings, so too the creatures, joined and coupled together, form various clauses and sentences, containing the science that is, before all, requisite for us.' This is from the Prologus to Raymond Sebond's *Book of the Creatures*, to be found in *The Essays of Michel de Montaigne*, ed. M. A. Screech (London: Allen Lane, 1991), pp. lv–lviii, at p. lvii. Galileo dissented; he took the Book to be written in mathematics.

86. Berkeley's favourite quotation, from Acts 17: 28. Strangely, it is also the last sentence in Malebranche's *Recherche* 3. 2. 6—the section expounding Malebranche's view that 'we see all things in God'.

87. The sense of this sentence is: 'it is still possible that matter, taken in this limited sense, may exist'.

88. This notion of an occasion is a reference to Malebranche's Occasionalism, for which see the Editor's Introduction, Sect. 14.

89. 'Meanest' here means 'least', 'slightest'.

90. 'Though in the lowest rank of probability': this shows that Berkeley's view is not that we have more reason to believe that matter does not exist than that it does; he thinks we have *no reason whatever* to believe it exists. See §19.

91. The passage of thought detailed in this paragraph ('first . . . second . . .) is remarkably similar to the structure of the first of the *Three Dialogues*.

92. The reference must be to §7.

93. Malebranche wrote in *Elucidations* 6, p. 575: 'Now in the appearance of Sacred Scripture and from the appearance of miracles we learn that God has created a heaven and an earth, that the Word was made flesh, and other such truths that assume the existence of a created world. Hence it is certain through faith that there are bodies . . . I believe that the above will satisfy anyone who is not overly demanding.'

94. In the *Three Dialogues*, however, Berkeley had to take seriously an objection that obviously had not occurred to him when he wrote the *Principles*. The wife of his friend Sir John Percival objected that he could not account, on his principles, for the biblical story of the Creation. The problem derived from the awkward fact that, as the Bible tells it in Genesis, God created the physical world on the fourth day, *before* he created animals (the fifth day) or humans (the sixth day) to perceive it. The question is: in what did the existence of the physical world consist during the fourth day? In being perceived? But by which minds? Berkeley's answer to this difficulty is at *Three Dialogues* pp. 250–6.

95. This is a reference to the miracle performed by Christ at the wedding-feast at Cana in Galilee, when the wine ran out and he turned water into wine.

96. For the remainder of the *Principles*, Berkeley lists awkward consequences of

materialism, and liberating consequences of immaterialism, as promised in §21.

97. We have seen all three of these questions before. The first is the one to which Descartes gave the answer 'no', and Locke the answer 'possibly'. The second was raised at §47, and will be discussed in §§123–32. The third is the old chestnut of mind–body interaction, which appeared in §19.

98. 'the sequel': this may be a reference to the intended Part II of the *Principles*, which never appeared; but more probably it refers merely to what follows in Part I, since Berkeley removed what looks like a reference to Part II from the first-edition version of §144, in the 1734 version (see the footnote to that passage). This would be consistent with the sentiments expressed at the end of his first letter to Johnson (p. 175), in which he makes clear that he had abandoned the prospect of ever writing Part II.

99. The terminology of 'self-evident or demonstrative knowledge' is from Locke's *Essay* 4. 2. 14, where Locke denies the possibility of any such thing. Self-evident knowledge is knowledge that stands alone, without needing the support of a reason. Demonstrative knowledge is knowledge derived from a proof or reasoning.

100. Like the similar addition to §142, the passage added in the second edition at this point contains important material. For the new, sharper distinction between ideas and notions, see the Editor's Introduction, Sect. 13. The doctrine that we know of our own existence by 'inward feeling or reflexion' is new. There are several passages in the first edition where Berkeley speaks of 'sense or reflexion' as two distinct sources of knowledge (§§13, 25, 35, 70, 73), and these remain in the second edition, despite their suggestion that reflection is a source of ideas rather than of notions. The present passage also adds the distinction between three objects of knowledge rather than the two of §§1–2—the addition being that of relations, for which see §142 and the note there.

101. The 'them' here refers to the corporeal substances created by God, not to the ideas of them. Berkeley is alluding to the view that even God is incapable of creating things *ex nihilo*, from nothing, as we see from the next paragraph.

102. The pre-Socratics generally assumed that matter was eternal. Aristotle explicitly asserted it (*De Caelo* 2. 1, 283^{b}26).

103. Epicurus (341–270 BC) and Hobbes both maintained that the universe is nothing but matter in motion. Neither explicitly denied the existence of gods or of God. But Epicurus thought that the gods did not concern themselves with mundane affairs, and Hobbes, though he wrote as if he was an orthodox Christian believer, was always held to be a secret atheist.

104. We would normally distinguish between fatalists and determinists. A determinist holds that every event is the effect of necessitating causes—causes such that, once they have occurred, the effect cannot fail to happen. A fatalist is someone who holds that it is already fixed what will happen tomorrow,

but not for causal reasons. (The reason will be either that God already knows what will happen, or that it is already true, of the things that will happen tomorrow, that they will happen.) It is not clear which of these doctrines Berkeley is referring to here, but since he is supposing that belief in the existence of matter encourages fatalism, it is probably what we would call determinism.

105. The resurrection of the body (the belief that in the afterlife we retain our own body) is a doctrine enshrined in the Christian Creed; it caused obvious theological difficulties, particularly on the point that Berkeley is discussing here, namely what makes it the case that the body we have after death is the very same one as the one we had in mortal life. Berkeley claims that this is only a problem for materialists; there may be difficulty in supposing that the later body consists of the same matter as the earlier one, but there is none in supposing that it has the same outward form—the same sensible qualities— which is all that his doctrine would require. It is not obvious that he has entirely escaped the problem. All that he seems to be offering is that we will have a similar body. He needs more to justify the claim that we will have the very same one. But see the remarks on identity in the *Three Dialogues* pp. 247–8. Berkeley makes a weaker claim in the first letter to Johnson (§6, p. 174); his views are compatible with the resurrection, but not the best way of defending it, as they are said to be here.

Socinians were the followers of Fausto Sozzini (1539–1604), an Italian whose religious views were idiosyncratic. They included the claim that Christ was not fully divine; he was God, but naturally human. A letter of Sozzini's dated 1563 rejects the doctrine of the natural immortality of man.

106. It is not clear what this phrase is supposed to mean. It probably refers to the sort of knowledge that is concerned with the nature of time, place, and motion. There is a contrast between real and ideal knowledge in Locke's *Essay* 4. 4. 6.

107. This must be a reference to St Augustine's remark: 'What is time? If nobody asks me this question, I know what it is. If I try to explain it to someone, I don't know' (*Confessions* 11. 14).

108. This thought derives from thinking of infinity in both directions, as in §47: see the note to that paragraph.

109. The possibility that one be annihilated every instant derives, presumably, from the difficulty of making sense of our existence continuing from one moment to the next, across the point at which one ends and the next begins.

110. This 'therefore' seems to be quite unjustified.

111. Berkeley wrote even more definitely in his second letter to Johnson: 'A succession of ideas I take to *constitute* time, and not to be only the sensible measure thereof' (p. 183).

112. This was the doctrine of Descartes (see his Replies to the Fifth Objections, in *Philosophical Writings*, ii. 246–7), but not that of Locke, who wrote: 'I confess

myself to have one of those dull souls, that doth not perceive itself always to contemplate *ideas*; nor can conceive it any more necessary for the *soul always to think*, than for the body always to move' (*Essay* 2. 1. 10). In his second letter to Berkeley (pp. 180–1), Samuel Johnson argues vigorously in favour of Locke's position.

113. This is a different twofold abstraction from that described in Intro. §§7–8; the first element here is the second there, and so the second element here is in effect a third stage in the process of abstraction. The phrase 'the entity of extension' means 'the existence of extension'.

114. Berkeley says little about morality in the *Principles* (but see §143). Here his point appears to be an instance of his more general view that we should abandon the abstractions of philosophy and get on with the practicalities of ordinary life and religion; see e.g. §156. He has the same attitude to the details of natural science (§109) and geometry (§131).

115. §§85–100 concerned general advantages of Berkeley's position, with respect to ideas (as opposed to spirits, which are discussed in §§133–56). §§101–32 are concerned with the advantages of Berkeley's view with respect to science and mathematics.

116. See here the note to Intro. §2.

117. Occult (hidden) qualities are contrasted with manifest (discernible) ones. Newton wrote that gravity and cohesion were manifest qualities, 'and their causes only are occult. And the Aristotelians gave the name of "occult qualities" . . . to such qualities only as they supposed to lie hid in bodies and to be the unknown causes of manifest effects, such as would be the causes of gravity and of magnetic and electric attractions . . . if we should suppose that these forces or actions arose from qualities unknown to us and incapable of being discovered and made manifest' (*Optics*, query 30, in *Newton's Philosophy of Nature*, 176).

118. Explanation by appeal to attraction, e.g. explanation of the movements of the tides, was thought to be far from satisfactory or ultimate by the physicists themselves, even by Newton, who wrote in a letter to Richard Bentley, 'It is inconceivable, that inanimate brute matter should, without the mediation of something else, which is not material, operate upon, and affect other matter without mutual contact' (*Isaac Newton's Papers and Letters on Natural Philosophy*, ed. I. B. Cohen (Cambridge: Cambridge University Press, 1958), 302–3; see also the introduction, pp. 1–9). Newton's response to this difficulty was to say that we do not know the cause of gravity; but that it must be something real but not material. This was to be an elastic and electric fluid which Newton called the 'aether', whose operations were the intermediate causes that explained gravitational effects and all other cases of apparent 'action at a distance'.

The philosophers agreed that real action at a distance is inconceivable. Here is Locke: 'The next thing to be considered is how *bodies* produce *ideas* in us; and that is manifestly by *impulse*, the only way which we can conceive bodies operate in' (*Essay* 2. 8. 11; see also 4. 3. 6). Locke's pronouncement reflected a sense that only mechanistic explanations really explain. Berkeley could not say that; but he agrees that appeals to attraction do nothing to tell us the nature of the force concerned. He goes on to make the same point about the other non-mechanistic phenomenon that troubled the mechanists, the cohesion of the parts of a lump of metal; this cannot be explained mechanically either. See Locke, *Essay* 2. 23. 26.

119. 'Drawing' here means 'pulling', 'attracting'.

120. In this sense, then, Berkeley does not object to scientific explanations in terms of attraction or cohesion. He only wants to say that such explanations do not identify efficient causes for the events they explain; the explanation is achieved by finding analogies and similarities between this event and others, not by finding its cause. We know its cause already, namely God.

121. 'Universal' is one thing, 'essential' another. The former means that all bodies in fact attract and are attracted; the latter means that no body *could* exist without being subject to attraction. Berkeley wants to rejects the latter, while leaving the former at best dubious; note the cautious phrases 'Whereas it appears . . .', and 'seems to show itself . . .'. Even the denial of necessity or essentiality can be read in more than one way, however. The sentence that starts 'There is nothing necessary or essential in the case, but it depends entirely on the will of the *governing spirit* . . .' might mean that there is nothing necessary or essential here, only the arbitrary will of God. But it might also mean that the only necessity in the case is one that depends entirely on God's will. For this possible use of 'but' meaning 'except', see a famous sentence in Locke's *Essay*: 'qualities which in truth are nothing in the objects themselves but powers to produce various sensations in us' (2. 8. 10). It should be noted that Newton himself did not claim that gravity was an essential property of bodies; see his *Optics*, advertisement II, 2nd edn., 1717.

122. 'Perpendicular' here means 'straight up'.

123. 'Become' here means 'be becoming to'.

124. Here, as elsewhere in this passage, 'philosopher' means 'scientist'. It was Descartes who most notoriously denied that science should concern itself with final causes: 'When dealing with natural things we will, then, never derive any explanation from the purposes which God or nature may have had in view when creating them, and we shall entirely banish from our philosophy the search for final causes' (*Principles of Philosophy* 1. 28, in *Philosophical Writings*, i. 202). See also Spinoza's *Ethics* 1, Appendix. Newton, however, wrote, 'it is not to be conceived that mere mechanical causes could give birth to so many regular motions [as those of the moons and planets] . . . This most beautiful system could only proceed from the counsel and dominion of an intelligent and powerful Being' (General Scholium added to book 3 of

Newton's *Principia*, in *Newton's Philosophy of Nature*, 42). See the Editor's Introduction, Sect. 12.

125. As the notes at the foot of the text show, Berkeley significantly changed the tenor of this paragraph and the next two in the second edition, removing the reference to the 'language of Nature' which reminds one of §§44 and 65, and almost all the thoughts that relate to it. Since he does not seem to have abandoned his general view that natural events are the language in which God informs us, given the elaboration of such ideas in *Alciphron*, it is not clear why he withdrew these remarks here, especially since he leaves the phrase 'perusing the volume of Nature' in §109. One possibility is that he thought them incidental to his main point, and a distraction; for another, see n. 49 to the Editor's Introduction. See also the note to §65, where the relevant passage from *Alciphron* is quoted.

126. Berkeley is referring to Newton's *Mathematical Principles of Natural Philosophy*, normally referred to as the *Principia*. On Berkeley's general attitude to Newton, see the Editor's Introduction, Sect. 14. Berkeley admits here that Newton explicitly asserts that absolute space, time, and motion have an existence outside the mind. He therefore has to undermine that claim without doing any general damage to Newton's physics. He does this by denying the possibility of absolute motion, and using that to deny the possibility of absolute space.

127. 'Perseverance' here means 'continuity'.

128. The remainder of this paragraph is a perfectly fair and often verbatim summary of the contents of the Scholium or note to Definition 8 of the *Principia* (in *Newton's Philosophy of Nature*, 17–25).

129. 'Ambiguity' here means 'uncertainty'.

130. This sentence means that even if motion means a change in a relation between one thing and another, this does not require that when such a change occurs, both things move.

131. The 'above-mentioned properties, causes and effects' of absolute motion are those mentioned at the end of §111; they are listed as such by Newton (Scholium to Def. 8, pp. 21–2).

132. In this experiment, a vessel (a bucket) full of water is suspended from a long rope, twisted round many times, and then let go to spin back. Newton held that at the beginning the bucket is moving and the water is at rest, as its flat surface shows. However, both are in relative motion with respect to each other. Only one has absolute motion. After a while, however, the absolute motion of the bucket communicates itself to the water, which begins to spin, i.e. acquires absolute circular motion. Since absolute circular motion is centrifugal (i.e. things going round in circles always try to move away from the centre) the water's surface becomes dished, i.e. lower in the middle than at the edges. This shows that it is moving absolutely, though it is no longer moving relative to the bucket.

Berkeley's description of the situation is quite different. He maintains that the water is at first at rest, not absolutely but relative to the bucket, while the bucket is moving. (He can say this because he takes the view, unlike Newton, that of two bodies one can move relative to the other without the other moving relative to the one; see §113). Later, the water is moving, though not relative to the bucket. It is moving relative to the earth, or some larger frame, considered as inertial for present purposes. This establishes, contrary to Newton's view, that circular relative motion has centrifugal force. For when the surface of the water is not dished, the water has no relative motion; and when it is dished, it has relative motion. Berkeley thus denies that one can appeal to centrifugal force either to distinguish relative from absolute motion, or indeed to establish that the notion of absolute motion makes sense.

133. Berkeley warned in Intro. §§21 ff. that we should take care not to be misled by language. This is perhaps the most important instance of that warning in the *Principles*; but see also §122.

134. See e.g. Locke's *Essay* 2. 13. 2: 'it would be as needless to go to prove that men perceive, by their sight, a distance between bodies of different colours, or between the parts of the same body, as that they see colours themselves'.

135. Berkeley's view, as we saw in §44, is that the ideas of space and distance are only possible when we have succeeded in correlating visual experiences with tactual ones. On pure space, see *New Theory of Vision* §126.

136. Entry 298 of the *Philosophical Commentaries* reads: 'Locke, More, Raphson etc. seem to make God extended.' Locke's *Essay* 2. 15. 8 speaks of 'the boundless invariable oceans of duration and expansion which comprehend in them all finite beings and in their full extent belong only to the Deity'. Newton wrote the General Scholium added to book 3 of the second edition of *Principia* partly in order to defend himself against this sort of accusation; he said there: '[God] is not eternity and infinity, but eternal and infinite; he is not duration or space, but he endures and is present. He endures forever and is everywhere present; and, by existing always and everywhere, he constitutes duration and space' (*Newton's Philosophy of Nature*, 43). Henry More (1614–87) wrote of space that it 'must of necessity be a substance incorporeal necessarily and eternally existent of itself; which the clearer *Idea* of a *Being absolutely perfect* will more fully and punctually inform us to be the *self-subsisting God*' (*Antidote against Atheism*, App., 2nd edn. (London, 1655), 338). But he did draw some distinction between space and God: 'mere space is . . . a certain rather confused and vague representation of the divine essence or essential presence, in so far as it is distinguished from his life and activities' (*Enchiridion Metaphysicum*, ch. 8, par. 14). See further the correspondence between Johnson and Berkeley, pp. 178–9 and 183.

137. This sentence means 'some have set themselves to show that space has the attributes of God—which it cannot have, since those cannot be shared'. This

is probably a reference to *De Spatio Reali* (1697) by Joseph Raphson, a Cambridge mathematician (*c.*1676–*c.*1715), which according to Berkeley, 'pretends to find out fifteen of the incommunicable attributes of God in Space' (second letter to Johnson, p. 183).

138. i.e. the arabic numerals 1, 2, 3, etc. The numeral names are 'one', 'two', 'three', etc. This paragraph and the next contain the kernel of Berkeley's philosophy of mathematics. For him there are numeral names, numerals, and things numbered. There are no numbers. We delude ourselves, therefore, if we think that mathematics has its own subject-matter, namely the numbers and relations between them. As §122 makes clear, what may seem to be theorems about numbers are really about particular numerable things (such as the inhabitants of London) or about names. If we study the theorems for their own sake, then, we have turned from things to words.

139. 'Multitudes' here means 'numbers'.

140. Berkeley is perhaps referring to the paradoxes of Zeno, which are indeed designed to test, among others, the hypothesis that space is infinitely divisible.

141. This belief is that the bread and wine consumed by the congregation in Holy Communion has been turned into the body and blood of Christ.

142. 'Scheme' here means 'diagram'.

143. Berkeley is suggesting that the belief in infinite divisibility derives from a mistake in the theory of general ideas, exposed in Intro. §12. We take a line an inch long to stand for all lines whatever. If it stands for all lines, it stands for some infinite ones, i.e. ones which are indeed infinitely divisible, since they have an infinite number of parts. By a natural mistake, we think of the sign, which is only an inch long, as having as many parts as any line that it is capable of signifying. And so we come to think of an inch-long line as having an infinite number of parts.

144. The ten-thousandth of the inch-long line is nothing at all, Berkeley says. But in order to use this line as standing for all lines whatever, we have to think of this line as having ten thousand parts, for otherwise we could not use it to stand for a line that does.

145. For a posteriori proofs, see the note to §21.

146. 'Root' here means 'a number which is to be multiplied by itself a certain number of times'.

147. The *minimum sensibile* is the smallest quantity that is capable of being sensed.

148. See Intro. §2.

149. Berkeley leads straight in with his main point. This is that his philosophy can explain what others cannot, namely our apparent inability to say anything much about the nature of the mind. (Malebranche wrote: 'our knowledge of [the soul] is imperfect. Our knowledge of our soul is limited to what we sense taking place in us' (*Recherche* 3. 2. 7. 4). Berkeley claims that we have been misled into treating the mind as just another part of the natural world,

which has merely the peculiarity of being especially difficult to pin down. In his own terms, this is to think that the mind is the sort of thing of which it should be possible to get a clear enough idea, and then to be disconcerted by the fact that no such clear idea seems to be forthcoming. Once we realize, however, that the mind is active, and not part of the natural world at all, we cease to look in the wrong place for knowledge of its nature. Berkeley would, I think, be particularly disconcerted by the mainstream modern view that his account of the mind is one of the weakest aspects of his philosophy.

150. This paragraph and the next were altered in the second edition in order to bring out more clearly Berkeley's point that we can perfectly well understand the word 'mind' without being able to have an idea of a mind: we can have a notion of a mind.

151. What does Berkeley mean by saying that our soul is the image or idea of others, when he has repeatedly told us that we cannot have any idea of a mind? The words 'in that sense' must bear considerable weight here. The point, presumably, is that our mind stands to others as our ideas stand to those of other minds, in relations of resemblance. But yet, we might think, the *sort* of resemblance at issue between two passive beings (ideas) must be different from that at issue between two active ones (minds).

152. The remainder of this paragraph was added in the second edition, for reasons discussed in the Editor's Introduction, Sect. 13.

153. This is an important doctrine which has not surfaced before, though a preliminary thought about relations was added to §89. The general idea here must be that relations occur when things (ideas) are related, and relating things is something we *do*, and therefore relations are at least partly active.

154. Berkeley seems to be thinking of Hobbes here; if everything in the world is nothing but matter in motion, as Hobbes held, so must the will be.

155. '*who works all in all*': 1 Cor. 12: 6; '*by whom all things consist*': Col. 1: 17. This paragraph recapitulates and extends the argument for God's existence originally given in §§29–32.

156. At *Dialogues* p. 257 Berkeley goes even further than this. He claims there that God's properties are 'as conspicuous as the existence of sensible things, of which (notwithstanding the fallacious pretences and affected scruples of *sceptics*) there is no more reason to doubt, than of our own being'.

157. Here Berkeley fails to see a serious difficulty to which he has no obvious answer. If the movements of my body are real things, they are ideas of sense, and as such caused by God, not by me. But if so, I am incapable of performing any physical action. Berkeley is unable to make out my status as a human agent. See Taylor, 'Action and Inaction in Berkeley'.

158. The quotation comes from Heb. 1: 3.

159. This is another reference to Malebranche.

160. Acts 17: 28 (again); see note to §66.

161. Acts 17: 27.

162. The word 'legible' is another allusion to the doctrine that the world is a book or text, or at least a linguistic object. See also 'speak themselves' in §36. See the note to §65.
163. 'Machine' here means 'created system'.
164. This is Berkeley's answer to the standard problem of pain: how can there be pain in the world, if everything in it is caused by an all-powerful and benevolent God? His answer is that in asking this question, 'our prospects are too narrow'; we should consider the whole system, rather than any single part of it.
165. Manichaeanism is named after its founder Mani (AD 215/16–276/7). Mani believed that the world is contradictory because it is the product of two opposing forces, light or good and darkness or evil. From this were derived demands for extraordinary self-denial, as devotees sought to expunge from themselves every sign of darkness. Manichaeanism flourished in the Later Roman Empire, and was still influential up until the 13th century in Europe. By then it had adopted various Christian doctrines; but it was incapable of accepting the divinity of Christ.
166. Gen. 28: 20.

NOTES TO THE BERKELEY–JOHNSON CORRESPONDENCE

1. 'ideal scheme': scheme of ideas.
2. 'subordinate natural causes': i.e. second causes; see *Principles* §32. A second cause is one that transmits causation from its cause to its effect, like the link in a chain that is pulled by the link before it and pulls the one after. Berkeley supposes that physical events cannot be first causes, since they have no agency in them, being entirely passive. But he also holds that they cannot be second causes, since they are incapable of transmitting the sort of agency that a mind has.
3. The archetype of my idea of the fire (the original of which my idea is a copy) is here supposed to be not an idea in the mind of God, but a real physical cause—which, of course, like everything else, exists in the mind of God in the sense that God is aware of it. Berkeley's reply should be that such physical objects would be material, and that he has sufficiently disproved the existence of material things; that no physical object can be any sort of cause; and that the supposition of real archetypes for our ideas of sense leads to scepticism (*Principles* §86).
4. Johnson urges that our senses represent the events we perceive as related to each other as cause and effect, rather than as sign and signified; so that if there are no physical causes, we are under a perpetual illusion. This is like the suggestion that our senses represent their objects as 'out there'; so that if there is no such thing as 'out there' the senses deceive us systematically (for which,

see *Principles* §42 ff.). Berkeley does not respond to this point, but presumably he would just deny the claim that the senses represent physical events as causally related, arguing that causal thoughts are the products of inference.

5. This objection concerns Berkeley's arguments in *Principles* §§60–6.

6. 'proper means of trial': the suggestion here is that God might be testing us by giving us thoughts and ideas which, as good Christians, we should suppress.

7. This objection asks whether, if God knows that his causing in us certain ideas will lead us into sinful acts, it would be consistent with his holiness to give us those ideas. Our wickedness may be our own fault because we have gradually become wicked by failing to resist temptation. But God would be to some extent complicit in our wickedness, since he does something which he knows will lead us to sin.

8. There seem to be two questions raised here. The first is whether on Berkeley's views the 'curious structure' of the eye is anything more than a fine show, since it is not at all involved in the process of vision. The second is that it seems to be designed as a instrument; so that if it is not one (i.e. if it is not involved in the process of vision as an instrument), God's creation is misleading.

9. This objection concerns the Christian doctrine of the resurrection of the body after death; in *Principles* §95 Berkeley argued that the difficulties in supposing that we had the *same* body after resurrection as we had before death derived from a materialist conception of what a body was. If we abandon that conception, there are no longer any difficulties about resurrection. The difficulty that Johnson is raising here derives from a special feature of the doctrine of resurrection, that resurrection would have to wait for a while. John 5: 28–9 reads: 'Marvel not at this: for the hour is coming, in the which all that are in the graves shall hear his voice, and shall come forth; they that have done good, unto the resurrection of life; and they that have done evil, unto the resurrection of damnation.' Johnson apparently takes this to mean that our bodies languish in our graves for a while, until the time of resurrection; but that we ourselves are in a 'separate state' during that period, bodiless but sentient. Johnson suggests that Berkeley cannot consistently describe this temporary state of being bodiless but sentient. In that state it will seem to us as if there are bodies, including ours. But this is the sort of appearance that on Berkeley's view counts as reality; so what difference could the supposed later resurrection of the body actually make?

10. Johnson's question about archetypes relates more to the discussion in the Third Dialogue than to the *Principles*. In both works, Berkeley was careful to avoid saying whether our ideas of sense are identical with, or only copies of, ideas in the mind of God. Johnson tentatively takes it that Berkeley's real view is that they are only copies of a divine archetype. I suggest in my Editor's Introduction, Sect. 9, that Berkeley probably took the other line. *In mente Divinâ*: in the mind of God.

11. '*toto coelo* different': literally, different by the whole world; i.e. completely and utterly different. The difference between visible and tangible ideas is not stressed in the *Principles* and *Dialogues*. It is more a feature of the *New Theory of Vision*. See *Principles* §43.

12. Johnson here suggests that if our ideas are to be thought of as copies of divine archetypes, and if a real physical object is therefore to be thought of as a collection of ideas in God's mind, we can properly be said to see the very thing we feel. We do this when the archetype of our visual idea is part of the same collection as the archetype of our sensory idea.

13. Grant that the thing I feel can be the same thing as the thing I see, when I touch and see the basket; because the archetypes of my ideas are parts of the same collection of ideas in God's mind. Still, Johnson is saying, there is a good sense in which the things I feel and see cannot be the very same things as the ones you feel and see, without this constituting any real objection to Berkeley's system. For though the ideas in my mind are not identical with any ideas in yours, my ideas and yours both correspond to (are resemblances of) the same ideas in the mind of God.

14. This is Halley's comet, which made a great stir on its first observed appearance.

15. Johnson's conclusion is that real existence is permanent existence in the mind of God. His conclusion here is at odds with the doctrine that Berkeley expounds in the Third Dialogue, that at the Creation 'things before imperceptible to creatures, are by a decree of God, made perceptible to them; then are they said to begin a relative existence, with respect to created minds' (p. 252). For the persisting existence of real things seems to be more to do with their availability to us, and so with their 'relative existence', than with their permanent existence in the mind of God. Chimeras and other fanciful creatures have a permanent existence in God's mind, but do not for that reason have a real existence. See the discussion in the Editor's Introduction, Sect. 10.

16. '*pro nostro modulo*': roughly 'in accordance with the natures of our senses'; the thought here is that God's ideas cannot be directly present to us in sensory form, since God has no senses; if an idea is to be present to our senses, it can at best 'correspond to' an idea of God's.

17. Berkeley's answer to this point should be that even if there is a divine archetype to my idea of the distance between two trees, that archetype is not external to all minds, but only to my mind.

18. 'Nor can I see how it follows': Johnson here alludes to the argumentation in the First Dialogue, pp. 188–90; here Berkeley argues that objects have various apparent shapes and sizes, according to the distance and angles from which we view them, and that none of these apparent shapes and sizes can possibly be identical with the real shape and size, there being no criterion by which we can tell which are the real ones. If all have an equal claim to be real, none can be real.

19. Johnson here suggests that since spirits have a real existence external to one another, they must exist in space, and there will either be some distance between them, or none. Berkeley need not allow Johnson's claim that the sort of existence that spirits have requires them to exist in space; the rhetoric of 'real' and 'external', to the extent that Berkeley would use it of spirits, does not require this. But suppose that he does allow that spirits exist in space. The question then is whether the spatial existence of spirits is anything like that of physical things. The natural answer to this is that spirits exist in space, since we see the world from a point within it; but that spirits do not *occupy* space as physical things do, to the exclusion of other things. It would be possible, then, for all spirits to be in the same place without their therefore becoming the same spirit.

20. Here Johnson approaches a difficult subject, the question whether real space is God. Samuel Clarke (1675–1729) argued in his *Discourse Concerning the Being and Attributes of God* (1705–6) that infinite space was an attribute of God. Newton falls not far short of saying the same thing; he says that God is not space, but constitutes space. See n. 128 to the *Principles*, where the passage that Johnson is referring to here is quoted. If God is space (which Berkeley denies at *Principles* §117), the absolute existence of space (i.e. its existence without the mind) follows from that of God.

21. These questions, thrown out at random by Johnson, are never tackled head on by Berkeley. But there are plenty of remarks in the *Principles* and *Dialogues* that seem to give us clues. In the Third Dialogue (p. 234) he writes: 'I know what I mean, when I affirm that there is a spiritual substance or support of ideas, that is, that a spirit knows and perceives ideas. But I do not know what is meant, when it is said, that an unperceiving substance hath inherent in it and supports either ideas or the archetypes of ideas.' Berkeley, that is, objects to talk of material substance as a support for primary qualities (see *Principles* §16), but allows that in some sense a mind supports its ideas, in that it perceives them. As for the second question, about whether ideas are modifications of minds, Berkeley says in *Principles* §49 that extension and figure 'are in the mind only as they are perceived by it, that is, not by way of *mode* or *attribute*, but only by way of idea; and it no more follows, that the soul or mind is extended because extension exists in it alone, than it does that it is red or blue, because those colours are on all hands acknowledged to exist in it, and no where else'. But this does not tell us whether the idea is a quality of the mind, or an object for it. On the first view, one mind is distinguished from another by its qualities; on the other, the difference lies rather in which things are present to which mind. Probably the safest view is that for Berkeley ideas are dependent mental objects, rather than attributes or modifications of minds. This makes it more sensible to suppose that one and the same object could be present to more than one mind at once.

22. This page reference is to the first edition of the *Principles*.

23. '*durare, etsi non cogitet*': to persist, even if not thinking.

24. '*perseverare in existendo*': a persistent or continuing existence.

25. John James and Richard Dalton travelled with Berkeley from England to America. James, a bachelor, eventually left all his fortune to Berkeley. But Berkeley vigorously rejected it, and had it returned to James's family.

26. The 'mechanical philosophers' are supposed to be arguing here as follows. All bodies fall equally fast in a vacuum. Momentum = mass × velocity. In a vacuum, everything falls at the same speed. So setting aside complications to do with wind resistance and so on, the mass of a body varies only according to its momentum. Matter (mass) is therefore proportional to gravity (momentum of falling body). Gravity exists. So matter exists. Berkeley's reply is to ask how the mass of a body is determined. It is not determined by volume (extent). Suppose it is determined by weight. But weight is the product of the mass of the body and the acceleration of gravity. The whole system, then, is little more than a circular definition, in which mass or matter is defined in terms of itself. There is nothing here for him to worry about—no suggestion that physics, by means of this rigmarole, establishes the existence of material things without the mind. See *Dialogues* pp. 241–2.

27. '*moles in celeritatem ducta*': mass times velocity.

28. For absolute space and motion, see *Principles* §§110 ff. and *Dialogues* pp. 192–3.

29. *natura naturans*: this untranslatable phrase means roughly 'nature conceived of as active, as cause'. When we think of nature as operating in certain ways, according to the Laws of Nature, we are thinking of nature in this way. Often 'nature' so conceived is given a capital letter, as when we say 'Nature dictates that . . .'. *Natura naturans* was contrasted with *natura naturata*, which, equally untranslatable, means roughly 'nature conceived of as effect'. Here we are thinking of nature as the sum total of how things are ('naturally', at least), and of Nature as (part of) the cause of their being that way. Berkeley's point in this paragraph is that he is far from alone in thinking of that cause as mind—as the mind of God. For a short account of the history of the contrast between *natura naturans* and *natura naturata*, see I. M. Gueroult, *Spinoza* (Paris: Aubier, 1968–74), i. 564–8.

30. divine conservation: the doctrine of divine conservation was the doctrine that God keeps the world going by an act that is no different from one of repeated creation. Berkeley agrees with the tradition that conservation and creation differ only in the *terminus a quo*—i.e. in the point from which they start; creation starts from the very beginning of things, conservation starts thereafter. But, as he says below, he gets this result in a rather special way, by understanding the continued existence of the world as God's continuing to make available to us certain ideas of sense. (At least, this is the account given in the Third Dialogue; another account would appeal rather to God's continuous awareness of all ideas.)

31. Durand de St Pourçain (d. 1332) was supposedly unusual in thinking of the

world as a great machine that God set up with its own laws, and then set in motion so that it would run on all by itself. Pascal accused Descartes of thinking in the same way: 'I cannot forgive Descartes; he would have preferred to keep God out of his philosophy altogether; but he needed God to flick his finger to set the world going; after that, he had no more use for him' (*Pensées* 1001 (p. 431); my translation). Pascal is suggesting that Descartes's mechanistic world would be one that required God only as a First Cause; once the whole thing was set up and working, God could retire gracefully into the background and rest on his laurels, like the dignitary who kicks off ceremonially at a football match. Whether this is a fair accusation is another matter. There is some justification for it in what Descartes says at *Principles of Philosophy* 4. 203 (*Philosophical Writings*, i. 288): 'mechanics is a division or special case of physics, and all the explanations belonging to the former also belong to the latter; so it is no less natural for a clock constructed with this or that set of wheels to tell the time than it is for a tree which grew from this or that seed to produce the appropriate fruit'. But in the Third Meditation, Descartes writes that 'the same power and action are needed to preserve anything at each individual moment of its duration as would be required to create that thing anew if it were not yet in existence. Hence the distinction between preservation and creation is only a conceptual one' (*Philosophical Writings*, ii. 33). Malebranche held a similar view (see his *Dialogues on Metaphysics*, quoted in *The Search after Truth*, ed. and trans. Lennon and Olscamp, 816); so did Gassendi.

32. '*Mens agitat molem*': it is mind that makes matter move.

33. Berkeley is suggesting that the thought that God is implicated in our guilt is the same for him as for anyone else. Johnson had suggested that if we think of our sinful thoughts and actions as the effects of 'certain irregular motions of our bodies', which are able to have this effect because we have gradually given in to them over the years, we ourselves will bear all the blame for those thoughts and actions. Berkeley points out that God is still the prime cause of those motions, and knows full well what they will lead to now. So he bears part of the blame either way.

34. Here Berkeley repeats a claim he makes in the Third Dialogue: 'I have no where said that God is the only agent who produces all the motions in bodies. It is true, I have denied there are any other agents beside spirits: but this is very consistent with allowing to thinking rational beings, in the production of motions, the use of limited powers, ultimately indeed derived from God, but immediately under the direction of their own wills, which is sufficient to entitle them to all the guilt of their actions' (p. 237). The trouble is that it remains a question how a movement of my body can be an action of mine rather than of God's. For a bodily movement is a real thing, an idea of sense, and such ideas are caused by God; in which case God seems to have more claim to be the agent than I do. See Taylor, 'Action and Inaction in Berkeley'.

35. See *Principles* §§60–6.

36. Johnson is very politely pointing out here that Berkeley's letter failed entirely to address these questions. There is a slight implication here that these are the hard ones, and they are Johnson's own. The others, which Berkeley had no difficulty in answering, really arose from the confusions of Johnson's friends.

37. The passages cited by Johnson occur in the *Dialogues* at pp. 212, 231, 235 and 254. It should be noted, however, that Johnson's citations are more like paraphrases than exact quotations.

38. 'not in the divine mind, but in our own': Johnson rightly says that he has 'gathered' that this is Berkeley's view; but it remains at best unclear whether Berkeley held any such thing. Johnson seems not to consider the possibility that our ideas of sense are divine ideas made available to, i.e. shared with, us.

39. '*unum et idem . . . ectypo*': one and the same in archetype, but many and diverse in ectype. The archetype is the divine pattern or original, the ectype the copy supposedly occurring in our minds.

40. Johnson has here described accurately *one* reading of Berkeley's position. He does not raise any question about it. In the earlier letter, he linked this reading with his question about space and duration, which now follows.

41. Here Johnson returns to his earlier worries about the relation between space, time, and God. He is still tempted by the view that infinite space and time are attributes of God, rather than elements of the created world. This is not exactly what Newton says; indeed he explicitly denies it; see n. 20 above.

42. '*Deus—durat semper . . . constituit*': God persists eternally and is present everywhere, and by existing always and everywhere he constitutes duration and space, eternity and infinity. The Latin 'constituit' normally, however, means 'constitute' as in 'constitute (i.e. set up) a committee' rather than 'constitute' as in 'eleven players constitute (i.e. make up or just are) a football team'. So the whole sentence might mean rather 'God persists eternally and is present everywhere, and so doing he brings it about that there is duration and space, eternity and infinity.'

43. '*God's boundless sensorium*': the sensorium was supposed to be the place in the brain where sensation occurred, or more generally the sensory apparatus as a whole, including the nervous system. So Newton is suggesting that space is the sensory aspect of God's mind.

44. The 'most beautiful and charming description' occurs on pp. 210–11; though the exact phrase that Johnson cites is not to be found there.

45. The *punctum stans* (the standing point, i.e. the extensionless point) and the τὸ νῦν (the now, i.e. the durationless instant) are to be understood in the following way. God himself has no duration; he does not exist in time, as physical things and events do. But he contains time, since all moments are equally present to him. Similarly, God himself does not occupy space, since he does not exist in space. He has no spatial dimensions, but is everywhere equally present. So God is a dimensionless point which contains all places, and he is a

durationless 'now' which contains all times. Johnson with some justice complains that he understands very little of all this.

46. Johnson is right in saying that there is no apparent connection between the doctrine of abstract ideas and his belief in external space. This is because his notion of external space is the same as (or at least part of) his notion of God. An ordinary belief in external space as something distinct from God might still be infected by the doctrine of abstraction. It should be noted that the topic that is worrying Johnson here is external space, not absolute space as Newton distinguished it from relative space. So it is not subject to Berkeley's claim that absolute space is identical with space 'as such', i.e. with the abstract general idea of space.

47. '*Actus*' is probably best translated as 'agency'; so '*Actus purus*' is 'pure agency'. God is pure agency because he is never passive; nothing happens *to* God. We are partly passive, though also active.

48. The word 'something' in brackets here refers to the 'something' of the previous sentence; the brackets are functioning as quotation marks.

49. Here and in the next three paragraphs Johnson puts sustained and justified pressure on Berkeley's claim that the existence of a mind or soul is its perceiving, so that it cannot exist unperceiving; see *Principles* §98: 'Hence it is a plain consequence that the soul always thinks: and in truth whoever shall go about to divide in his thoughts, or abstract the *existence* of a spirit from its *cogitation*, will, I believe, find it no easy task.' If Berkeley's claims about abstraction are as I have suggested (in the Editor's Introduction, Sects. 7 and 8), his thought should be that we can consider a mind without considering the ideas it may be having, but we cannot consider a mind as existing entirely devoid of ideas.

50. '*Perseverare in existendo*': see n. 24 above.

51. Berkeley's argument for the natural immortality of the soul is found at *Principles* §141: 'We have shewn that the soul is indivisible, incorporeal, unextended, and it is consequently incorruptible. Nothing can be plainer, than that the motions, changes, decays, and dissolutions which we hourly see befall natural bodies . . . cannot possibly affect an active, simple, uncompounded substance: such a being therefore is indissoluble by the force of Nature, that is to say, *the soul of man is naturally immortal.*' Berkeley's view would be that God could destroy a soul, but death, which is a natural event, could not. In this he agrees with one of the doctrines expressed by Plato in his *Phaedo*.

52. 'some principle common to these perceptions': a principle here is a source, ground, or base for the perceptions that happen to the soul.

53. Locke's *Essay* 2. 19. 4: 'since the mind can sensibly put on, at several times, several degrees of *thinking* and be sometimes even in a waking man so remiss as to have thoughts dim and obscure to that degree that they are very little removed from none at all; and at last in the dark retirements of sound sleep, loses the sight perfectly of all *ideas* whatsoever: since, I say, this is evidently so

in matter of fact and constant experience, I ask whether it be not probable that *thinking is the action and not the essence of the soul?* since the operations of agents will easily admit of intention and remission; but the essences of things are not conceived capable of any such variation.' The basic point is that thinking is a matter of degree, and existence is not.

54. '*Intellectus intelligendo fit omnia*': literally, the intellect, in understanding, becomes everything. This is a doctrine of Aristotle's; see his *De Anima* 3. 5, 430 a9. Johnson's thought is that if our ideas are modifications of our minds, then in coming to understand the way things are we, as it were, absorb that way into our minds, which take on the guise of the world as we understand it. Aristotle's views survived in the scholastic doctrine that when we perceive an object, its form enters our mind.

55. It is not clear that Johnson's suggestion here, that ideas are the mind, is compatible with what he says in the previous paragraph, where the mind is a principle common to all perceptions. It looks as if the claim that ideas are the mind is not very different from what Hylas says in the Third Dialogue (p. 233): 'Notwithstanding all you have said, to me it seems, that according to your own way of thinking, and in consequence of your own principles, it should follow that you are only a system of floating ideas, without any substance to support them.'

56. Does Berkeley here admit that our ideas of sense are copies of ideas in the mind of God? Probably not. He does not really engage with Johnson's talk of resemblances (in Sect. 1 of his second letter). Berkeley is here only concerned to distance himself from any suggestion that *as well as* there being ideal archetypes of our ideas in the mind of God, there are real archetypes existing in a material world, and acting as intermediate causes of our ideas. Johnson discussed this possibility in Sect. 2 of his first letter.

57. The argument that all space, time, and motion are relative occurs in the *Principles* §11 and §§110–17; also in *Dialogues* pp. 192–3.

58. This is Joseph Raphson, for whom see nn. 128–9 to the *Principles*.

59. Not all the supposed attributes of God are negative: there are omniscience and omnipresence to be considered. But infinity is 'having no limits'; unchanging is 'not changing', and so on.

60. The view expressed here is stronger than, though not incompatible with, the remark given to Philonous in the First Dialogue (p. 190): 'And is not time measured by the succession of ideas in our minds?' See also *Principles* §§97–8. For Locke's views, see *Essay* 2. 14. 12: 'So that to me it seems that *the constant and regular succession of ideas* in a waking man *is*, as it were, *the measure* and standard *of all other successions.*'

61. This is not quite candid. In Intro. §§10 ff. Berkeley argues that we cannot have abstract ideas because they are impossible. To be true to what he says there, the present sentence should read: 'I find that I cannot have any such idea, and this is my reason against it.'

62. Here Berkeley is responding to Johnson's argument (taken from Locke) that existence is not a matter of degree, but that perception is; so the existence of a mind cannot *be* its perceiving. He suggests that the fact that there can be more or fewer perceptions does not show that perception is a matter of degree; each perception is as much a perception as any other. Perceptions may vary in degrees of various qualities, as Locke says, without perception itself being a matter of degree. The same is true of existence.

63. This is a slip. Berkeley should have written 'nothing without your mind'. The reference is to §2 of Johnson's second letter.

64. This college later became Yale University. Berkeley here alludes to the question whether a college established for Puritans would accept the works of Anglican theologians. He eventually sent nearly 1,000 books to the college, worth the huge sum of £400. (For the value of this today, see n. 8 to the Editor's Introduction.) For a list of the books sent, see *Yale University Library Gazette*, 8 (1933), 9–26.

Index

Index

Index

Index

Index

Index

Index

space *19*
  absolute *vs.* relative 143–6, 183
  empty, pure space an abstract idea 146, 170
  its relation to God 146, 178–9
  the idea of space not furnished by sight 146
  external 117, 169–70, 180, *225*
  see also extension; infinity
speed *see* swift/slow
spirit, spirits *54–8*
  consists of understanding and will 112
  active *55–6*, 112, 122, 170
  partly passive? *55*, 180, 184, *203*
  agents 157, 158–9
  the only substance 105, 112, 154, 155
  how spirit interacts with matter 109, 120, 133
  an object of knowledge 135
  known by reflection, inner feeling *55*, 135
  our knowledge of others *57*, 135, 155, 157–8
  knowledge of the meaning of the word *57*, 112, 156
  the only (efficient) cause 112–14, 124, 140, 141, 173
  no idea of, imperceptible *56*, 112, 154–5
  completely different from ideas 156
  their existence is thinking 138, 170, 180–1
  are things 135
  must exist in space? 170
  not to be abstracted from its powers and acts 138, 157, 170
  advantages of immaterialism with respect to 154–9
  see also mind; notion; soul; spiritual substance
spiritual substance *14, 57–8, 59*, 115, 135, 155 ; *see also* immaterial substance; incorporeal substance
stand for 94–6, 99, 101, 112, 117, 139, 150–1, 148; *see also* representation
Stoics 173
subject 108, 112, 119–21
subjective *16n.*
subsistence *see* existence
substance *14*, 115, 120, 127
  vulgar *vs.* philosophic sense 115
  spirit the only substance 105
  not an idea or sensation 154
  see also material substance; spiritual substance
substratum *25*, 105, 108, 129, *199*
suggestion 94, 99, 117, 149, *204*
support *25*, 108, 112, 115, 120, 127, 129, 154

swift/slow 92, 106
Swift, J. *203*

table (example) 104
tastes 103, 108
teleology *see* explanation
texture 126, 156
theorems 141, 147–53
things 103, 104, 115–16
  as combinations of qualities 103, 115
  meaning of the word, includes spirits and ideas 135
  vs. ideas 116, 132, 134
  vs. words/signs 149, 151
  scepticism arises from the distinction between ideas and things 134
  see also real things; sensible things
Three Dialogues 26–7, 40–1, 43–4, 48, *57–8*, 177, 198, 201, 209, 217, 220
time 138, 143, 170, 178–9, 183–4; *see also* infinity
τὸ νῦν 179, 183
transubstantiation 150

understanding 104
  a spirit consists of will and understanding 112
  weakness of human 89–90, 139
uniformity 113, 123, 125, 128, 129, 138, 141, 142, 157
unity 107, 147–8, *201*
universal notions, ideas 96–7, 150–1, *196*; *see also* general ideas

variability arguments 47–8, 107–8, 169, *201*
veil of perception *46, 48*
virtue 139, 156, 162, 167
vision 117, 118, 146
  language of 117, *205*
vividness 110
volition 113; *see also* will
volume of Nature 142
  legibility of Nature 160
vulgar 115, 117, 120, 122, 132, 136, 154, *204*
  vs. mathematical 110
  see also meaning

waste 160–1
watch (example) 124–5
weakness of human understanding, senses 89–90, 119, 132, 134, 139, 154
  see also understanding
weight 140
will, willing 103, 112–13, 155, 173

236

(LOCKE)->if you can experience it, it exists

Simple ideas   (table, book)
•common sense ideas^that are broken down to complicated ideas
• They must be specified (ex-> this table, this red)
•a whole bunch of steps must be taken before you can even produce a be
•pg 130-> you cannot destroy an idea, you cannot have an idea of
Somthing that you do not sense
• Locke sudgests that the world is just a big empty space filled with things
• 5 qualities make things exist
  ① extension ② shape ③ mobility ④ Number ⑤ solidity
•Secondary qualities are Mind dependent, they are subjective ideas
    -ex (sharp knife)

Representative Realism?
•The mind represents the external world, but does not duplicate it.
•memory is the ability to re-recieve it <-Locke

Complex Ideas
a) made up of modes   •modes->combos of 1 kind of simple idea (12)
b) made up of substances   •combos of different kinds of simple ideas (be
c) made up of relations   •Substance->•simple
                                          •colective
                             • Relation -> "husband", "father"

Primary & and ary qualities
  Chocolate
  PQ   SQ   In order to have any of these ideas, you
-shape   -brown   must relate them to somthingelse,
-the space it   -soft/hard   there has to be a underlying concept
takes up (extension) -texture
-number
-motion

•Where does substance come from?
  -locke claims that substance is a complex idea
  -if you think of substance in general, we cannot preceive it
  -you cannot experience substance, it is an idea
  -essence is extension.
• priori->logiclly independent ideas
• pest eriori -> refutable independent ideas
•The sound of a word is a sign of an idea in the mind & has to be convay
 to other people
   •words are attached to an idea in your mind
   •There is no way to prove that the word you say to someone is going to
    be linked to the same idea
•Kowledge is the perception of ideas
   -it is not the connection of ideas to the world.
   -ideas are connected to objects in the world.
•Primary qualities resemble the world
• pg 544->when it comes to our ideas of substances. ....

| Berkley | -›existence is perception

• Locke & Berkley were impurists
• "   " believed the mind is born & blank page
• "   " believed knowledge comes from experience
• Single abstraction -› single quality & we consider it itse by itself (ex -› blue)
abstract the (color) from the object

Abstract General Ideas
1) all words stand for ideas in the mind
2) communication wouldn't work if we diddnt use certain words to expl⁴
ideas & the ability to understand them
• precieveing = thinking of something
• exictence is perception b/c in order for semthing to make a sound, it must be
heard by someone
• if you were to take away someone's somthings primary & 2ⁿᵈ ary quality,
you ce would have nothing.

• Everything we know about reality is mind dependent
  ˙: the metaphysics of Locke & descartes does not work

Idealism vs. Realism
• There is no such thing as mind independent reality ‹- Zdealism
• Realism/materialism -› beleives there is a mind independent reality

⊙ Qualities that are primary are ideas that exist in a precivers mind